INSIDE PRIVATE EQUITY

BILL FERRIS is regarded as one of the fathers of the venture capital industry in Australia. He formed the country's first venture capital company in 1970, having studied the then emerging sector in the United States while completing his MBA at the Harvard Business School.

Ferris teamed up in 1987 with close friend Joseph Skrzynski to form Australian Mezzanine Investments Pty Limited (AMIL), a venture capital and private equity funds manager and one of the outstanding successes during the 1990s expansion of the venture capital sector in Australia. Its investments in companies such as Datacraft, Austal Ships, LookSmart, Fingerscan, Seek and many others yielded high returns to the AMIL funds' investors. Since 2000, Ferris has been the executive chairman of the successor company to AMIL, the CHAMP Private Equity Group. CHAMP has pioneered the development of the management buy-out business in Australia. Its successful investments in companies such as Bradken, AUSTAR, Study Group International, United Malt Holdings, Manassen Foods, among many others, have yielded impressive returns to investors in the CHAMP funds from Australia and around the world.

Ferris has been chairman of both the Australian Trade Commission (Austrade) and the Australian Venture Capital Association, and in 1990 was made an Officer of the Order of Australia for services to the export industry.

In the health and medical research sector, Ferris has been active as chairman of the Garvan Institute of Medical Research since 2000. He is also chair of the $5.5 billion National Health and Hospitals Fund, one of the Federal Government's Nation-building Funds. In 2011 he was appointed by the Federal Government to a national panel to review and recommend funding for the health and medical research sector.

In 2007 Bill Ferris received the nation's highest civic honour, Companion of the Order of Australia, for his philanthropy and services to the medical research sector and his support for venture capital and private equity.

INSIDE PRIVATE EQUITY

Thrills, spills and lessons
from the author of
Nothing Ventured, Nothing Gained

BILL FERRIS

ALLEN&UNWIN
SYDNEY•MELBOURNE•AUCKLAND•LONDON

This edition published in 2013
First edition published in 2000

Allen & Unwin
Sydney, Melbourne, Auckland, London

83 Alexander Street
Crows Nest NSW 2065
Australia
Phone: (61 2) 8425 0100
Email: info@allenandunwin.com
Web: www.allenandunwin.com

Cataloguing-in-Publication details are available from
the National Library of Australia
www.trove.nla.gov.au

ISBN 978 1 74331 329 9 (paperback)
ISBN 978 1 74331 598 9 (hardback)

Index by Trevor Matthews
Typeset in 12/15 pt Granjon by Post Pre-press Group, Australia
Printed in Singapore by KHL Printing Co Pty Ltd

10 9 8 7 6 5 4 3 2 1

To Lea, Ben and Ira, Willea, Jojo and Hugh
(with whom nothing gained compares)

Acknowledgements

The writing of *Nothing Ventured, Nothing Gained*, the precursor to this book, was made possible by taking 'sabbatical' leave from my Australian Mezzanine Investment responsibilities midway through 1999. This three and a half months' absence from the office placed an increased load on friends and colleagues whom I named at the time.

In completing this expanded volume I now wish to thank Aja Manu, CHAMP's research associate, for his tireless chasing of details, and my personal assistant, Anthea Pegum, for her professionalism in producing draft after draft of my 'old technology' handwritten text.

As usual, all errors, omissions and shortcomings rest squarely and only with the author.

WDF
October 2012

Contents

List of Abbreviations

AME	Australian Multimedia Enterprise
AMIL	Australian Mezzanine Investments Pty Ltd
ARPU	average revenue per user
ASX	Australian Securities Exchange
AVCAL	Australian Venture Capital Association
CRC	Co-operative Research Centre
EBIT	earnings before interest and tax
EBITDA	earnings before interest, tax, depreciation and amortisation
EMA	Enterprise Management of Australia Corporation
FMCG	fast-moving consumer goods
GFC	global financial crisis
GIRD	Grants for Industry Research and Development
GP	general partnership
IIF	Innovation Investment Fund
IPO	initial public offering
IRR	internal rate of return
IVC	International Venture Corporation Pty Ltd
LP	limited liability partner

MAC	material adverse consequence
MBO	management buy-out
MIC	Management and Investment Companies
NIES	National Industry Extension Service
PDF	Pooled Development Funds
PE	private equity
R&D	research and development
REM	remuneration committee (CHAMP)
SKU	stock-keeping unit
SMEs	small- and medium-size enterprises
SWF	sovereign wealth fund
VA	voluntary administration
VC	venture capital

PART ONE:

Venture capital, good and bad

I am on the deck of a 16.5-metre Robert Ladd–designed ketch, sailing down the coast of Turkey with my wife. The crew has just served us an aubergine and lemon salad with a side dish of yoghurt and olives. We are washing this down with a cool Bordeaux. The temperature is 27°C, the wind is from the north at about 15 knots apparent and we are making 7 or 8 knots, heading from Bodrum down to Simi. Indeed, we are hoping to arrive in time for dinner on that beautiful island, which used to boast the world's premier shipbuilding industry in the days when the ancient Greeks were all-conquering.

I am part way through a well-earned sabbatical: three months of relaxation and exploration, together with work on the first edition of this book.

After 30 years in the venture capital business I had begun to wonder whether my investing experiences, successful and unsuccessful, would be interesting and even instructive for others, especially those contemplating a career in this most exciting and creative segment of the capitalist system. Finally I decided they might be. So, let me take you now on a sort of picaresque journey replete with venture capital adventures. Hopefully the stories will convey various lessons, some amusing and others sobering. For reasons that will become clear, in a few cases the names of individuals and companies are codenames.

Introduction

Since founding Australia's first venture capital company in 1970, I have been intrigued by the sector, with what it stands for and what it has and will achieve. Since those early days, the venture capital sector has grown in fits and starts, in recent years maturing into a better organised but still under-resourced segment of the capital markets with approximately $1 billion presently under management.

Unlike its private equity buy-out cousin, the subject of Part Two, the VC segment is still struggling to demonstrate credible financial returns for its investors. As a result, VC has not yet reached the scale or momentum that will be needed if Australia is to meaningfully capitalise on the inventiveness of its people.

During the 1990s, the venture capital activities of my firm Australian Mezzanine Investments Pty Limited (AMIL) assisted in the creation of more than 50 millionaires throughout the country. In doing so we played a role in the creation of many thousands of jobs and the generation of hundreds of millions of dollars in exports and taxes. We enjoyed many wins and some losses. Always interesting and often exhilarating for those of us involved, the venture capital business is quite different from any other capital-investing activity. Yet this venture capital process has rarely been analysed as compared to the other segments of the capital markets.

What is venture capital? As the name implies, it is capital ventured by investors willing to take, and capable of taking, the risks associated with young and rapidly expanding businesses. Venture capital is provided by professionally staffed and managed venture capital funds that typically take an equity (a shareholding) position in their 'investees', the entrepreneurial companies. This form of investing clearly differs from that of banks and other institutions, which lend their funds and expect their clients to return the loans with interest. In terms of security, lenders rank ahead of the shareholders; in the event that a company is unsuccessful, the lender may still recover all or most of its loan, but the venture capital equity investor is likely to lose all. Venture capital is thus the essential risk capital required by entrepreneurs seeking to start new companies, expand existing businesses or try out new technologies or products.

The major suppliers of venture capital in Australia have been a mix of large Australian superannuation funds, high net-worth investors, and government-funded initiatives called Innovation Investment Funds (IIF). In return for the extra risk involved in early stage companies, these investors expect to earn above average returns, never less than 5 to 10 per cent per annum above what they might expect from simply investing in listed stock exchange securities. Since the impacts of the 2008 global financial crisis, institutional investors in Australia have withdrawn from the VC market, unconvinced that potential returns justify the risks they see ahead. In Part Four, I reflect on this 'capital strike' . . . does it constitute a continuing market failure or is it a rational and inevitable supply-side response? And does it matter for Australia anyway?

The venture capital process is a quintessential blend of art and science in commerce. It is *art* in that it involves judgement of people (the entrepreneurs and their team executives) along with assessment of their integrity, their drive, and their thirst for financial and product success. And it is also art in the sense of timing—is the tide of economic and other events right for this innovation, or is the whole project premature, and swimming against an ebbing flow?

It is *science* in the sense of analysing what it is that is truly distinctive and competitive about each project. Is there innovation in product or service? If so, is it sustainable and, in any case, will consumers pay for the difference? And what else is coming out of the laboratories in California or Tel Aviv or Perth that can blow this apparent competitive advantage away?

Thus venture capitalists have to be both artist and scientist. Once they have made an investment, the other two ingredients required during the life of the investment are hard work and a measure of luck.

The venture capitalist will normally require a seat on the board of directors of each investee company. This enables the investor to closely monitor the operating performance of the business and, importantly, to contribute as an involved partner to the actions of that business. The venture capitalist will often act as an objective sounding board for the entrepreneur chief executive on issues such as salary levels, recruitment of key personnel and strategy development. This can sometimes simply take the form of good listening and handholding skills on a range of issues that the CEO may feel are too sensitive or inappropriate for discussion with his or her own employees. At other times it will involve the venture capitalist in a detailed understanding and analysis of the company's strengths and weaknesses, of acquisition and divestiture opportunities. The venture capitalist may arrange a refinancing, and may often ultimately find a buyer for the business. The venture capital investor may also occasionally need to step in to run the company, replacing an underperforming chief executive. The venture capitalist's role is obviously a very hands-on one from time to time during the life of each investment.

In my experience, throughout 40 years or so as a practising venture capitalist, hard work helps to avoid losses but luck is probably more important in generating truly exceptional profits. The stories that make up Part One of this book illustrate this experience and perhaps provide a guide for others seeking to enter the world of professional venture capital.

In the case descriptions that follow I make repeated reference to three key components of investment analysis that venture capitalists typically focus on:

- CORE PROPOSITION: What is the core proposition of the deal? Why can we expect to make exceptional returns from this investment? What is so different or superior about this product or service that ensures above average profits and a sustainable competitive position? Is there protectable intellectual property? (Each core proposition must be capable of articulation in less than one page.)
- KEY PEOPLE: Who are the key executives who will make all this happen? Do they have their lives on the line for this? What experience, contacts and existing business opportunities do they bring to the table? Are they people of integrity?
- NUMBERS: What do the numbers look like and are they credible? If the core proposition is exciting and the people check out, just how good are the numbers anyway? If everything goes to plan, what are the likely financial returns? And how disastrous will they be if things go badly? How do these various upside and downside cases or scenarios correlate with the nature of the risks involved? In other words, does the risk/reward profile really warrant the exposure of time and money?

In the following case descriptions, each of these three components are examined with the clinical benefit of hindsight. Success or failure can usually be sheeted home to the degree to which the pre-analysis of the critical components actually applied in practice—always acknowledging that luck invariably plays a key role too, sometimes wonderfully and sometimes horribly. In every case, nothing ventured, nothing gained.

Some deals that went badly wrong

Associated Bitumen Sprayers

It seems so long ago—an investment in the early 1970s—but it offers some wonderful lessons in what not to do. I can't remember the exact amount of money involved—about $200 000—but I do remember that we lost the lot! And in fairly quick time, too.

I had just returned to Australia in 1970 having obtained my MBA from the Harvard Business School. I had become fascinated by the venture business in the United States and had decided to start my own, and Australia's first, venture capital company. I remember receiving lots of advice (in retrospect, I now realise, very good advice) from people such as Rod Carnegie and Bryan Kelman, who said that I should work for a US venture firm for some years prior to starting an enterprise of that sort in Australia. Sir Roderick was then head of McKinsey's practice in Australia and later the chairman of CRA; Bryan ran CSR's concrete and quarrying businesses and subsequently became CEO of the overall group.

I was 25 years of age, impatient and genuinely fearful that if I did not then launch out on my own I would never do so. I feared that I would go to Wall Street and never emerge from that wondrous jungle. I decided to return to Australia since the prospect of pioneering venture capital in my own country was irresistible: perhaps it was a case of heart over head.

From my pre-Harvard days of working as Bryan Kelman's assistant at CSR, I knew a bit about the road aggregates contracting business. Peter Nagle had been referred to me by someone in the industry and he presented me with his plan to commence a 'renegade' road aggregates and bitumen spraying business in New South Wales and in Fiji. Why Fiji, you ask? Well, I will come to that soon.

The road surfacing business in those days 'belonged' to just a few companies: Boral, Shell, Mobil and Blue Metal Industries (BMI). There was no Australian Competition and Consumer Commission in those days, otherwise its chairman Alan Fels would have had them all for lunch, so widespread and blatant were the arrangements for geographic sharing and pricing. These circumstances made it interesting for a renegade operator to enter the market.

Peter Nagle's business proposition was as follows. His new company, Associated Bitumen Sprayers (ABS), would bid on New South Wales country town road contracts at prices approximately 20 per cent below the majors. ABS would win some of these and complete them profitably, given its much lower overhead cost structure; it would then threaten to enter the big city markets where the majors made most of their monopolistic profits. Nagle's CORE PROPOSITION was that not only would the majors be unable to meet ABS's prices on contracts bid by ABS, but they would also have to drop their prices on *all* tenders. Otherwise ABS would easily win a predatory pricing action in the courts and the majors would be fined big-time and suffer public humiliation to boot.

Thus ABS's entry might well cost the industry 20 per cent across the board—many millions of dollars each year. The idea was to cause enough havoc that one or other of the majors would bid to take over ABS at a massive profit to Nagle and his financial partners.

I was attracted to this core proposition. In my concrete and quarrying days, I had seen similar successful sorties with entrepreneurs enjoying takeouts by big ready-mix concrete groups like CSR, BMI, Boral and Pioneer. Each of these corporations had invested heavily in the infrastructure of quarries, crushing plants and fleets of delivery

vehicles. Steady pricing was critical to the bottom line; an upstart operator with a secondhand truck and a source of river gravel and sand
could cause havoc. Such upstarts were invariably run out or bought
out. I had participated on the heavyweight side of this game and had
seen some of the renegade operators' profits at firsthand.

The ABS game plan fitted this experience. In other words, I was
happy that the core proposition made sense.

Next, checking the KEY PEOPLE. Nagle had worked as a fairly senior
sales executive with one of the major oil companies. He therefore had
a reasonably good knowledge of the industry players and dynamics—
the 'mud map', if you will. We had satisfactory industry references,
although, when I now look back on the checking process, there's no
way that Peter could get through our screening today. He had no track
record of money making; he was a sales guy, not an operations executive; and we were aware of reports of alcohol abuse in years gone by.
But leopards can change their spots, can't they?

At least we had enough sense to immediately supplement the management team in the New South Wales business with a competent
young financial accountant.

Turning to the third component of the venture capitalist's trilogy,
the NUMBERS looked pretty good. It was a high-risk game plan requiring
enough firepower to seriously take on the majors for at least a couple of
years until a takeover offer might be forthcoming. The upside case reasonably suggested three times our money back in two years and maybe
a lot more if we could cause enough damage to the market.

What happened? It was a great, swashbuckling adventure. ABS
won several tenders and managed to break even on most of them. This
was in spite of the efforts of the majors to bully some of the suppliers
into delaying deliveries to ABS. These efforts reached farcical propor-
tions when one morning ABS found all its spraying equipment vehicles
with flat tyres, including the foreman's utility.

Well into the second year it was clear that our CEO was not an
operations man. Costs were uncontrolled, tenders were badly priced,
man-hours never properly measured and so on. We were still burning
cash—at about $10 000 per month. The company had leased most of

its equipment and we had invested about $150 000 in cash as the 'fire-power' working capital needed to sustain the campaign.

I calculated that ABS had maybe another 60 days before it ran out of cash. Still no takeover offer in sight. Through the trade press, Nagle announced ABS's ambitions to expand its activities into the metropolitan centres of Sydney and Melbourne and a joint venture with a CSR subsidiary for similar activities in Fiji. Still no response from anyone! So, at fifteen days before D-day, my good friend and co-director at the time Rodney O'Neil (from the famous O'Neil Hymix concrete empire), rang Sir Elton Griffin to make an appointment for me to visit.

Sir Elton had a formidable reputation in Australian business circles as a tough, driving bull of a man. He had breathed life and then fire into Boral, building it entrepreneurially into a well-respected industrial enterprise across Australia. Sir Elton was a hands-on, no-nonsense operations man. He was not an MBA yuppie like me. His office was austere and, from memory, rather bare. He sat on his side of a large desk and leered down at Rodney O'Neil and me in our lower seats. His eyes fixed discerningly on me and seemed to anticipate my words even before I uttered them.

Nonetheless, he gave me a fair hearing as I explained the wonderful opportunity ABS had in Fiji and that we were presently weighing up whether to invest more heavily into the New South Wales business or move everything into Fiji. I thought that, given his experience, he might have some advice, some ideas . . .

Sir Elton smiled at Rodney and then at me, leaned right across his desk and, pumping his right-hand index finger up and down on an imaginary spray can, said, 'Do you know what this is? Psst, psst—it's a bloody Mortein payment. I'll pay you $100 000 to get rid of you insects out of this business—psst, psst—take it or leave it, here and now.'

Needless to say, we tried over the next few days to negotiate a better deal, but Sir Elton was true to his word. We accepted the Mortein payment, Boral took over the equipment and ABS never made another spray in Australia.

ABS now had all of its cash back, but no profits, only bruises to show for its trouble.

During this time, Nagle had been approached by a former Mobil colleague, now working for Mobil in Fiji, to consider entering the asphalt spraying business in that tropical paradise. Fiji was opening up with a major thrust on tourism in a frantic bid to compensate for the decline of the sugar industry. In the sixties, the aptly named and wonderfully imperial Colonial Sugar Refining Company Limited (now more modestly badged CSR Limited) had announced its intention to withdraw from the sugar business in Fiji. CSR was the largest employer in that country and had made a spectacular and positive impact on the economy over many decades. It had not been an easy decision for the company, emotionally or politically, but one which commercially could no longer be ignored. The end of an era had come when one of the greatest plantation owner–developer models of all time had run its course.

In the exit transition, CSR very responsibly set out to find other economic activities that it might stimulate in the Fijian economy; that is, activities about which it had some direct knowledge in Australia, such as concrete and quarrying. In the early seventies, a joint venture in quarrying was established between CSR and a local Indian operator, Sethi Narain. Mr Narain operated the only two licensed quarries on the island, one on the Nadi side and the other on the Suva side. Both quarries were ideally situated close to the developing markets for road and concrete aggregates and both were monopoly supply situations. In short, they were licences to print money, weren't they?

My early boss at CSR, Bryan Kelman, confirmed that Nagle had been chatting to Narain about extending the joint venture's quarrying activities into bitumen spraying. CSR had really only been acting as a catalyst to get this enterprise up and going in Fiji and did not see it as a long-term strategic fit, given its overall withdrawal strategy. And so it was that ABS was presented with an opportunity to join as a shareholder in the Fijian company operating in quarrying, ready-mixed concrete and asphalting services. ABS would provide approximately $200 000 for asphalting equipment and would manage the operations.

During my apprenticeship years with CSR between 1962 and 1966, I had the good fortune of visiting Fiji on a number of occasions.

My task was to learn from and 'keep an eye on' the company's special quarry consultant, Arthur Harrison. I should give Arthur his proper title: Group Captain Arthur Harrison. Arthur had been a fighter pilot based in Darwin during the war years, had no love for the Japanese, great love for a gin and tonic and an insatiable love for anything in a skirt. He was a very handsome, upright roué in his early sixties. He would swan into CSR's senior executive floor on O'Connell Street in a seersucker suit with a red carnation in the button hole. Bryan Kelman was his patron and so he got away with this behaviour, even at a time when Colonial Sugar did not hire Jews or Catholics, when only men were allowed to smoke and when an old school tie was not just a help but de rigueur.

I remember Arthur was always positive, always fun, and his feasibility studies were always sound. That was why Kelman kept him around. Kelman had an extraordinary ability to work with all sorts of personalities, to get the very best out of them, and usually to have fun doing so.

So, to get back to Fiji, Arthur had previously shown me the Narain quarries, had analysed the quantity and quality of the reserves and was convinced of their commercial viability. He still found time to show me every bar and nightspot worthy of a group captain on both sides of the island.

We decided to take the Fijian plunge and our hero, Peter Nagle, eagerly relocated to Suva.

At this stage I married my wife, Lea, and I arranged for the tail end of our honeymoon to be in Fiji. I had apparently overlooked telling Lea about our prospective business venture in Fiji and the need for me to hold one or two meetings while we were there. This omission, plus a large helping of *kava* which she obligingly consumed when visiting our new partners at the Suva quarry, created a cocktail of tears and illness for the balance of our honeymoon. It turned out that she was also pregnant at the time—come to think of it, that may be why our son Ben decided on a filmmaking career with the exciting Sydney Film School instead of becoming a venture capitalist.

Perhaps the more important meetings were in the offices of our Indian partner, Sethi Narain. Sethi was a sophisticated, successful and quite charming man in his early forties. His grandfather had arrived from India as an indentured labourer sometime in the nineteenth century. Most indigenous Fijians did not choose to cut cane in the blazing heat; curiously they preferred to swim, catch fish, lie around and basically have a healthy good time. So something like 20 000 Indian slave labourers were 'temporarily imported' into the country to work the sugar plantations. These 'temporary' inhabitants stayed and multiplied and today outnumber the native Fijian population. Sethi's family had prospered in a variety of trading activities and had shown vision and dexterity in securing the monopoly stone supply position.

Sethi's finance director was a young man with twelve fingers—more specifically, eight fingers and four thumbs. During our discussions, he would constantly stroke the smaller of his thumbs. I found that whenever I spoke to him I actually addressed his thumbs. I simply could not take my eyes off them, hard as I tried. I am sure you have had a similar experience when, try as you might, you cannot take your eyes off someone's eccentric habit or marking.

Peter and I, in the grand Australian tradition, came to give this fellow a fetching nickname: Thumbs Down. This proved entirely appropriate over the next two years. Not only did he have more thumbs to point down than any other man I've met, he also gave us the thumbs-down on any request for better trading terms from Sethi's trucking contractors, for better dividends or, frankly, for anything.

So what happened? The company did win tenders from the Suva City Council, but at prices well negotiated by the British and Australian advisors to the bureaucracy. Nagle's operating skills were certainly no stronger in Fiji than they had been in New South Wales. Plant breakdowns were numerous and, unlike in Australia, repairs took unfathomably long and were rarely complete. Parts and mechanics were equally scarce.

First year losses were unwelcome, but as Thumbs Down said to the board, 'What could you expect?' Year two losses deepened our problems. Our man Nagle's drinking problems had apparently re-emerged and, on one visit to Fiji, we eventually located him unconscious in the Suva gaol. It transpired that Nagle had instructed the company's oil broker to pay 15 per cent 'commissions' on all oil purchases into a special account, a very special Peter Nagle account. He subsequently told police that this was a 'bridging arrangement' only and had enabled him to settle some personal debts and the money would of course be repaid, etc., etc.

This 'bridging arrangement' grossly exacerbated the company's cash flow problems, and the game was up unless more cash was injected into the business. We had no more cash, CSR had no further appetite for this non-core activity, our entrepreneur was bankrupt and in the Suva gaol, and Thumbs Down gave the thumbs up to the liquidator by purchasing all the assets for a nominal consideration that cleared out the remaining trade creditors.

So there it is. We lost the lot from this 'no-brainer'. The lessons are no doubt obvious, but let me summarise what the key ones were for me.

Lesson one: *Having high-profile shareholders/partners doesn't necessarily make a deal a good one.* They can and may help, but over-reliance on the strength and credibility of such partners can bring you undone. I knew that the project was weak in terms of executive skills, but I thought the strength of the core proposition and the calibre of the partners would combine to make it work. This was sloppy thinking.

Lesson two: *Leopards don't often change their spots.* Our leopard was always and only a salesman, not an operations executive. We expected him to do an operations job. This was at best naïve on my part and at worst unfair to everyone. No doubt Nagle's reversion to alcohol abuse was in part a direct outcome of this misfit between the job at hand and the skills in place.

Lesson three: Fiji is a great place for a venture capitalist's first honeymoon, but not for his first deal. In spite of this experience, *I don't believe that a venture capitalist's returns are directly correlated to the distance between his office and the investee company's office.*

Rumentek Industries

For some years I had read and known a little about the Rumentek technology developed by the CSIRO. Ruminants—animals like cattle and sheep—have digestive mechanisms with multiple stomachs that enable them to eat and live the way they do without requiring bucket-loads of Alka-Seltzer each day. A cow has four rumens (stomachs): the first stomach is a massive bacterial chamber that gets rid of much of what comes in directly out the back door without any opportunity for meat or milk conversion. For example, anything higher than about 5 per cent fat intake is toxic to the animal and is rejected by the first stomach—or otherwise proves fatal.

Have I lost you? In retrospect, I would have been less poor and had fewer grey hairs if I had given up at this point also. But sometimes venture capitalists cannot help themselves. You see, the CSIRO had come up with a patented process for feeding animal supplements in a way that bypassed the animal's first and grossly inefficient stomach, allowing the supplements to be digested by the fourth stomach where immediate conversion to meat and milk occurs. So what? Well, if it worked, this could change the entire cattle feeding paradigm in Australia and worldwide, that's what!

The CORE PROPOSITION was that the technology enabled a 15 per cent better feed conversion, so providing enhanced economics for the commercial cattle feedlot industry. Furthermore, in one particular application, the Rumentek process allowed the production of healthier meat and milk. Feed supplements low in saturated fats (for example, canola-based supplements) could bypass the first stomach and result in low-fat meat and milk production—low cholesterol foods naturally produced by the animal itself.

Extensive laboratory and field trials had been conducted by the CSIRO and the Rumentek company over several years and the results appeared very convincing, if still preliminary. The Rumentek company had a pilot feed production plant in Moree, close to the supply of requisite raw materials such as cottonseed. The company had negotiated worldwide rights to the CSIRO process and, if the economics worked in Australia, then markets such as the United States should also prove attractive.

The veracity of the proposition depended on assumptions about alternative feeding regimes and commodity prices and about the future direction of the cattle feedlot business in Australia and elsewhere. Assumptions about the important export markets of Japan and Korea were also key factors in the analysis. Lots of variables, lots of risks—in the technology, in the production economics, in the markets.

Rumentek was to be one of the early stage and riskier investments in the first investment trust managed by AMIL. This first trust, AMIT No. 1, comprised $30 million subscribed by four large superannuation funds. It was the first institutionally subscribed VC/PE fund in Australia. By definition its investment performance would be critical to a demonstration of whether VC and PE should be included in the investment allocations by superannuation funds, endowments and other institutional entities.

In mid-1994 a colleague at Australian Mezzanine, Paul Riley, and I reckoned that this was a most exciting new technology and we were convinced that the upside was truly exceptional. This was a world-class project considered suitable for the AMIT No. 1 portfolio. We accepted that the downside could be a total wipeout—in this assessment we were to be proved remarkably accurate, as I will show.

But first, what about the KEY PEOPLE? The CSIRO scientist inventors, John Ashes and Trevor Scott, were and are very impressive men. Trevor joined the board of Rumentek and was passionate in his belief in and hopes for the process. Recognised worldwide as a leader in the science of animal nutrition, Trevor was fundamental to our belief in the veracity of the science. And, as it transpired, the low saturated fat claims for the process are now undeniably proven. In that respect, the scientists have been vindicated.

The real commercial leadership in Rumentek came from a mercurial animal nutritionist whom I will codename Micawber, after the famous optimist in Charles Dickens' *David Copperfield*. Micawber and his father had some prior and unprofitable experience using the CSIRO process to produce lamb for the Japanese market. It turns out that the Japanese don't like the smell of lamb. Micawber was successful in using the Rumentek process to remove the smell, but the margin wasn't there. In fact the meat smelt more like fish than lamb. So the project turned out to be 'on the nose' for the investors and the company went into bankruptcy.

Micawber was a high-energy man, entrepreneurial and a workaholic. It took us a year or two to realise that his optimism ran way ahead of actual results. Worse still, Micawber genuinely believed his own BS. He liked to see himself as a scientist, yet his scientific method was one that always selectively fitted the 'facts' to his preferred outcome. I do not believe this was ever other than unwitting on his part, but I stress the experience because it was a salutary one for all of us. When you want something so badly, you can rationalise all sorts of facts and figures; this was Micawber all over!

Early positive results masked this process of self-delusion. The number of cattle on Rumentek feed accelerated from about 10 000 at the time of investment to more than 30 000 within eighteen months—right on business plan. This appeared to justify our initial $3 million investment in plant and equipment and accelerated our approval of the second $3 million tranche to fund subsequent working capital requirements.

Micawber's (and others') interpretation of these early commercial trials were very upbeat; subsequent analysis by the clients proved that the costs of the process exceeded the benefits derived.

Apart from Trevor Scott, to whom I referred above, three other key executive directors were involved. Ian Reid, a successful cattle breeder and farmer (and part beneficiary of the Reid family fortune), was a strong financial supporter and friend of the company. John Macphillamy had been infected by Micawber's optimism and was a live and active carrier. Macphillamy was responsible for the finances of the group—as it turned out he was better at raising it than at spending it. Still, all of us were guilty of that attribute in this particular venture.

Finally, there was Dr Doom, aka George Karhan. George was well known to me as a fellow member of the Young Presidents' Organization. This is a US-based non-profit body formed to provide a unique opportunity for 'education through idea exchange' among young chief executives. CEOs must be under 40 years of age, running businesses of a certain minimum size in terms of sales and employees. The organisation has proved to be a very effective one for its members and has expanded around the world. In Australia there are now active chapters in Sydney, Melbourne, Perth, Adelaide and Brisbane.

George has successfully built and run his own plastics injection machinery business and has also been an astute investor from time to time in companies such as Memtec, when it was starting out in life. He had money in Rumentek and, while a great believer early on, he grew increasingly sceptical of Micawber's claims, so earning the title of Dr Doom. A man of integrity and wry, self-deprecating humour, George could smell something fishy, a bit like the Japanese previously.

I must also mention a young man who, in 1997, was appointed general manager, charged with a brief to redirect the company and attempt to salvage value. Aged 26, Stirling McGregor came from a distinguished and experienced pastoral family. He put some fresh money on the line and introduced a hardnosed approach to the difficult task of stemming the cash hæmorrhage running at about $30 000 per month.

By the time McGregor got his hands on the reins, the damage to the company's reputation and to its resources were such that a turnaround would very likely prove elusive. Indeed we came to write off more than $6 million!

How did experienced venture capitalists like us get into such a mess with this project? Let me stick to my format and describe the basic NUMBERS before dealing with this painful question.

Over a period of more than a decade prior to our involvement, not less than $20 million had been spent by the CSIRO and two research and development syndicates. This investment had facilitated the fundamental R&D, the early laboratory and field trials and the costs of a worldwide patenting process.

The Rumentek entrepreneurs had already invested about $1 million of their own money when we committed to a $3 million first mortgage loan to build a new plant; we also conditionally committed another $3 million equity for working capital. For this we acquired a 50 per cent interest in the Rumentek company and its intellectual property. Sales volume was an annual $1.5 million prior to our investment, rose to about $5 million in year three, and subsequently collapsed.

Given that we dropped more than $6 million down this agribusiness hole, what went wrong and what are the important lessons?

Lesson one: Our analysis of the core proposition was flawed in one important regard: we allowed ourselves to be overly impressed by the science and spent too little time on the marketplace analysis. In fact, what we had was a solution looking for a problem—rather like the laser beam technology that sent so many people broke in the sixties and seventies before the market was ready for laser-based solutions. Beware of solutions looking for problems!

To be kind to all the Rumentek players, no one could have predicted the collapse that occurred in the cattle industry, in particular in the feedlot business. Prices dropped, export markets dried up, oversupply of cattle in the United States led to further pressure in the Japanese market, and drought conditions in northern New South Wales added to the woe. Clients who had previously been open to experimentation and field trials could no longer afford such risks and distractions. They were concentrating on downsizing and survival.

Furthermore, when we proved to the major retailers such as Coles Myer that Rumentek beef, milk and cheese were lower in saturated fats, they said, 'We like that but we cannot pay you any premium; oh, and we want you to pay for the promotion costs as well.' Until and unless there is a sufficient consumer pull for this sort of healthy product, our Rumentek solution will not be commercially viable.

So I guess the first lesson is: *Be sure your inventor's solution is solving a problem that the marketplace will pay for now, not in ten years' time.*

Lesson two: A related lesson is: *Know when to stop flogging a dead horse*—or in this case, a dead cow. Have the courage to call it quits.

Perhaps a more elegant and useful expression of this maxim is to insist on specific deliverable milestones against which to incrementally invest in these kinds of high-risk projects. We fell into the trap of approving too much money too soon, based on overdependence on apparent company results that were in fact not repeatable and sustainable in the marketplace. Hindsight is a convenient lens with which to magnify the entrails one originally read, but how much better we and indeed the project would have been had we required more disciplined and objective outcomes for our first $3 million tranche. We should also have insisted that the company invite other investors at that point, rather than our chasing the original investment so aggressively. Easy in retrospect, isn't it?

Lesson three: Another lesson is this: *Never let a pathological optimist be the CEO.*

Entrepreneurs and venture capitalists need to be optimists, otherwise they would never get up in the morning. But I am referring to the likes of Mr Micawber who suffer self-delusion, who fit the facts to the outcome they so desperately want for you and themselves. Pathological optimists actually believe that what they are telling you is true and deliverable. These people are dangerous to themselves and everyone else around.

Lesson two is actually the most important one for me, going forwards. Of course, I hope to identify the Micawbers in future but, even if I don't, a rigorous regime of incremental investment, with drawdowns conditional upon clearly agreed project milestones, will better protect all concerned.

William Shakespeare must have foreseen my fate with Rumentek when he wrote in *Julius Cæsar*:

> There is a tide in the affairs of men,
> Which, taken at the flood, leads on to fortune;
> Omitted, all the voyage of their life
> Is bound in shallows and in miseries.

Specialty Jewellery Australia

Diamonds may be a girl's best friend, but the retailer Specialty Jewellery Australia (SJA) turned out not to be one of ours!

SJA, in fact, began life as a chain of small stores selling relatively inexpensive gold jewellery to a young female market. The company was brought to our attention early in 1988 by a very old friend of mine, an incomparable networker, the unique and anything-but-shy character John Walton. Himself a retailer from the business empire started by his father, John had been mightily impressed by the performance of the SJA business and was keen to introduce the CEO to me.

John reminded me that back in 1970 I had interrupted him in the middle of a shower to secure his signature on a commitment to my very first venture fund. His introductory fee for the SJA deal would turn out to be three times the amount of his 1970 investment! With this fee negotiation out of the way, John introduced us to the SJA players: the CEO, Howard Previn; the accountant, Andrew Allbright; and the chief jewellery buyer, John Pope (all three players, as well as the company, are codenamed).

Previn explained how his company had grown rapidly to now being a chain of 25 jewellery stores, each averaging sales of $1 million per annum. This growth had come partly at the expense of established competitors and partly, in Previn's view, through SJA's creation of new demand in the young female market.

The CORE PROPOSITION was as follows: SJA's small store retail format could be rolled out nationally, allowing economies of scale in terms of television advertising spend and in terms of the top management overheads. Pitching directly at the 16- to 30-year-old female office and factory worker, SJA would continue to expand its market share in this niche by dedicated product ranging and by a price discounting strategy that consolidated its position as the 'best value' jewellery retailer in the country. Furthermore, SJA's growth would be fuelled by its demonstrated ability to create new demand.

The average purchase at SJA was $100 and Previn believed that the competitors for his customers' discretionary dollars were not just the jewellery stores like Angus & Coote and Prouds but all the clothing boutiques as well. This was his opportunity to convince the young female to treat herself to $100 worth of jewellery rather than to a new skirt or blouse. Previn would roll out new stores in key shopping centres across the country and also identify acquisitions to accelerate the company's growth path towards a public listing.

If the people and the numbers stacked up, we agreed that this was a reasonable core proposition, given that the team had already success-fully progressed from one store to 25 stores in the space of three years. How could we go wrong? Read on . . .

Of the KEY PEOPLE, Previn was the main author and proponent of the core proposition. He was key to the aggressive store rollout strategy. Previn and his leading jewellery maker, Ben Isaacs, and a marketing executive, David Faber, had all emigrated from South Africa five years earlier. Previn had been a chartered accountant in South Africa and had managed to get some of his funds out of the country with which to start the SJA business. He seemed hungry to build a successful busi-ness, but clearly did not have previous experience in managing a large number of employees in multiple locations. Nonetheless, he was tena-cious and competent and our references checked out satisfactorily.

During the early growth phase of his company, Previn had met up with an importer/wholesaler who was also the owner of a display case and retail fitout business. This was the pipesmoking, mercurial John Pope. A lean protestant from the northern suburbs of Sydney, Pope was a quite different personality from the two South African Jewish found-ers of SJA and from the tubby Catholic accountant, Andrew Allbright. Come to think of it, we had quite an ecumenical team on our hands!

Pope had sold his shop fittings business into SJA and continued to design and supply all of SJA's store fitouts. Equipment was also sold to other retailers. From the start, Pope struck us as always having a highly inflated view of the value of SJA and, in particular, of his personal con-tribution to that value. During our deal-structuring discussions, he quickly adopted 'take it or leave it' positions. He would fix you with a steely glare, suck on his pipe and wait for you to say something. I think Pope was a believer in the negotiation principle that says you should listen rather than talk and never be embarrassed by silences.

Subsequently, Pope inserted and asserted himself into the senior position on the 'buy' side of the business. This was a fundamentally important position, sourcing gold, diamonds and other such materials and components for the company. For all his eccentricity and prickliness, we concluded that Pope had been a reasonably successful businessman to date and would be a good, hardnosed operator to have in the business, going forward. Like Previn, Pope also had his own money in the business and this comforted us.

Andrew Allbright was the external accountant with his own private practice. He had been helpful in supplying us with the financial information we needed and agreed that we needed to quickly recruit a full-time finance director.

We liked the other South Africans, Ben Isaacs and David Faber. Isaacs was a long-time friend of Previn and a talented jewellery designer. Quietly spoken and in his early thirties, Isaacs was an equal shareholder with Previn and Pope. David Faber was also an important player, being the key to the retail format, the product offering.

It is fair to say that we had some reservations about how this team would work together if the going ever got rough. But on balance we believed they could deliver the business plan in the five-year timescale envisaged. By July 1988 we had completed the documentation and Joe Skrzynski joined SJA's board as AMIL's representative.

The NUMBERS were straightforward enough. In the year to June 1988, SJA achieved sales of approximately $25 million from 25 stores, producing a profit after tax of $980 000. Our first fund, AMIT No. 1, acquired a 10 per cent interest for $1.5 million, valuing the company at $15 million. The gross profit margin on sales ran at a healthy 50 per cent level.

The initial period of operations was encouraging. The existing SJA stores continued their strong performance and the new store rollouts were basically on schedule. By mid-1989 the chain had grown to 62 stores and revenues were $62.5 million for that year. Management had achieved this impressive expansion not only by growth in the number of stores but also by increasing sales in the rollout stores to an average of about one million dollars each.

At this point Previn came to his board with a proposal to acquire the Prouds jewellery store business. This business was a long-established industry leader with 104 stores and revenues of $116 million. Previn believed the company would be sold at a knockdown price since its holding company, the real estate empire Hookers, was headed for bankruptcy. Prouds would be 'on the block'. Previn was highly motivated, not only because he saw Prouds as a desirable acquisition opportunity but also because he was most concerned that it should not fall into the hands of someone who knew what to do with it. In other words, he argued that the acquisition was an important defensive move.

For as long as Prouds was run by a real estate owner, Previn did not view it as a threat to SJA. Run by a savvy jewellery merchant, it would be dangerous competition, he reasoned. Previn talked excitedly about the opportunities for economies of scale in management and marketing, and especially in purchasing. A combined SJA and Prouds would be the largest jewellery business in Australia, straddling demographics other than just the SJA niche of young females. Once consolidated, the Prouds and SJA chains would represent an attractive public float. By 1992 consolidated sales were projected to reach $300 million, producing earnings before interest and tax (EBIT) of $35 million. An initial public offering (IPO) at that time would provide an excellent exit opportunity. We decided to back management's acquisition plan.

The lenders to the Hooker empire did appoint a liquidator and the Hooker chairman subsequently went to the 'slammer' for various offences. Wardleys was appointed by the liquidator to sell the jewellery business—in a process that ultimately saw SJA emerge with the winning bid of approximately $50 million. This required us to arrange a further equity syndicate provision of $10 million, which we led with an incremental AMIT No. 1 investment of $3.5 million. Senior debt of $40 million and mezzanine debt of $20 million completed the funding package to provide the necessary working capital. Upon the merger of SJA and Prouds, AMIT No. 1's shareholding increased to 18 per cent.

As I look back on this experience, it is clear that from the day the Prouds acquisition was completed the game was over for SJA and for our investment. What went wrong?

Fundamentally, the acquisition was ill-conceived. SJA was a jewellery discounter to a young female market. Prouds was an old established name selling 'upmarket' giftware and jewellery to an older and more conservative customer mix. Quite different business cultures existed in these companies. Attempts at rationalising or merging product ranges were misguided, resulting in the cannibalisation of each other's sales, confusing customers and employees alike. The purported economies of scale proved illusory. The advertising budgets needed to be totally independent to ensure that the two brands survived and prospered. There were no savings there. Prouds had been a steadily declining business; its main stores were shabby and in need of significant capital expenditure for refits. This cash requirement diverted SJA and sank the original SJA store rollout plan.

The original attractive core proposition had been replaced by a fundamentally unsound one. An overstretched management team was very quickly out of its depth. The struggle to deliver rationalisation and economies ensued for several years; sadly, this struggle diminished the effectiveness of both organisations rather than creating an integrated new one with hybrid vigour.

I recall an experience five years earlier when I was CEO of Barlow Marine, a yacht fittings manufacturer. I was contemplating the merger of a profit-making division of Barlow with what was then the unprofitable Windsurfer Australia company. At Barlow, we had established a sailboard importing subsidiary that had proven to be a very profitable business at the expense of the Australian manufacturer of windsurfers. I thought that the combination of the businesses could make good sense and so I raised the concept with Barlow's principal supplier of sailboards, Will Fischer of the Dutch Ten Cate company. Will was quite negative about my plan and told me of a Dutch expression that translated into: 'If you mix a bucket of clear water with another bucket of muddy water you usually finish up with a bigger bucket of muddy water.'

We knew how to import and market sailboards, but we had no experience in making them. Will was right and we did not proceed with the merger; the Windsurfer company subsequently proceeded into liquidation.

In retrospect, when SJA and Prouds came together they were destined to become one big 'muddy bucket'.

After a debilitating and drawn-out downhill slide, the merged company eventually went into voluntary administration, with the appointment of Ferrier Hodgson. Ferrier Hodgson did a competent job settling with creditors and procuring buyers for the businesses. Basically, Angus & Coote picked up the SJA business and Patons from New Zealand acquired the old Prouds assets.

Of our total investment of $6 million, we eventually received back $2.2 million, proving among other things that not all that glisters is gold.

Lesson one: The first lesson from our misadventure is a very old one: *In acquisitions, one plus one sometimes equals less than two.* Critically examine the assumptions about economies of scale and, in particular, carefully inspect the impact of an acquisition on the core proposition that underpins the acquirer.

We had been naïve in backing the management team's merger plan. We assisted in raising the necessary acquisition finance, including approximately $20 million in expensive subordinated debt. This sort of leverage can work extremely well when acquisitions produce results where $1+1 > 2$; the same debt leverage is a nightmare when the arithmetic comes out at well under two, as in the SJA/Prouds union.

Lesson two: This important lesson emerged during our extended exit process.

The enlarged business continued to deteriorate in terms of bottom-line performance. The acquisition had been heavily leveraged with senior and subordinated debt totalling $60 million. The interest service covenants were breached and the lenders were on the brink of taking over control.

Long before this point, we had realised that we needed to replace the management team and/or sell the business. Sadly, our shareholders' agreement did not permit us to do either of these things. This was one of the earliest shareholders' agreements in the first AMIT fund; the form of such agreements has since evolved considerably.

So, *always have an exit timetable agreed with the company's owners before you invest*. In the event that the timetable is not achieved, ensure that the shareholders' agreement provides a process for the sale of the company.

Absence of such provisions in our SJA documents resulted in unnecessary procrastination and further erosion of shareholder value. We squandered the opportunity to sell the businesses as separate going concerns.

As usual, hindsight is a great instructor. Had we stuck with the original core proposition and organically grown SJA, would the investment have proved successful? Probably yes.

Some deals that went wonderfully right

Austal Ships

Early in 1993, in my privileged role as non-executive chairman of the Australian Trade Commission (Austrade), I had the pleasurable task of leading a trade mission to China. Actually, the then minister for trade, John Kerin, was really the boss man and his presence meant that wherever we travelled our entourage received the full treatment.

Our start in Hong Kong proved somewhat humbling. The entire trade mission of about twenty business executives, plus the minister, were caught between floors in a lift at the Hong Kong wharf, the lift having decided that further movement was out of the question. Its security phone didn't function and, since it was only 7.30 in the morning, there was no one yet on duty who could hear our best Cantonese calls for help.

The minister, an immense bear of a man at 193 centimetres, commanded that since we were all reasonably large people we should synchronise a jump off the lift floor. This, he explained, would briefly release approximately two tonnes of Western weight from this Eastern floor, to be followed by a reapplied two tonnes as we synchronously returned.

We all thought this was a breakthrough idea, but in practice it proved to be yet another ministerial initiative without results. Happily, but 45 minutes later, our shouts and tapping led to a rescue and the mission began.

We boarded a high-speed ferry bound for Foshan, the nearest port to Ghangzhou. This proved to be a fascinating entry into mainland China, travelling up the ever narrowing and busy Pearl River.

So what has all this got to do with Austal Ships and venture capital? Well, I was standing in the stern of the ferry gawking at the huge wash our craft was sending over both sides of the river bank, the water cascading through the houses. Pointing to this embarrassing and blatant abuse, I turned to the fellow standing next to me and said, 'Hell, I'm glad we're not flying an Australian flag on this vessel.'

He replied, 'Oh, I don't know. I built this boat and it's the twenty-fifth one I've sold to China.'

Such was my introduction to John Rothwell, the founder and chairman of Austal Ships. Austal was then emerging as a key player in the fast-ferry business and, along with Bob Clifford's company INCAT, is now a world leader in this exciting and high-growth segment of the transportation industry.

When we arrived at Foshan, we attended a ceremony at the Bundy Tube Mill's plant where Minister Kerin formally opened this new installation. Lunch was attended by a variety of Chinese dignitaries including the Mayor of Foshan and related luminaries. All of these gentlemen insisted on sharing a toast, a *campai*, with the minister. One by one during lunch they would come up to the minister and fill his glass with the clear, strong liquid, swallow theirs in a single gulp and invite (insist) the minister to do likewise. To the Chinese delegation's amusement and awe, John Kerin obliged with nine such gulps!

Later during the lunch, I watched him scribbling an important note, which he handed across the table. It read: 'Legend travelled through the land, Kerin of the nine campai.'

Rothwell told me of his ambition to extend his shipyard facilities in Fremantle to enable his company to develop a new product, an 80-metre ferry to carry vehicles. Until this time the company had been building 40-metre passenger ferries like the housedrowning one we'd been on coming up the Pearl River.

The CORE PROPOSITION for an expanding Austal was this: fast ferries propelled by jet engines were changing the paradigm of water transportation. As they could travel at speeds greater than 40 knots, these vessels offered cheaper and better solutions than building long bridges or tunnels and were competitive with aircraft over distances less than 200 kilometres. And if the largest vehicle-carrying vessels could be developed, additional commercial demand would be generated. This industry was where aviation was in the 1930s and the prospects were truly exciting.

But why Australian? Why not? The construction was aluminium, lighter than steel, and Australia had the welding and fabrication skills. In hull design, our marine architects were already at the cutting edge. The jets and the materials were at world parity prices wherever the yards were located and, since labour was only around 20 per cent of total costs, Austal could expect to continue to be world competitive.

Furthermore, waterfront land was a key ingredient. The West Australian Government showed considerable foresight many years ago in designating Jervoise Bay, just south of Fremantle, as a shipbuilding precinct. There is now a cluster of companies with outstanding launching facilities and immediately available waterways for sea-trials prior to delivery. I have visited many shipyards around the world and I don't believe there is any other natural facility on the planet that competes with this.

Almost always when I have attended a board meeting in Austal's handsome head office perched right on the waterfront of Jervoise Bay, dolphins swim by as if to check the minutes of the meeting. I have always taken their presence as a sign of good fortune and, so far, fortune has indeed shone on this deserving company.

Now, the KEY PEOPLE we would be backing in the proposed venture.

John Rothwell (born in Holland as Rotteveel) migrated to Australia with his family in the early fifties. As a young lad he mucked around in boats and built furniture for pocket money. Later on he tried his hand building a small sailboat and then graduated to fishing boats. With a couple of colleagues he started a small aluminium fishing boat business and sold that to a larger company, part of the soon to be infamous Christopher Skase group.

John did not last long working for others and left to start Austal Ships Pty Ltd in 1987. Curiously, this was the same year that I incorporated Australian Mezzanine Investments with my fifty–fifty partner, Joe Skrzynski. While 1987 is notorious for the spectacular stock market crash, I think the stars were somehow well aligned for those of us forming new businesses that year.

The Austal founding shareholders were the same team that had worked together previously. In addition to John there were two hands-on aluminium welding and fabrication guys, Gary Heys and Kevin Stanley, plus a brilliant young naval architect, Chris Norman. A few years later they were joined by the fifth key player, a very quiet, very modest and very savvy financial accountant, Michael Atkinson.

Heys and Stanley had no formal qualifications, but were graduates from that famous 'hard knocks' school with boat-building skills learned on the job with Rothwell. Heys came to work in jeans and ponytail and on a Harley Davidson. Stanley was the more conservative quiet-achiever type, but both were likeable, competent young men who loved building and launching boats . . . on time.

Chris Norman had recently graduated top of his class in naval architecture from the University of New South Wales. Young, clean-cut, with great people skills, Norman had been recruited by Rothwell to help Austal find faster hull designs and to head up a sales and marketing function within the company. Selling a $15 million passenger ferry, or a $50 million vehicle ferry, calls for more than just a telephone call or an e-commerce transaction. It is a long and complex process, given the high technology involved in the jet engines and the instrumentation, and the fact that safety and insurance regulations vary from one country to the next. The finance structuring, with performance bonding and progress payment drawdowns, further complicate an already difficult sale process.

Michael Atkinson, the finance director, had arrived in Perth from Zimbabwe and had only recently joined Austal. He was the main source of financial information for Andrew and me; we found him to be polite and open, tending to understate rather than overstate.

This was the team we would be backing with $15 million in expansion capital. Could this team build the larger facilities, produce and sell a new product (the vehicle ferries) and recruit and manage a workforce four times larger? And could they do all this inside five years, with sufficient profitability to justify and organise an IPO so that we, the financial backers, would have a way out for our investors? Well, art and science might provide some clues.

From the time I first met Rothwell on the back of that ferry on the Pearl River he impressed me with his drive, his confidence and his passion for what he was doing. He was focused—he is still focused! He wants to build a billion-dollar shipbuilding business that is not just one of the best but is absolutely *the* best in the world. He was consistent in his representations about the company to me and my colleague, Andrew Savage, and handled all discussions and negotiations with the utmost integrity.

Each of the executive team was impressive in his own right and they all unquestionably accepted JR as their leader. So, there was depth, commitment, loyalty, ambition and, of course, they all had their own money in the business too. Our judgement was that this was a special team: they certainly have not disappointed us. Although we did have a short-term scare, which I will come to shortly.

I should mention that Rothwell did not have to accept our offer of financial support. He had other venture capital investors to choose among and other offers on the table. He chose us because he wanted more than just the money: he wanted professional and fresh input at board level, a personal sounding board for himself on issues like salary levels and incentive schemes, and strategic planning; and he expected networking assistance with government and clients.

I believe we have worked hard to deliver our side of the bargain, but you will need to ask Rothwell if you want an objective view!

Now, let's look at the NUMBERS.

Austal mandated us to raise $15 million in equity capital to facilitate their expansion plans. For this we were offered a 20 per cent interest in the company, valuing the company at $75 million.

As is so often the case, the venture capitalist and the founders/ entrepreneurs had a difference of opinion about this starting valuation. Our negotiations on this issue were strident, but never heated. We settled on a formula that was largely driven by future results rather than by past achievements. We have learned that this approach to valuation can avoid unnecessary disputation about present values; future performance is obviously the key to the outcomes for all participants.

We therefore happily agreed to invest via convertible preference shares, convertible into a maximum of 30 per cent and down to a minimum of 20 per cent of the company's ordinary equity, the conversion dependent upon the future profit performance.

We decided to be the lead investor, with a $7.5 million investment by our AMIT No. 2 fund in an investment syndicate we managed. We introduced Prudential Asia out of Hong Kong with $6.5 million and Foundation Capital from Perth with $1 million to complete a strong syndicate of financial investors.

Prudential Asia was an experienced venture capitalist in the region, with a network we believed would assist Austal's sales efforts. Prudential's managing director, Douglas Fergusson, was well known to us and agreed to join the Austal board. He brought loads of energy and multiple networks with him, probably flying more kilometres each month of his life than most jets do. Foundation Capital had recently been established by Ian Murchison as a Perth-based venture capital firm and we were keen to see them succeed, not only because Western Australia needed a local source of venture capital but also because we liked Murchison and his colleagues and believed they would assist Austal locally and keep an ear to the ground for us. This they did.

As events transpired, our shareholding adjustment formula did assist us in securing a fair return for the risks we took. The first year of our investment was a tumultuous one. It was a baptism of fire for my younger colleague, Andrew Savage, who had worked so hard on the project and had championed it with me. It was a year in which the shipyard moved to newly completed premises and in which the first of the new product, the vehicle ferry, was to be delivered. The employees more than doubled in number, the design office worked around the clock and, in short, the organisation was overstretched.

I must say that I enjoyed the year immensely. The new ferry, larger than a Boeing 747, was called 'The Supercat' and was to be delivered to the big cross-channel operator in Britain, Sea Containers Limited.

Andrew rechristened the vessel 'The Slug' when, in sea-trials, it failed to achieve the minimum contract speed of 38 knots. Sea Containers refused to take delivery and rescinded their contract. We were now the proud owners of a $35 million vehicle ferry sitting at the wharf in Fremantle! Welcome to the world of venture capital.

But Rothwell and his team never lost faith in themselves. They were determined that the engine problems would be fixed, that a redesign of the underwater foil section at the stern of the vessel would enhance performance, and that an alternative buyer would promptly be found. It was a galvanising experience for all of us, and when the problems were solved and the vessel was successfully sold at a better margin than we would have realised with Sea Containers, I knew we had a winning team for the long haul. The hackneyed phrase 'When the going gets tough, the tough get going' was an apt description of Austal during the early period of our investment.

Table 1 illustrates Austal's impressive growth and financial performance before and after its IPO in 1999. Table 2 summarises the gain of approximately 4 times AMIT No. 2's original investment.

Table 1: Austal's financial performance

	Pre-investment year, 1994 ($'000)	IPO prospectus year, 1999 (forecast) ($'000)	Year ending 1999 (actual) ($'000)
Sales	87 665	195 681	212 088
EBITDA	9 208	36 234	43 091
Net profit after tax	6 046	21 703	39 832
Employees	500	1 000	1 600

Table 2: Financial outcomes, Austal

	($m)
Investment, 1994	(7.5)
Dividends received	3.5
Sale of 50% shareholding, 1998	17.2
Residual shareholding at market, 1999	15.8
Net gain to AMIT No. 2	**29.0**

Expressed in terms of an internal rate of return, this investment has produced better than 40 per cent. (The internal rate of return is approximately equivalent to the compound annual yield achieved on the cash outlay over the life of the investment.)

An important element in these financial returns was the successful IPO of Austal in October 1998. For years I had been encouraging John Rothwell and his colleagues to think about and plan for an IPO. John had been reluctant. He saw himself as a hands-on operations guy and did not want to be distracted and frustrated by public participation in his company. Hard to argue with that—unless you want to access capital for expansion, or provide some liquidity for existing investors, or create the opportunity to make acquisitions using your own company's negotiable shares. John slowly came around to appreciating these benefits and ultimately embraced the IPO wholeheartedly.

Austal listed its shares at $1 each in October 1998; one year later the shares were tracking at $2—a high-speed performance. Particularly pleasing in this IPO process were the profits enjoyed by the several hundred members of Austal's workforce who acquired stock.

Lesson one: *If you back high-quality people you are more likely to get a high-quality outcome.* This sounds trite, I know. Perhaps a less banal way of putting it is this: You must assess your entrepreneur and the team in terms of how you think they will cope with unexpected setbacks. You want them to hang in there, not just because their money and reputation are on the line, but because they actually love the challenge. And Rothwell and his team, I'm glad to say, thrive on it.

One of the real joys for me in this venture capital business has been the experience of successfully working through good and bad times with entrepreneurs. Without the bad times, you don't know how good 'good' is; the lessons learned through the bad days are often more valuable than those of the good days.

Lesson two: This lies in the analysis of the core proposition. We were right in the analysis that suggested that this fast-ferry sector should enjoy a high-growth decade or so and we were right about Austal's competitive position. *Pick a fast-moving stream and hop in where the current is with you.*

Lesson three: This lesson relates to *structuring the deal with a future-performance-based shareholding formula*. This clearly helped us to cope with the risks, with the huge uncertainties involved in plant relocation, new product introduction and pioneer marketing. The willingness of the entrepreneurs to share this risk rather than insist on a fixed valuation upfront made it possible for us to step up. They now have a smaller share of a much larger and more successful pie.

At IPO in 1998 Rothwell's equity was worth about $80 million. Post the impacts of a divorce and the global financial crisis, his equity value in the enterprise is probably no greater. But, importantly, Austal's expansion into high-speed littoral combat vessels for US naval defence purposes has positioned the company with every chance of landing multi-billion dollar contracts.

Austal has continued to innovate in design and manufacturing to maintain its world number one position in this high-speed-vessel niche. The company has recently acquired a shipbuilding facility in the Philippines to complement its capacity in Fremantle, Western Australia, and in Mobile, Alabama.

Austal's distinctive success has recently attracted the notice of the Harvard Business School faculty, who have prepared an Austal case study for inclusion in their famous MBA course curriculum. Given nostalgic memories of my high-speed journey in the Harvard MBA class of 1970, I live in hope that I may get a footnote reference somewhere in this unique Australian story!

Education and Training Australia

This deal came to me from an old and close friend, the lawyer Peter Kemp. PK, as he has always been known among his large and diverse group of friends, built up a very successful corporate legal practice over many years in Sydney. Kemp Strang is a second-tier firm with a solid reputation for liquidation work, conveyancing and general corporate practice.

PK and I once owned a turf farm on the Colo River, about an hour and a half from Sydney. Nestled in the calm and beautiful Colo Valley, this property was the source of much fun during the seventies and eighties. It turned out to be more successful at growing losses than growing turf, for shortly after our purchase of the farm the valley suffered a one-in-100-years flood. Exacerbating this hard luck story was PK's indefatigable practice of ploughing. He loved to plough. He would roam over the fields with the tractor, in the process ploughing over most of our underground sprinkler outlets and ultimately destroying much of the tractor and its ancillary equipment. Libel laws restrain me from offering further anecdotes about my farming partnership with PK; let me just say that I would not hesitate to send you along to his firm for legal advice, but I would send you elsewhere for investment advice.

So you will understand my apprehension when PK rang one day saying that he had a 'great deal' for me to look at. PK had a client called Barry Tilley, a powerfully built man with a do-or-die, fear-nothing style in the way he conducted himself. Both Barry and his wife were very entertaining company; one quickly came to the view that he would always lead a 'colourful' life. Barry and another colleague had invested some 'punt money' in a business called Careers Business Colleges Pty Ltd (Careers). Careers had been started in 1986 by a Canadian entrepreneur I will codename Hank.

Careers was like a private TAFE (TAFE being the government-funded Technical and Further Education system). It was a privately owned enterprise offering certificate and diploma courses in a range of vocational studies such as tourism, hospitality, computers and word processing, commerce and marketing. It also provided English-language training for overseas students.

The CORE PROPOSITION was this: while the TAFE system would continue to provide vocational studies on a heavily subsidised basis—for example, a diploma course costing $5000 at Careers might cost only $500 at TAFE—the demand for such services would outstrip the government's willingness and ability to fund them.

Furthermore, the relatively bureaucratic and inflexible TAFE system would never suit certain candidates: mostly young people who preferred to be treated like a customer rather than as a student number, and who expected to get a job as soon as they graduated.

Careers had been successful, in each of the three years prior to our investment invitation, in placing more than 90 per cent of their students into jobs.

Another part of the core proposition related to the market for foreign students. It was projected that more and more overseas students, particularly from Asia, would travel to Australia for English studies and subsequently for a vocational qualification. The playing field was level in this market in the sense that, unlike the TAFE domestic students market, Australian taxpayers were not subsidising the fees of the offshore students and so Careers was free to compete.

I needed little convincing with respect to this prospect of rapidly expanding foreign student business. One of the early successes for Austrade when it was created in 1985 was its push to open up Australia to foreign students. Prior to that time, apart from a small number of postgraduate students, there were virtually no visas available for overseas students. The Austrade team completed a persuasive analysis that demonstrated the size of business being lost at the time to Britain, Canada and the United States. Australia had the credibility, reputation and teaching resources; it also had the geographic advantage of proximity to the Asian market, where English-language training was the highest-growth product in the region. What was needed was the political will to relax our temporary-immigration laws and to persuade the Australian community that the foreign students would not displace Australians from education and training opportunities.

The first minister during my term as chairman of Austrade was John Dawkins, who had become minister for education. Dawkins was a prime mover in Cabinet in getting the necessary changes through and, as a result, Australia now has an industry in foreign student education worth $1 billion and more per annum.

So, although there was significant private and government competition, we liked Careers' core proposition. The company had established a profitable business with strong cash flow, had an enviable record in achieving job outcomes for its student customers, and was in a fast-flowing river.

And what about Careers' KEY PEOPLE? We used to refer to them as the Three Musketeers, all likeable, highly entrepreneurial, swashbuckling characters. I have already described Barry Tilley. His investor partner was a very experienced retired lawyer, Tom Cahill. Tom had been a schoolboy boxing champion, was still very fit at 65, and was now a skiing enthusiast. I liked him from the start and, although he was always a non-executive director, he turned out to be an important player—as I will explain later.

The key man, however, was the founder, the Canadian-born entrepreneur Hank. In his late forties, Hank was a handsome and hard-driving operator, the quintessential salesman with that motivational can-do North American style. Hank could make his salespeople feel as if they had filled their quotas even before they left the weekly sales meetings. He believed, so they believed. Hank's wife featured in the television commercials promoting the company's services, and she was actively and effectively engaged in sales and sales training. They were a formidable team.

The Three Musketeers had done pretty well building the business in five years to a $10 million sales enterprise. Some of my investment committee colleagues, Joe Skrzynski and Professor Jeremy Davis in particular, had doubts about the Musketeers' ability to develop a large corporation when organisational challenges of structure, management information systems and so on could prove beyond Hank's skills and experience. Joe said he had a 'bad feeling in his *kischkas*' about all of this.

Earlier in our twelve-year partnership, Joe and I had agreed that we would not invest in anything that left either of us feeling uncomfortable. The deal had to feel right for *both* of us in our *kischkas*—a Yiddish reference to somewhere in your guts. In the end Joe's discomfort dissipated, but in the meantime it influenced our ultimate structuring of the transaction.

Nick Greiner, AC, former premier of New South Wales, accepted our invitation to join the board as chairman. Nick and I were classmates from Harvard Business School days and I knew of his interest in and knowledge of the education sector. His skills and contacts turned out to be all-important when this investment hit choppy waters.

But first the NUMBERS. We were invited to subscribe $3 million, providing $1 million to the existing owners and $2 million for new capital to expand the business. After much 'argy-bargy' with the Three Musketeers, and in part to settle down Joe's *kischkas*, we subscribed only $2 million for 25 per cent of the company's capital. Three years later we subscribed for a further $0.8 million and advanced an additional $5.4 million to facilitate an acquisition. In 1997 we sold our $2.8 million equity stake to a larger competitor for $8 million. A summary of these flows is shown in Table 3.

This surplus produced an attractive IRR over our six-year investment period of 29 per cent.

But, oh, what a roller-coaster ride this deal turned out to be! For the first year or two after we made our investment all seemed to be on track. Student numbers grew, good profits were earned and cash surpluses expanded. Note that this is a business with no inventory and no receivables. Students pay a portion of fees upfront and the balance during the course of their studies. This makes the business largely self-funding. Of course, investment in the infrastructure of lecture rooms, computer networks, curricula development and advertising was significant; hence the need for our involvement.

But then the numbers began to slide. The company had been supporting a subsidiary in Indonesia that did two things: it acted as a sales

Table 3: Financial outcomes, Education and Training Australia

	($m)
Original equity, 1992	(2.0)
Additional equity, 1995	(0.8)
Loan, 1995	(5.4)
Dividends and interest received	2.6
Loan repayments	5.4
Sale proceeds	8.0
Net gain to AMIT No. 2	**7.8**

office to secure Indonesian students (primarily Chinese Indonesians) to study in Australia; and it also conducted English courses in its small college located in a suburb of Jakarta. This Indonesian operation was a cash hole, but because Indonesian student numbers at Careers' Sydney campus had expanded to more than 500, the company had been reluctant to close down the loss-making Jakarta office.

I asked my colleague, the experienced AMIL executive director Su-Ming Wong, to visit the Jakarta operations and to make immediate recommendations. Su-Ming was disappointed to find a mess: the financial records were non-existent; the Australian general manager had resigned, leaving the business in the hands of untrained local employees; the furniture had been seized by police on the grounds that certain business licences had not been properly applied and paid for. These licence payments were in fact a form of 'protection money' that had previously been administered by the expatriate general manager but which the local employees refused to go along with. One of the local employees was hospitalised following one of these 'police' visits. All in all, Su-Ming concluded that we had to either significantly expand the operation in terms of numbers and quality of both management and teaching staff, and relocate the campus to the Chinese district, or otherwise immediately close the present operations. We chose the latter course of action and made alternative arrangements for attracting Indonesian students to Australia.

The next problem was more serious and systemic. Following the Tiananmen Square riots and killings in June 1989, Prime Minister Bob Hawke granted amnesty to some 25 000 Chinese students who had been studying in Australia and had 'gone missing'. Political and community pressure concerning the maladministration of foreign students in Australia intensified. There were numerous examples where the student visa process was being roundly abused. Asian students might pay their enrolment fees to a private college, obtain entry to Australia, attend classes for maybe two or three weeks and then go AWOL. There was evidence that some private college operators were quite active in this trade; after all, this was an attractive, high-margin business for dodgy operators—fees upfront and no students to bother the teachers!

Against this background, we were advised at a board meeting called to review declining numbers that several of our key sales agents were redirecting business to colleges where the rules and protocols were more 'lenient' than ours. We became concerned that this competitive pressure might lead to a slackening of our own protocols. (Records had to be rigorously maintained and the immigration authorities immediately advised if a student fell below an 85 per cent attendance rate. Strict legal obligations applied, with serious consequences for the company directors if breaches were allowed.)

Therefore we commissioned an independent firm of accountants, Mann Judd, to review our practices and protocols and to make any necessary recommendations to ensure that Careers complied with the relevant regulations. Shortly thereafter, Hank received a call from a television company saying that they were going to run a story on the 'foreign student visa scams' and wanting to do an interview on the Careers campus. The team was from *A Current Affair*, a leading prime-time current affairs program.

Hank declined the offer to appear on the show and called a meeting to discuss the development. It became clear that the program people had the chairman of Careers, former premier Nick Greiner, in their sights for maximum impact and controversy. To a lesser extent they also had me lined up, as the immediate past chairman of Austrade, the organisation that was one of the architects of the foreign students program.

We had two big concerns. The first was the immediate commercial one. It was September and we were coming up to the peak selling season in the domestic market, when school leavers and their parents would be making the decision on what college to select. Then, in the December–January period, came the peak enrolment period for off-shore students. Negative press could not come at a worse time and might even prove fatal.

The second concern was whether there might be some truth in the allegations and whether Careers could be implicated in the story about manipulation or abuse of the visa laws. We asked Mann Judd, the accounting firm, to complete their report as a matter of urgency.

Nick Greiner agreed to have an initial 'off the record' discussion with the television journalist in order to get a fair understanding of what was being alleged. Unfortunately, however, the program was run that night, prior to any discussion with Greiner or the company. It was a terrible story, full of innuendo and unsubstantiated allegations, and replete with pictures of the directors and so on. Welcome once more to the world of venture capital!

We became very angry. The accountant's systems review came to us the next day and, while we were relieved that they'd found no evidence of regulatory abuse, we were shaken by their comments about the many *opportunities* for abuse and the insufficient checks and balances in our current data collection and reporting systems.

In spite of our formal protests to the television channel and requests for right of reply, the program was aired again and trailers were run heralding a follow-up report for the following week. The damage to our business was becoming substantial. We briefed legal counsel, applied for an injunction to prevent any further programs being aired and threatened to sue the television company for damages to our own company and to Nick Greiner's personal reputation. Finally we had the television company's attention.

Nick Greiner was unflappable and resolute throughout these drama-packed three weeks. He and I held discussions with the television executives and a settlement was rapidly agreed. No more programs, and a formal apology by the channel went to air.

This put out the fire, but as we were to learn over the ensuing six months, we were left with fire-damaged goods. Domestic enrolments collapsed to less than 50 per cent of the previous year's numbers, although we were able to hold the foreign student numbers at about 80 per cent. The impact on cash flow was immediate.

But there was more bad news. Following the television show, we received a note from a student alleging that falsification of attendance and academic records had occurred in one of the college's diploma courses. The board confronted Hank with the letter and its evidence and simultaneously instructed the accountants, Mann Judd, to investigate the matter. To cut a long story short, one of the head teachers was guilty on all counts and furthermore had, in our view, obtained Hank's tacit cooperation in that endeavour. While only ten students' records had been manipulated in this fashion, out of perhaps as many as 3000 in that year, nonetheless it had happened. If that sort of cancer appears in an organisation, you have to cut it out, there and then. If that means the top has to go, then all the more important that the surgery be swift and decisive.

It is said that the life of a venture capitalist is incomplete until he has had the task of replacing a portfolio company CEO. This experience was an awkward one. Hank was the founder and he was still the single largest shareholder, with 40 per cent of the company. His leadership had been found wanting but he would argue that the matter was grey, not black and white—that he had not personally pocketed anything, that he was just meeting the competition, that it would never happen again, and so on. However, our unequivocal view was that he had placed us all at risk, jeopardising the entire company in the process, and that we were not prepared to live with a 'grey' code of ethics.

Furthermore, the company was now going to need a further cash injection from the shareholders or otherwise collapse. It came down to a shootout at high noon—either Hank had to buy us out or we had to buy him out. In the event, Tom Cahill and Australian Mezzanine Investments together purchased Hank's shareholding and obtained his immediate resignation as CEO.

Tom Cahill was another exemplar of the old saying 'When the going gets tough, the tough get going'. Tom still believed in the business and its core proposition. He was as angry as we were about the way it had been mismanaged. He put in some more money with us when it was needed. He and I effectively ran the business for the next three months, co-signing every cheque, selecting new advertising formats, and generally keeping the show on the road until such time as a new CEO could be found.

The task of finding a CEO fell to me. As luck would have it, I stumbled on the right person at just the right time in his career. By extraordinary circumstance, the new CEO, Arvid Petersen, was also a Canadian. I had met Arvid in the Young Presidents' Organization in

Sydney. He had just completed a five-year contract as CEO of Pepsi-Cola in Australia and was now looking for a fresh opportunity where he could make an investment in a smaller business that he could build up. Why not Careers?

Arvid negotiated a good entry price, investing several hundred thousand dollars of his own money to buy an equity stake of 20 per cent. He hopped into the fray as CEO and began the tough job of rebuilding reputation and share. The Careers name, for so long an asset, had become a liability. Such is the power of a prime-time television story!

We needed a bold move to re-establish the business in its rightful place as a leader in the private college sector. I had known Lorraine Martin for some years, having arranged for her appointment to the Board of Austrade. She had successfully built a Queensland private college business that enjoyed a market leadership position and a well-deserved reputation. Lorraine had previously raised with me her desire to sell her interests one day and perhaps pursue other activities. After discussions spanning a year and a half, we completed the acquisition of Lorraine's business, which effectively doubled the size of the company and provided it with campuses in Cairns and Brisbane together with a high-quality network of offshore agents.

Arvid set about the challenge of capturing the best from both organisations and driving for economies of scale. This involved a transitional change of trading name to Martin College, which today has campuses in Cairns, Brisbane, Gold Coast, Sydney, Parramatta and Melbourne.

To facilitate this acquisition and rebuilding strategy, we had by December 1995 increased our investment by $6 million.

Midway through 1997 we received an approach from British Study Group, the education arm of London Daily Mail Co., to buy the business. The CEO of British Study Group, Andrew Colin, was a bright, articulate, no-nonsense young man who got on famously with Arvid and wanted him to continue on as the CEO of an enlarged group encompassing some of BSG's Asian activities as well.

As the venture capital providers, we had concluded that, given the hiccup in earnings and growth of the enterprise during the adverse television phase, an exit via public flotation was no longer an option.

The attraction of a trade sale was therefore compelling and we moved promptly to close a fair transaction with British Study Group. This sale realised $8.2 million for our shareholding, against a cost base of $2.7 million.

Lesson one: *If the time comes when you need to fire the CEO, don't procrastinate.* When the problem became clear, the one thing we did right was move quickly and efficiently, so limiting the opportunity for ongoing damage to the enterprise. We found a new CEO with integrity and drive, one who was given the benefit of the doubt by the media, the sales agents and the employees. This gave us a breathing space to enable the company to deliver on its original core proposition, a proposition that was always valid and ultimately delivered a very profitable outcome.

Lesson two: This point relates to the composition of the board. *It is almost always best for the new money to have the right to appoint the chairperson.* From the outset, we insisted that Hank step down from the chair in favour of our appointee. When things become difficult, when fundamental disagreements among the shareholders emerge, a strong chairperson has a very important role. Nick Greiner played that role with skill and courage.

Lesson three: *Before you invest, always be sure that you have at least two realistic and alternative exit tracks.* Had we relied only on an IPO exit, we would have been frustrated by the media damage inflicted on the company. That experience would have rendered an IPO, at best, deferred and discounted and, at worst, impossible. A trade exit, by way of a sale to an existing competitor or a new entrant, was always a prospect for this business—that is, if the core proposition was valid, somebody would want our market share and our established infrastructure and distribution set-up. As it happened, selling the business was not difficult.

Lesson four: A further lesson based on this venture (and many others) is: *The opportunity for a venture capitalist to truly add value to a portfolio* *company is directly proportional to how badly that company is doing.* The company that is travelling well, with a strong management team in place and the tide of events going with it, presents relatively limited opportunity (or need) for significant value to be added by the venture capitalist. If it works, don't fix it. If it doesn't work, move quickly to see what you can salvage and rebuild. The art here is, on the one hand, not to give up without a thorough assessment of your salvage chances and, on the other hand, not to go on flogging a dead horse.

In the present case, we were able to make a realistic assessment of what could be done to save and rebuild the business and we were able to add value significantly. We replaced the CEO, we identified and executed a smart acquisition opportunity, we arranged the necessary incremental funding and we negotiated a very successful sale price on exit.

And we sold just prior to the Asian meltdown of October 1997, so I should add that Lady Luck was on our side too. The venture capitalist who tells you that luck has never played a key part in his or her successful deals is either a liar or about to have a real bad day.

Cuppa Cup Vineyards

For more than a decade we had searched for a venture capital opportunity in the exciting Australian wine industry—always without success. Typical reasons were the capital intensiveness of the business, the land development costs, the time to first commercial-volume vintage, and the investment required in brand building. These factors usually combined to produce negative cash flows and low investment returns.

Frustration after frustration! We love to drink wine, we love to pretend we know something about it—you know, the *terroir*, the late picking, the length on the palate and all that—and we certainly believed that this industry represented the best agribusiness opportunity for Australia since the merino wool innovation of over 150 years ago.

During my years as chairman of Austrade, the organisation worked with the wine industry and developed an export business plan predicting that Australian wine export sales would reach $1 billion per annum by 2000. This was sceptically received by many at the time, but the prediction has proved pretty accurate. Wine exports in fact topped $1 billion in 1999, a remarkable achievement by the industry.

In 1994 Paul Riley and I met with the past chairman of the Australian Wine and Brandy Corporation, Robert Hesketh. Robert had been a partner with two other wine men, James Herrick and Mark Swann. These three pioneered the exporting of Australian wine to California, eventually with some success. They sold their export distribution business to a larger Australian group and embarked on their own grape production enterprise in South Australia. They purchased 200 hectares in the area of Bordertown adjacent to the now world famous Coonawarra district. Enjoying similar *terra rossa* over limestone, and Murray River irrigation, the vines prospered and successful harvests of cabernet, shiraz and merlot were achieved. The group signed a take-or-pay style of contract with Penfolds, providing a steady cash flow that was intended to fund the realisation of a far more ambitious and innovative vision.

Encouraged by James Herrick's prior experience in the French wine business, the group developed a bold plan based on three premises:

1. Wine country in the Languedoc region of France was very cheap when compared with prices in the famous *appellations* such as Bordeaux, Champagne, Burgundy and Chablis. This was in spite of its high-quality soils and generally very favourable conditions for wine growing. The region suffered from a *vin ordinaire* reputation, with a veritable sea of red grape production. The team believed that this relatively cheap land could produce high-quality grapes and wines.
2. Australian wine-growing skills and wine-making techniques could be applied to the Languedoc district, involving broadacre farming (with high trellises and frost controls) where previously only small (four-hectare) sub-economic plots existed, and using stainless steel tanks in production, where old and cracked concrete vats were the norm.
3. Varietal wines could be successfully promoted, still with the 'Made in France' cachet, where *appellation* geography had until

now been the prevailing product description. In particular, Herrick was convinced that a chardonnay could be marketed. Believe it or not, there were no French chardonnays available on the market. Indeed, of approximately one million hectares planted to wine worldwide, by 1991 fewer than 100 000 hectares had been planted to chardonnay!

The group believed that a French wine marketed as a chardonnay varietal would be very popular in Britain. Australian varietals had already proved successful in this large market; why not a 'Made in France' chardonnay produced by Australians?

These three premises formed the CORE PROPOSITION for their French enterprise.

Five years and many millions of dollars after embarking on the pursuit of this vision, the group needed more money—and so my story really begins here. Robert Hesketh explained the good news and the bad news to Paul Riley and me; we had to work out whether the core proposition had ever made sense and whether it could still make sense.

But first—what about the KEY PEOPLE?

Hesketh, a likeable and knowledgeable identity in the Australian wine industry, gave us a straightforward pitch with negligible gilding of the lily. His steady and usually phlegmatic behaviour (at least by comparison with many others in the industry with whom we had dealt over the years) was to prove important. The industry has a healthy share of prima donnas, winemakers who regard customers as somewhere between ignorant and irrelevant, accountants as oozing carbuncles on all human progress, and financiers as leeches to be spoken to only when all else fails.

Hesketh's colleagues, Herrick and Swann, occasionally stray (or is it swagger) into this prima donna profile. At such times, Hesketh is fairly artful in running around with buckets of water to throw over everybody until temperatures can be reduced to talking levels.

Actually, Herrick beat up on me only a few times; what's amazing is that, every time he did, I realised afterwards that he was more right than wrong. James Herrick is a handsome man in his mid-thirties with an attractive personality and a good degree of style and joie de vivre.

It is his name on the bottle, his heart and soul in the product inside and his anatomy on the line. James *is* the company, in the sense that he runs the French vineyards and winery and is the key executive to whom all the distributors, wine writers and creditors wish to speak.

I first met James at his winery at the La Motte vineyard just outside Narbonne in the Languedoc. Someone had to go to the south of France to do the due diligence work and, as is often the case, this onerous task fell to me. A flight from Paris to Toulouse, followed by an easy two and a half hour drive on the motorway, takes you past the walled mediaeval town of Carcassonne, alongside the Canal du Midi and into Narbonne. Along the way, you go through wine country with vines that have been providing the peasantry with jobs and hangovers for over 1000 years.

After my long trip from Sydney, James received me politely if a little perfunctorily. After all, he had a lot of wine to make and sell; besides, the essence of his business plan was so bloody brilliant that one would have to wonder why any venture capitalist wouldn't just do the deal over the phone. James didn't actually say these words, but I saw them in the body language.

It was that evening which provided me the best due diligence, the most relevant insights into Herrick and his colleagues. We were all invited to share a cassoulet and a wine-tasting at the country house where James and his family live, on the La Boulandiere estate owned by the company. The cassoulet prepared by James's American wife, Simone, was delicious. The wines had been selected and masked by our host. Dinner guests were the venture capitalist and potential financier, namely *moi*, Robert Hesketh, Mark Swann, and a man who turned out to be very important for the ultimate financial success of the company, Trevor Mallett, the finance director.

The wine-tasting proved great fun if a little embarrassing for me. I was able to tell the difference between a red and a white, and I did pick the one Australian bottle from all the rest, which were French. I was amazed that Hesketh and Swann could actually identify vintage years, grape varietals, winemakers and the *appellation contrôlée* in each instance.

But more important than these skills was the camaraderie, the strength of the personal relationships, the respect for and enjoyment of each other, and the obvious fondness and high regard with which Herrick was held by all of them. I reckoned that if these relationships had survived and strengthened through the difficult financial period they had experienced in recent years, this was indeed a good sign.

I should add, lest you think that sipping wines was the extent of my due diligence, that I was thoroughly impressed by the quality of the engineering of the vineyards and the winery. Both were beyond my expectations—the company clearly had outstanding assets.

On a subsequent visit to the winery, this time as a director and one year after our initial investment, I was accompanied by Ken Allen. Ken was an external director appointed by us and someone who we believed would assist the process towards corporate governance and ultimately public flotation. During this important board meeting at the La Motte winery, Herrick accused Ken and me of not having read the board papers, of unreasonable delay and obfuscation in approving a red wine expansion project, and generally of being unhelpful. Ken has had a successful career in investment banking and, while he had in fact read the board papers, it is fair to say he kept his focus on the big picture issues, not on all the details. A big man of disarming charm, he handled the contretemps admirably: his suggested adjournment for lunch proved to be deftly timed.

Two years later, when we were planning the IPO, it was Ken's idea that we should invite the wily investor and experienced businessman Grahame Mapp to be the company's independent chairman at the time of the IPO. Ken had been a key player for County NatWest when it successfully floated the Petaluma wine company and was well equipped to assist our IPO efforts. Thankfully, Grahame accepted the invitation, adding experience, discipline and credibility to the float process. He insisted on improved corporate governance, but in a manner that kept the entrepreneurial essence of the company intact.

(A quick aside about the IPO prospectus. During the extensive and painfully slow due diligence process involved with the offering document, the solicitors required objective verification of 165 different statements made by the directors. One of these related to the opening statement in the offering memorandum: 'The chairman is pleased to bring this opportunity . . .' But was the chairman actually pleased? This we had to verify! Happily, Grahame Mapp *was* pleased, and he continued to be pleased as the share price of Cuppa Cup settled sensibly above the offering price.)

Trevor Mallett was the other key figure. Trevor was really Herrick's right-hand man; a softly spoken, somewhat shy person, Trevor knew the numbers inside out and spoke up firmly and unhesitatingly when he needed to. With the company's borrowings in Australian dollars and French francs, with domiciles in France, the United Kingdom, the Netherlands and Australia, with sales revenues in sterling, French francs and Australian dollars, with principal assets in Australia and France, Trevor had his work cut out hedging the exchange risks and managing the various accounting consolidations. For a small company, it had big complexity and the group was fortunate to have a man with Trevor's experience and talents.

Which brings us to the NUMBERS.

The costs, delays and frustrations in the establishment of the French operations had more than offset the previous three years' $5 million profits from the Australian vineyards. Indeed, shareholders funds of about $2 million had been eaten up and the company was technically in default of various loan documents with its Australian and French bankers.

At the time of Hesketh's invitation to us, the company had borrowings of approximately $18 million, assets of around the same and annual revenues of approximately $4 million. The company urgently needed working capital in the order of $5 million to fund its growth plans and to settle down some sceptical bank lenders.

After long and difficult negotiations with the Herrick/Hesketh team, we agreed on a $1 million redeemable convertible preference share arrangement entitling us to a 50 per cent shareholding, accompanied by a subordinated loan of $1.5 million and a guarantee to support a UK overdraft facility of $2 million. All of this was conditional upon the company first securing an agreement to a 'haircut' (debt forgiveness) of approximately $1.5 million from one or more of the principal lenders.

Three years later, at the time of its successful IPO in July 1998, the company was capitalised at $27 million and our shareholding was worth approximately $9 million. We sold back half our shareholding in a company buy-back arrangement concurrent with the IPO.

During the sabbatical I had in part taken to write the first edition of this book, Lea and I chartered a 54-foot ketch in June 1999 to explore some Turkish coastline. This coincided with a takeover offer for Cuppa Cup from the very much larger Southcorp beverages group. My mobile phone took a thrashing; after the usual amount of argy-bargy, the board decided to recommend the Southcorp bid at $1.35 per share, subject to no higher bid being received.

At this price, our internal rate of return on the investment jumped to 50 per cent—a very successful vintage indeed!

Now, let's return to the core proposition.

When James Herrick arrived in Narbonne in the late 1980s and announced that he was looking to buy some properties, or *domaines*, the local people were somewhat bemused. But he found three separate *domaines*, in aggregate some 200 hectares, with appropriate soil and water rights. These were *domaines* with long-established vines, all of which Herrick proceeded to remove. He also fumigated the soil. At this point, the locals' mood of bemusement shifted to one more of agitation. Then, when Herrick finally had 200 hectares of broad-acre chardonnay vines in full leaf, complete with fencing and trellises, things turned rather nasty. Guns were fired at and through the vine-yards, sheds and equipment were graffitied, and threats were made against Herrick himself.

This behaviour of the locals mystified Herrick until one day in a Narbonne bar he learned that the annual district *chasse* had been effectively ruined by the Cuppa Cup development. Shooters and their dogs were unable to pass through the property. Herrick rapidly made it known that during the two- or three-week hunting season the shooters would have free access into and through the vineyards. End of problem.

After some other project delays, the first and second pieces of the core proposition had been delivered: Herrick had demonstrated that this Languedoc land could be bought at an economic price and was indeed capable of supporting a high-quality chardonnay varietal.

Herrick then had to prove the third part of his proposition—that a demand for wine from this region could be established in the UK market. Not surprisingly, convincing the key buyers in the specialty chains like Oddbins and Victoria Wines took longer than first thought. The 1993 vintage was small and somewhat experimental; it was really not until the 1994 vintage was available that the buyers became confident of the sustainability and quality of the James Herrick label. The big retailers Tesco and Sainsbury's also bought the product as it began to establish a position at the then premium price point of £3.99 a bottle.

The fundamental pieces of the core proposition were beginning to work. There was only one problem—the company was now running out of money. Hence the possible opportunity for AMIL. Was the project ever really going to work or, once again, was the industry just too competitive for us, too capital intensive? This was the stumbling block that had thwarted our previous attempts to find a venture capital opportunity in the wine industry. The returns were always too far off and too low. But in Cuppa Cup's case we reckoned that most of the hard vineyard and wine development program had been completed, and very professionally so. If the lenders would take a realistic view of their debt and provide some debt forgiveness, the returns could still be there. So we agreed to provide funding for the company, including some for debt retirement, provided that Herrick and his colleagues could first convince one or more of the banks to agree to a 'haircut'. This was eventually negotiated and so the company was provided the wherewithal for a final chance.

The company used our money well. Extension of winery capacity, new product introductions including a shiraz, Cuvée Simone (named after the cassoulet chef), and an investment in promotion were all successful. Case sales grew from 25 000 in 1995 to almost 100 000 in 1998. The core proposition was bold and it was right; our funding assisted the realisation of Herrick's vision and the IPO allowed the development to continue.

So, is there anything to be learned from this intoxicating investment tale?

Lesson one: *Patience is still a virtue.* I mean this in two senses. First of all, we waited for many years to find the right opportunity in the wine industry. Those years were not wasted, since we had gathered together some worthwhile industry data and contacts that were useful in gauging the Cuppa Cup project. This patience equipped us to recognise value when it came along and when others did not see it.

The second reward derived from our patience with a talented and at times mercurial chief executive. James was difficult and perhaps precious from time to time. Yet we never doubted his integrity or his commitment; we learned to bite our lips occasionally (I think my colleague Paul's lips are still bleeding), because James actually does hear the other points of view—eventually.

Lesson two: *Timing is more important than analysis.* I must say I'm not sure my close friend and partner Joe Skrzynski necessarily agrees with this point. Joe has a powerful intellect and, in my experience, unmatched powers of analysis across a broad range of industries and technologies. And when he's firing, cerebral sparks fly. I remember one day when we were flying to New York together. On the runway at Mascot before take-off he was giving me a headache with an animated description of a technical software business. The flight attendant was at the same time asking passengers to turn off their mobile phones, laptops and other such equipment that interfere with aircraft instrumentation. Finally, I had to say to Joe, 'For God's sake, stop thinking until after take-off!'

Joe's cerebral energy notwithstanding, I believe timing is all-important. And it happened that when we were encouraging/requiring Cuppa Cup to achieve a debt forgiveness, one of the lenders was closing its European office and seeking to close off all receivables. This fortuitous circumstance played to our advantage.

A second piece of fortunate timing was the strength of the equities market and the voracious appetite for new issues during the first half of 1998. This also played well to our hand for, although Cuppa Cup was of small capitalisation (approximately $30 million), the IPO was well supported. And the takeover offer from Southcorp at $1.35 per share represented a 50 per cent premium over the issue price of 90 cents just twelve months after the IPO.

Lesson three: *A well-structured shareholders' agreement never needs to come out of the files.* One of the key points in our agreement with the founders was the timetable for realisation of the investment. A timetable and a commitment for realisation are important for all shareholders but especially for the minority non-executive shareholding of the venture capitalist. Otherwise, the venture capitalist is exposed to the whims and passions of the majority holders.

Our bargain with Herrick and his colleagues was unambiguous in this regard: here is our money with which to finish the job you have so impressively started, but let's have it back within five years or the price goes up. Needless to say, the legal talent (in this case Andrew Stevenson at Corrs Chambers Westgarth) expanded this understanding into innumerable pages of complex clauses!

Andrew Stevenson said to me several years ago, no doubt trying to justify his fees, 'The better your transaction documents, the less likely it is that you will ever need to pull them out of your desk.' This homily has proved to be correct over the years. (It proves painfully true in the reverse also.)

The Cuppa Cup founders were true to their word. Although James referred to our shareholders' agreement as the 'Australian Mezzanine Sword of Damocles', it did act as a sensible discipline for everyone in the value-creation obligations we shared.

Lesson four: *Personal 'money up' focuses the mind.* Nothing you haven't heard (or perhaps felt) many times before, but well worth repeating. The executives and founders of the company had a very high percentage of their individual net worth in this deal; in at least one case, that percentage was greater than 100 per cent.

Success in this venture, particularly in turning it from the brink of insolvency to a profitable public company, required risk taking, good luck and loads of hard work. Whether at harvest time (when Herrick literally works around the clock), or at wine promotions, or at investor meetings, the fact that the founders have their own money in the venture has maintained their focus, their commitment and their energy level. And the same has happened in our case, I might add.

Looking back, now fourteen years after the takeover of our listed Cuppa Cup company by Southcorp Wines, what has happened?

James Herrick was and always will be the quintessential Antichrist to large corporations and bureaucracy. I was not surprised (nor could James have been) when he and Southcorp parted company not long after the takeover. Subsequently, Southcorp was itself acquired by the successful Foster's Group.

The James Herrick wine business languished under the new owners and may be one of the early examples of a very successful beer business never making a success of its wine assets. Foster's sold their Cuppa Cup inheritance to a local Languedoc farming group. This group dropped the Herrick label but has continued to successfully integrate the vineyards and winery operations into their own branded products and distribution. The vines have returned to their French roots. *Plus ça change, plus la même chose!*

Datacraft

Datacraft was a great success story for us and for the venture capital industry in Australia. We invested $3.5 million and received back more than $30 million over our seven-year engagement with the company.

Established in 1974, Datacraft was already a publicly listed company when it was first brought to our attention by the well-known and highly respected stockbroker Gilles Kryger. Gilles' company, Ord Minnett, had been broker to the IPO of Datacraft shares in 1985. In 1989, the company was in need of funds for expansion, but an attempted rights issue had failed to achieve support. The shareholders had become disenchanted with the company's variable performance, and small technology companies had about as much appeal to the institutional investors as a Rumentek beef steak has to a vegetarian.

Datacraft had ridden an early wave of demand for modems, 'black boxes' enabling computers to speak to each other remotely by transferring large volumes of data down telephone wires. These black boxes were in high demand and Datacraft was successfully manufacturing and selling them throughout Australia. When we were invited to consider supporting the company's rights issue in 1989, the business was roughly $60 million per annum in sales and making a modest profit.

The problem was that modems were rapidly becoming commodities, with declining margins and prospects. Still, something caught my partner Joe Skrzynski's eye about this particular company.

Since starting the first AMIT fund in 1988, we had identified the IT and telecoms sector as a high priority. We believed it was a sector that could offer higher than normal returns for venture investors. This belief was founded partly on the predicted explosive growth for the sector as a whole in Australia over the decade of the nineties. It was also based on our own direct experiences and contacts confirming the significant research and development base in Telecom, CSIRO, Department of Defence and elsewhere. There would have to be opportunities for smaller companies to commercialise some of this work and to obtain profitable niche positions in the coming market explosion.

Joe was convinced that Datacraft could be one such company. Not because of what it presently made and sold, but because of what it could do building on existing expertise and credibility.

The CORE PROPOSITION was as follows. The requirement in the corporate world for local area networks (LANs) and wide area networks (WANs) was an immediate and escalating one. There was a proliferation of equipment suppliers, computers, telephones, routers, modems and so on. What would be needed in Australia and in Asia was a credible company to be a systems integrator to design and implement these communications networks. Customers were bewildered by the choices, alternatives and complexities—a credible and independent operator (one independent from any one hardware supplier) could charge handsomely if it could deliver systems integration that really worked. Furthermore, such an operator might also derive very attractive maintenance fees to keep these systems live. Such a maintenance business might prove particularly attractive in the disparate economies of Asia if a multinational company could call a Datacraft help desk and know that the same screwdriver would be used in Bangkok or Kaoshung or Guangzhou.

This was an exciting proposition that, if successful, would see modems represent only 10 per cent of Datacraft's business within five years compared with 90 per cent in 1989. Joe believed the founder and CEO, George Kepper, was on the right track. What was important and became our opportunity was that nobody else seemed to understand Kepper's concept or believe in it. As a consequence, Datacraft's 20 cents issue price had sagged to 14 cents and the rights issue at 20 cents had no chance.

We were able to negotiate a funding alternative to the proposed rights issue whereby we advanced $3.5 million to the company by way of a 14 per cent interest-bearing note, convertible into shares at our option at 20 cents each within five years.

There were several KEY PEOPLE in the Datacraft team—in research, manufacturing, finance and sales. The two key players, however, were George Kepper and the boss of the Hong Kong-based Asian subsidiary, Des Althorpe.

George Kepper is a charming, phlegmatic, careful and clever man. His only non-business activity that worried me (apart from his lack of interest in golf) was his passion for flying. He owned his own plane and I was alarmed to learn that occasionally he would fly himself from Melbourne to Sydney for board meetings. The centrepiece of our core proposition was at 12 000 feet in a small owner-operated plane! Fortunately, George brought the same meticulous planning and operating style to his flying as he did to his business.

Prior to starting Datacraft in 1974, George's career included five years in Europe as an electronics design and project manager at Ericssons and then a period as general manager of a division of Fairchild Semiconductor back in Australia.

George was always the majority shareholder right up until the day the company was sold in 1998. After full conversion of our convertible note, he would still own in excess of 51 per cent of the company.

Des Althorpe, the other key player, was an Englishman and a chartered electrical engineer. Des had worked with British Telecom and then Telematics International in Europe. Kepper recruited him in 1987 to be the managing director of a wholly owned Datacraft subsidiary, Datacraft Asia. I believe this was the single best action Kepper took as chief executive, as Althorpe proved to be a real winner. Of medium build, Althorpe was a dynamo, ambitious and hardworking and a tireless motivator of others. He told Joe and me of his plans to establish Datacraft offices right through Asia, from the top of China all the way down through Indonesia. He believed that the data collection and transfer requirements of Asia were immeasurably large and that Datacraft Asia would have to grow at 40 per cent per annum compound just to keep up.

By the time we were completing our due diligence, Des had established profitable offices in Hong Kong, Singapore and Kuala Lumpur. He was well advanced with the planning for Beijing, Bangkok and Taipei. It was difficult not to believe that here was a man in the right place at the right time.

In short, we were impressed by the core proposition and by the two men vital to the delivery of that proposition. But what about the NUMBERS? In 1988, the year immediately prior to our investment, the Datacraft performance was as shown in Table 4.

With approximately 77 million shares on issue, the company had a market capitalisation of just $10 million. We agreed to advance $3.5 million by way of a 14 per cent interest-bearing note, convertible into 17.5 million shares or roughly 20 per cent of the company. Kepper remained the largest shareholder with a controlling 70 per cent diluting to 55 per cent upon conversion of the AMIT notes.

In the year immediately prior to the company's acceptance of a takeover bid in 1998, the figures were as shown in Table 5.

Table 4: Datacraft financial performance

1988	Sales ($m)	Profits ($m)
Australia	38.4	3.3
Asia/NZ	22.3	3.4
Unallocated expenses	–	(2.5)
Group	**60.7**	**4.2**

With approximately 110 million shares then on issue, the company was capitalised at $330 million at the offer price of $3 per share. Kepper's holding was worth about $160 million. Consistent with our philosophy of realising profits on the way up, we had achieved the outcome set out in Table 6 for our investment.

This provided us with a very satisfactory internal rate of return of approximately 40 per cent over the seven-year life of our investment.

The outstanding value creation occurred in Asia. The Australian manufacturing activities had continued to show poor margins and the systems integration business began to suffer from an invasion of international participants. Kepper's core proposition had been right, but he no longer had it to himself in Australia.

As a consequence, the long-suffering Datacraft shareholders in Australia again lost patience and the stock price sagged. This sagging price was a concern since the company needed more funds to fuel the continuing high growth of its Asian business. The trick was how to uncouple the two companies and access the price divergence that existed between the valuations enjoyed by Asian IT companies and those suffered by small Australian IT companies.

Joe hit on the idea of a partial float of the company's Asian subsidiary on an Asian stock exchange. This would enable us to access earnings multiples closer to twenty times on the Hong Kong and Singapore

Table 5: Financial performance prior to takeover bid, Datacraft

	Sales ($m)	Profits ($m)
Australia	66.2	3.2
Asia/NZ	183.9	16.2
Other	20.5	(3.7)
Group	**270.6**	**15.7**

Table 6: Financial outcomes, Datacraft

	($m)
Initial outlay	(3.5)
Dividends and interest received	2.4
Share sales, 1993–97	7.6
Sale at takeover, 1998	18.4
Net gain to AMIT No. 1	**24.9**

stock markets, compared with the single digit multiples then afforded to companies such as Datacraft in Australia.

Althorpe was red-hot for this idea. He could see that unless he could uncouple from the Australian parent he would never be able to realise the growth potential of the Asian business, nor could he achieve personal wealth for himself and his management team. Des enthusiastically supported Joe's plan and together they eventually convinced George of the wisdom in the idea.

George was understandably nervous about having *two* stock exchange listings, and about issues of control, transfer pricing and other responsibilities complicated by the existence of two separate groups of shareholders. We assisted in the design of appropriate protocols and governance procedures for all these matters and enlisted George's now enthusiastic support.

The offshore listing proved to be a milestone in the value creation process for all Datacraft shareholders. We selected a venture capital group well known to us in Hong Kong and Singapore who could help in the process of the Asian float. This was the Transpac group headed by Christopher Leong. Transpac subscribed for a private placement of approximately 10 per cent of the capital of Datacraft Asia and subsequently introduced the Development Bank of Singapore as the sponsor for a public listing twelve months later on the Singapore stock exchange.

In March 1995 Datacraft became the first US$-denominated listing on the Singapore exchange. The IPO was priced at US39 cents a share, valuing the Asian subsidiary at US$71 million. Des Althorpe and his team always hit their prospectus forecasts and continued to grow the company at 40 per cent compound. Offices were opened in mainland China, South Korea, Japan, India, Thailand, Taiwan and Indonesia. Datacraft Asia thus became the only systems integrator that could offer a multinational company an Asia-wide maintenance and quality control service for its data networks.

By early 1997, less than three years from the Singapore listing date, Datacraft Asia's shares had moved past the US$2 mark; that is, more than five times the listing price. The Asian subsidiary, then 60 per cent owned by the parent, was valued at approximately $500 million on the Singapore market, while the Australian parent was valued at only $133 million on the Australian stock exchange. One of the markets had to be wrong and we held firm in our view that eventually Australian investors would recognise this arbitrage opportunity. Arbitrage refers to a divergence in price that can occur for the same product on different markets at the same time. Such apparent imperfection in the markets may create opportunity for investors to make an 'arbitrage profit'.

In order to create more liquidity in the Australian share register, I had begun to sell several million of our shares into the market during 1994 at prices between 50 cents and $1.10. This practice was also consistent with our philosophy of bagging some profits on the way up.

While this partial selldown created more institutional interest in the Datacraft Australia shares, the large arbitrage position between Asia and Australia was still unresolved. The riddle remained: how were we and the rest of the Australian shareholders ever going to be able to capture any benefit from this arbitrage?

The Datacraft board advised shareholders that it was actively analysing various scenarios: reverse takeovers, sale of the Asian company with return of capital, and other recapitalisation schemes. In the end, a takeover offer was received from the large South African group, Dimension Data. Dimension Data bid $3 a share for 100 per cent of the company and were successful in obtaining the board's positive recommendation to shareholders. This recommendation was forthcoming, among other reasons, because the bid was at a price that once and for all solved the arbitrage riddle.

AMIT sold its shareholding on market at the bid price, realising $18.4 million for its residual shareholding. This investment was a success on many counts: in terms of jobs created, exports generated, millionaires created in the management teams in Australia and Asia, and returns to the investors.

The lessons learned from all of this were many; the two most important for me were as follows.

Lesson one: This point has been made already but, in spite of its obviousness, deserves emphasis. *High-quality people get you high-quality outcomes.*

Kepper never lost faith in himself or in his company even during serious setbacks and even when the public investors deserted the stock. In 1996 the company had missed its budgets badly, the Australian company racked up abnormal losses of $6.5 million and the company's bankers had become concerned with the group's lack of cash flow. This was a time when Kepper personally provided extra collateral to keep the bankers at bay and to provide the company the time it needed to prove itself.

Althorpe, of course, proved to be a quite exceptional chief executive. He moved seamlessly from being a private subsidiary CEO to being a public corporation CEO. Leading by example, he delivered 40 per cent compound growth in sales and profits and ultimately created outstanding value for both Asian and Australian shareholders.

Lesson two: The second lesson was *the importance of thinking beyond just the Australian markets when planning the investment exit.* This point underscored by our experience with LookSmart is discussed over the page. In the case of Datacraft, I'm referring to the listing of the Asian subsidiary in Singapore, not the ultimate sale of the holding company. The Asian float captured an earnings multiple twice that available at the time in the Australian market. This facilitated an efficiently priced expansion of the Asian company enabling it, among other reasons, to purchase more equipment and services from its Australian parent.

I mention this aspect because of the concern, often negatively expressed in the Canberra bureaucracy and elsewhere, about Australian companies moving offshore. Much of this discussion is unbalanced, in my view, if the alternative would be stunted growth and a failure to access global markets. If such an alternative is the Australian solution, then badge me un-Australian.

LookSmart

LookSmart was the salvaged wreck of a Reader's Digest division. It began as a far-sighted internet initiative by Reader's Digest and sadly lost its way and all of its champions within that group. Then in 1995 along came a bright and energetic McKinsey IT consultant, Evan Thornley, and his wife, Tracey Ellery, who offered to take it off Reader's Digest's hands in return for taking on the responsibility of ongoing funding.

In the same year that Evan and Tracey made their purchase, Sequoia Capital, a leading Sandhill Road venture firm in California's Silicon Valley, completed a $1 million investment for 25 per cent of another internet company that had no business plan, no revenues, and nothing that it could sell. This company was a search engine business called Yahoo! and by early 1999 Sequoia's $1 million was worth $8 *billion*. Albeit since challenged by Google, Sequoia's investment is still probably the most spectacular venture return of all time. Sequoia was obviously not put off by strange names, as it had earlier financed a little company called Apple.

Thornley's vision, which became the CORE PROPOSITION for the company, was simple. Although influenced by Yahoo!, the proposition was different. Thornley believed there was plenty of room for a search engine that could get people to where they needed to be on the internet in a quicker and friendlier way than the other available search engines could. Furthermore, Thornley felt that LookSmart could deliver higher quality information by the prior editing of websites and other databanks. Given enough editors, he believed, LookSmart's buildup of information would ultimately constitute a proprietary franchise of considerable value to users and hence advertisers. He would build an internet media company with a proprietary database.

Okay, but how was LookSmart so different from, say, Yahoo! or Lycos or Alta Vista, all of which had such a head start? Why would they allow LookSmart into the game?

The core proposition involved the following ambitions:

- The company's category-driven (as compared with word-driven) search was aimed at maximising e-commerce usage by also capturing user data such as prior purchase behaviour. LookSmart would continue to build on Reader's Digest's direct marketing skills. LookSmart's proprietary dynamic server architecture was built around the need to capture, analyse and respond in real time to user behaviour data to optimise e-commerce revenue performance. This same user data would also assist the company's ability to attract quality advertisers.

Thornley's advertising model was to some extent borrowed from Yahoo!. In an interview with David Kaplan (*The Silicon Boys*, Allen & Unwin, Sydney, 1999), Sequoia's Mike Moritz reflected on his decision to invest in Yahoo!. Moritz said, 'Maybe too simply, I just felt you're in your car listening to radio for free or you're at home watching CBS for free. So why will the internet be any different? The trick, strategically, was to get an audience and retain the audience and at some point the advertisers would come.' And come they did.

- LookSmart was unique among navigation services in adopting a 'syndicated and distributed' traffic strategy. This distinguished it from the big-brand competitors like Yahoo! and would enable the company to quickly reach profitability.

- LookSmart had invested for two years in a team of 25 editors to provide it with a proprietary database targeted at consumers over 30 years of age. By rapidly expanding its investment in the editing process, LookSmart intended to establish the largest proprietary database of edited websites in the world. This database could be licensed to the likes of Microsoft and Excite, so providing a secure revenue stream additional to the less certain advertising revenue.

LookSmart's pursuit of these ambitions would provide it with a defensible and profitable position in a dramatically expanding internet market. If the proposition was sound, LookSmart could occupy this space alongside much larger players such as Yahoo! and Excite because its product was sufficiently differentiated.

The KEY PEOPLE who would make all this happen had mightily impressed one of my co-directors in AMIL, Paul Riley. Paul was the first believer and had to work overtime convincing the rest of us that LookSmart could really be a winner in such a competitive business. Like most successes, there is no shortage of champions who emerge after the event. I can nonetheless claim that I did encourage Paul to bring the project forward to the investment committee. Paul was the one who really stuck his neck out, as much because of the calibre of the key people as his belief in the core proposition.

Paul's quiet speaking style is sometimes mistaken for uncertainty of view and resolve. In fact, he has a steely 'dog with a bone' approach to many things, one of which was the LookSmart proposal.

He was very impressed with Evan Thornley, as were Joe Skrzynski and I. Thornley had spent four years with McKinsey in that firm's tele-communications, consumer goods and energy practices. He became a leader in the global online advertising practice group and led internet training programs on strategy and corporate finance. Evan had formed LookSmart in 1995 and had been its leader ever since. The big question for us was: could he make the step from successful consultant to effective chief executive officer?

Being a McKinsey alumnus myself, I was naturally predisposed to liking Thornley. Unlike Thornley, who had earned his McKinsey stripes the hard way, I can only lay claim to a good fun 'summer job' at McKinsey between years at the Harvard Business School. I had been recruited into the firm by two of the school's illustrious Australian graduates, Roderick Carnegie and Dr Timothy Pascoe. Rod and Tim were brightly shining comets in the McKinsey galaxy at that time and I was excited by the opportunity to learn more about the firm. In 1969 I worked the three-month holiday break in the New York office. The main assignment was for a new McKinsey client, Mr Kerkorian, then the owner of MGM. He was trying to work out how to improve the probability of producing profitable movies. It turned out that after the smash hit of Dr Zhivago, MGM's next 50 movies were all unprofitable. All 50 had been over budget on cost and under budget on revenues. So Kerkorian called in McKinsey.

We prepared an elaborate matrix of all the studio's movies for the previous 30 years. Love stories against revolutionary backgrounds were the top-scoring category—over westerns, comedies, spy dramas and so on. Kerkorian already knew this and so, while this piece of work was intellectually rigorous, it did not by itself take the client very far.

Thornley had more success with his clients at McKinsey and deserved his star reputation in the firm.

Evan's wife, Tracey Ellery, was the co-founder of LookSmart and had overseen the development of what was widely regarded as the best subject index on the web. With previous experience in computer retailing, market research and publications development, Tracey was obviously a key player from the start.

Thornley had recruited Brian Cowley as vice-president of sales and distribution. Cowley had headed advertising sales for the Netscape website and brought directly relevant experience to the LookSmart challenge.

The chief operating officer was Martin Hosking, who was also a McKinsey alumnus. Like Evan and Tracey, Martin was from Melbourne where he had completed his undergraduate and MBA studies.

This was the team we would be backing. Thornley was the boss and he was the face to the external market. Articulate and intellectually vigorous, he preached the LookSmart story to any and every audience. My first experience of Evan's oratory powers was at a meeting in our George Street office in The Rocks, Sydney.

Paul Riley had badgered me to come to this meeting. 'At least say hello and have a brief meeting with Thornley, who is in Sydney today and on his way back to San Francisco,' Paul had insisted. Well, what was intended to be a fifteen-minute hello and goodbye became a fascinating hour and a half presentation about LookSmart, its problems and its prospects. Thornley rarely drew breath and made a lasting impression on all of us. He told us that he had at least six weeks' working capital because the company's cash burn was 'now only $400 000 a month'. Talk about life on the edge!

Which brings us to the NUMBERS.

When we were in discussion with the company during the last quarter of 1997, the actual daily page views generated by the LookSmart engine had begun to demonstrate rapid acceleration. From fewer than 250 000 daily page views in September, LookSmart enjoyed over one million in December 1997. These were projected to grow to eight million by December 1998 if the company delivered on its core proposition.

Of great interest to me were two other important operating numbers. The advertising revenue per visitor was already a high 13 cents compared with a competitor average of 4 cents. And because of its leveraged distribution strategy, the company had achieved these revenue results with a cost base equal to one third that of Lycos and one fifth that of most others.

Monthly losses of approximately $500 000 in December 1997 were projected to fall progressively towards break-even midway through calendar 1998, as advertising revenues responded to the positive direction in page-view usage. The company's balance sheet showed only six weeks' working capital remaining; shareholders' funds had fallen from just under $7 million to approximately $2 million.

The company wanted to raise US$4 million and was offering a 25.40 per cent shareholding for this amount, valuing the company in the range of US$10 million to US$16 million. When I think back to the difficulty I had in justifying this valuation to myself, it seems amazing that only twenty months later, in August 1999, Goldman Sachs priced the IPO on NASDAQ at US$12 per share—a capitalisation of almost US$1.3 billion. At the end of its debut trading on Friday, 20 August 1999, LookSmart was valued at US$1.7 billion or A$2.5 billion! This proved to be the highest IPO capitalisation of a technology company in the history of Australia. By October 1999 the company's share price had doubled again and the market capitalisation stood at an astounding A$5 billion.

Available benchmarks for valuations at the time of our initial investment were internet company trade sales and IPOs, which were priced at multiples ranging from ten times revenue to 45 times revenue. Annualising December 1997 monthly revenue of $250 000 valued the company at between $2.5 million and $12 million. On projected December 1998 revenue the company could be worth between $20 million and $100 million. If the investment market's interest in internet companies was sustained, we could see a prospect for making ten times our money if LookSmart delivered on its core proposition.

So we agreed with Paul that there ought to be a place somewhere in our portfolio for an investment in LookSmart. We decided it was best suited to our recently formed innovation fund, AMWIN, which was a partnership fund with the Walden International Investment Group of San Francisco and the Australian Government. We decided to invest US$1.5 million via AMWIN, provided that our Walden colleagues were happy and that not less than another US$1.5 million could be found from another investor.

There was little time left as LookSmart was scheduled to run out of cash within a matter of weeks. We therefore pushed the Walden Group to complete their due diligence rapidly. Walden's CEO is a nuclear physicist and a trusted friend of ours by the name of Lip-Bu Tan. Like AMIL's executive director, Su-Ming Wong, Lip-Bu is a Malaysian-born Chinese and has an outstanding record of success in the early-stage venturing business in the United States, Asia and Israel. One of his colleagues just happened to be a key player in organising the IPO of Yahoo!. This was Steve Eskenazi who, at the time of the Yahoo! IPO, was working for Morgan Stanley.

Steve was well placed to understand the valuation templates and to gauge market appetite. While he liked the LookSmart people and its story, it is fair to say that Steve was less than enthusiastic. He was concerned that LookSmart might be too late and too small to make the impact that it envisaged for itself. Nonetheless, Lip-Bu decided to back his new Australian partner's judgement and so the AMWIN participation was approved. Securing the balance of the monies proved to be more difficult.

We had hoped and expected that our friendly venture capital competitors Allen & Buckeridge would be our co-investor. Roger Allen and Roger Buckeridge became disenchanted with one aspect of the terms sheet and rejected the final position drawn in the sand by Evan Thornley and LookSmart's lawyers.

Notwithstanding this disappointment, we decided to go it alone and we remained optimistic that LookSmart's discussion with the big US cable group Cox Cable might soon lead to a co-investment by this strategic player. Management and we also considered Cox the likely trade buyer in the event that the stock markets for internet companies did not hold up long enough for us to succeed with a LookSmart IPO on NASDAQ. Such an IPO exit for us would be reliant on the dotcom boom continuing to run for another year or so. But just how serious were Cox likely to be and would they come on board before the cash ran out? As circumstance would have it, the CEO of Cox, Jimmy Robbins, was a long-time friend of mine, having been my roommate in our Harvard Business School days. Jimmy was a 193-centimetre, no-nonsense guy who had been in cable all his business life. 'Ferro,' he boomed over the phone, 'our guys really like this LookSmart thing and we'll be there despite Aussiemezz beating us to it!'

Indeed, Cox went on to provide the extra money to LookSmart and proved to be a strong and supportive shareholder. Especially sad for me was to see Jimmy subsequently lose his fight against brain cancer. This followed on the loss to cancer of my other HBS roommate, Perry Haines, then head of the largest meat packer in the world, Iowa Beef. Jimmy and Perry were both groomsmen at my wedding in Marion, Massachusetts, and two of the very best I have been privileged to know as close friends.

And so what happened with this LookSmart deal? My colleague, Paul Riley, is still smiling from ear to ear, if that is any clue.

Six months after AMWIN's initial investment of US$1.5 million, we followed up with an AMIT No. 2 investment of another US$3 million. The company aggressively pursued its commitment to a proprietary database, increasing the number of editors from 25 to 65. Accompanied by content and a style that proved especially attractive to female navigators, and a business model offering syndicated links on a co-badging basis, LookSmart was succeeding in consolidating a position in the top twenty websites worldwide.

We were delighted when the company recommitted its navigation service to exclude all pornographic and hate material. It was not only a morally sound position but also one that was important to women and to parents.

Perhaps the key decision in 1998 was whether to pay US$6 million to Netscape to be designated one of their premier search sites. We worked on this analysis, with Paul Riley supporting Evan in

LookSmart's board decision to make what was then a major capital expenditure decision. This move was to result in a rapid increase in traffic to LookSmart.

All of these developments were being successfully undertaken by Thornley and his team during 1998 and captured the very close attention of Microsoft. Towards the end of calendar 1998, Microsoft negotiated an access arrangement whereby it would license LookSmart's proprietary database of URLs (universal resource locators) for a fee of approximately US$80 million over five years. This was a non-exclusive licence and did not lock LookSmart into Microsoft.

This arrangement was consummated in the first quarter of 1999 and it was then clear to all that LookSmart was headed for an IPO.

LookSmart's board invited formal proposals from Goldman Sachs, Hambrecht & Quist, Morgan Stanley and Robertson Stephens. Once again we at Australian Mezzanine were able to provide valuable input to Evan Thornley in the IPO process. The managing director of Morgan Stanley in Sydney, David Kent, was a long-time acquaintance of ours. He introduced Paul Riley to Rex Golding, then visiting Sydney from the Menlo Park office of Morgan Stanley. Rex liked the LookSmart story and persuaded his colleague in the New York office, Mary Meeker, to meet Thornley. Meeker was regarded as something of an internet guru in investment banking circles and her endorsement was valuable to the IPO underwriting process. Morgan Stanley's interest and enthusiasm stirred similar emotions in others. Ultimately, the mandate was given to Goldman Sachs as lead underwriter, who indicated an IPO valuation of approximately US$1.2 to 1.5 billion.

While this selection process was going on, we decided to lay off some risk by selling our free warrants in LookSmart for approximately $8 million to the Gresham Media Fund. We did this not out of any concern for the company as such, but rather from our anxiety about the stock market generally and the internet company valuations specifically. The dotcom boom was beginning to look like a vulnerable bubble. Our creed over many years has been 'Never be too greedy'. Expressing this another way, a handsome book profit always takes on an especially welcome flavour when converted to cash. As a result, the numbers at the time of the IPO in August 1999 were as shown in Table 7.

A gain of between $95 million and $279 million on an outlay of $5.4 million in a period of less than 24 months is not too shabby! It was not until the six months post-IPO 'lock up' had passed, in March 2000, that we were free to trade the shares and realise an actual cash gain of $245 million ... 100 times our initial investment plus 15 times the follow-up investment.

Once again, timing emerges as highly important factor in these outcomes.

When the buttons were pressed by Goldman Sachs for Evan Thornley to commence the LookSmart roadshow in the first week of August 1999, market conditions looked propitious. Some internet stocks had shown a few wobbles, but overall the Dow Jones, the S&P100 and NASDAQ continued their stellar performances of the record 1999 year. Thornley marched off with his presentation kit on a tour that would take in London, Frankfurt, San Francisco, Los Angeles, Phoenix, Chicago, Boston and New York. As each day progressed, so the market grew more volatile and weaker. The issue was due to be priced on Friday, 13 August 1999 in New York, but that turned out to be the 'week from hell' for internet stocks. The first three days of that week witnessed significant falls in the leading internet companies, including AOL, Yahoo! and Amazon. Of 40 scheduled IPOs that week over 30 were withdrawn, including ours. The market then picked up again on Friday and we all held our breath over the weekend. If Monday the

Table 7: Financial outcomes, LookSmart

	At August 1999 IPO value (A$m)	At March 2000 exit value (A$m)
Initial investment	(2.2)	(2.2)
Follow-up investment	(3.2)	(3.2)
Sale of warrants	7.9	7.9
Current shareholding	92.2	245.0
Net gain to AMWIN and AMIT No. 2	**94.7**	**247.8**

sixteenth was strong, then just maybe the IPO could be reinstated in the week ending 20 August. Well, luck was with us and the demand for LookSmart's offering firmed up rapidly, enabling Goldman Sachs to price the IPO on Thursday and establish a listing on Friday the twentieth.

This day turned out to be one of amazing timing for Paul Riley. The critical board meeting of LookSmart directors to authorise the IPO and fix the pricing, attended by representatives of the underwriters, Goldman Sachs, was set for 6.30 a.m. on Friday, Sydney time. This happened to be exactly the time Paul was scheduled to attend the birth of the Rileys' first baby. Paul took the conference call in the hospital while his wife, Irene, was entering the delivery room. He rang me at 6.55 a.m., to report the good news, namely that 'both IPOs were on track'. Goldman Sachs had committed themselves to get the LookSmart IPO completed that day at US$12 per share and Irene was on target for the IPO (Irene & Paul Offspring) of a baby girl, Eden. Now a most intelligent thirteen-year-old, Eden is heading for a career in medical research and may one day have her own biotech IPO to boast about.

Of course, many others had been eagerly awaiting LookSmart's market debut. Every LookSmart employee had a stake. About six weeks after the IPO I visited Evan Thornley, who showed me around the five buildings that LookSmart then sprawled through in the South of Market area of San Francisco. Once a garment and mixed manufacturing precinct, this area was then a hotbed of internet startups occupying converted warehouses and employing thousands of young people in occupations that had not existed two years before.

Hundreds of these young graduates sat at their screens researching and editing websites and databases for LookSmart. I was struck by the quiet and professional focus of these people, few of whom even met my gaze as we strolled by. Evan asked me how it could possibly be otherwise when every single person on the LookSmart payroll had stock and/or stock options in the company. 'No better way to make sure people are motivated and focused, and likely to stay with you,' Evan remarked.

When Evan was called off to another meeting, his assistant Teresa wanted to know what I thought of the about-to-break US$35 million

LookSmart television campaign. She ran the video featuring the Beatles song 'Help!' and encouraging family viewers to solve their diverse information needs through LookSmart. 'Help!' was a my-generation hit and the commercial looked perfect to me. But why, I asked, was the song delivered by a female rather than by the Beatles? A reasonable question given that the company had paid US$3 million for the rights, Teresa reminded me that LookSmart was the first-choice search engine for a majority of female users in the United States and the company intended to entrench this support.

By 2000, LookSmart was well underway with its bold adventure to establish its brand and accelerate the growth in numbers of users. The only Australian company that had established any sort of internet brand position internationally at that time, it has since lost its mojo and effectively been eclipsed by the more innovative and universal search models like Google.

Nonetheless, there ought to be some worthwhile lessons from such a happy outcome for us as a successful early investor, ones which might lead us to the next LookSmart deal.

Lesson one: *The venture capitalist needs to think globally when it comes to exit time.* If you have a business that is global, in terms of its markets and its competitiveness, then you must think of the capital markets in a similarly global context. It is not un-Australian to arrange an Australian company's IPO offshore. Upon listing on NASDAQ, LookSmart had a market capitalisation of A$5 billion and an additional $150 million in the bank. It established new high-water marks in the history of Australian technology companies by these achievements. Such numbers would not have been achievable from the local markets.

There is a fair amount of fuzzy thinking on this issue in Canberra and elsewhere. The Australian fear of losing technology offshore is understandable, given our nation's long history of outstanding inventiveness but poor commercialisation.

However, the surest way for us to fritter away the benefits of Australian innovation would be to deny Australian entrepreneurs access to the deepest and best-priced capital markets. Companies that are unable or unwilling to exploit their innovations widely and rapidly are likely to be swamped in the marketplace or by technological obsolescence or both.

Converting intellectual property into bottom-line outcomes is more about timing and the dominance of a niche marketplace than it is about patents and lawsuits. The successes of Australian companies like Cochlear, the 'bionic' ear implant business, and ResMed, the sleep apnea treatment business, have obviously been assisted by the original breakthrough research done by Graeme Clark and Colin O'Sullivan respectively. Their science and the patents arising from it formed technology platforms for these great companies. But it was the pioneering marketing work done by Paul Trainor and Michael Hirshorn that established Cochlear's sustained leadership position in the United States, Japanese and European markets. And the energetic, even frenetic, marketing accomplished by Dr Peter Farrell is what established ResMed in its leading position in the sleep disorder markets of North America.

While Cochlear successfully arranged its IPO in Australia and enjoys strong investor support, ResMed chose to IPO on NASDAQ, where the appetite among investors for this type of company was so much stronger. Farrell still runs ResMed, the Australian production plant has been expanded to cope with bigger export volumes, the number of Australian employees has increased and, importantly, the sustainability of the company's market position has been enhanced.

'Born global' high-technology businesses, especially internet ones like LookSmart, are sporadically well supported by NASDAQ. Ideally, an Australian company should have a significant proportion (probably not less than half) of its revenues derived in US markets and should be prepared to relocate its CEO and head office to the States should it seek a North American public listing. This is a prerequisite for the considerable information flow expected by US analysts and for achieving necessary investor interest and support in that market.

It will not always be the IPO markets in North America that offer the best outcome to Australians. Back in 1995, as noted in the previous case study, we arranged the IPO of the Asian subsidiary of Datacraft Limited. We were forced to look outside Australia as the local market had lost interest in the listed parent company. The US market was not really suitable since Datacraft's US activities were only nominal. Therefore we turned to Hong Kong and Singapore as alternatives.

Often the Australian stock markets will be the *right* IPO solution, as they were for other portfolio companies of ours such as Cuppa Cup Vineyards and Austal Ships. But whether or not this is the case, at all times the venture capitalist must think globally when it comes to exit time.

Lesson two: *Don't be greedy!* Unlike entrepreneurs' budgets, things don't always go up. Markets don't always stay in bull cycles and not all surprises are happy ones. In short, to use a current American technical phrase, shit happens.

At AMIL we have always adopted the approach of leaving something on the table for the next investor and of taking some profits on the 'way up'. We have seen many examples over the years where fortunes have been made and lost, where markets have collapsed more quickly than they rose and where extraneous events have devastated values in spite of blameless and dedicated performance by management teams.

When the opportunity presented itself in 1999 for us to sell our free warrants in LookSmart and bag an $8 million cash profit, we took it. This decision retrieved our total capital outlays twice over and left us still holding all of our shareholding in the company.

More importantly, we later made the right decision to sell all of our LookSmart shareholding immediately our six months IPO escrow period lapsed. It was just a few weeks later in March 2000 that the dotcom boom came to an end with the crash of technology stocks worldwide.

Lesson three: Again, *timing is more important than analysis.* As sound as our analysis of the LookSmart opportunity and core proposition was (and I think Paul Riley will reluctantly agree), we never really expected the interest in internet companies to explode in the way it did. When we committed to LookSmart we thought our upside could be ten times our investment, if everything went to plan. As it happened, we realised more than 100 times on our initial $2 million investment.

Since those heady days twelve years ago, LookSmart has struggled to find its place in the internet search space. Describing itself today as a provider of 'search advertising network solutions', LookSmart's sharemarket value is approximately $13 million, somewhat shy of its $5 billion debut on NASDAQ.

The venture capitalist who does not admit to luck playing a significant part in his successful deals is either a true genius or deluding himself. How many true geniuses do you know?

Of course, we had looked at several internet investment opportunities prior to LookSmart. We had built up a certain level of understanding and confidence before we took the plunge. This experience and sensible analysis helped us to avoid some internet lemons, but I have no doubt that timing and luck will be a key to finding the next LookSmart.

The twenty most important lessons—so far

What follows is a summary of the twenty major lessons I have learned from the various investment adventures described in Part One. On balance, I have probably learned more from the disappointing investments than from the successful ones. Perhaps that mirrors life generally: you learn quickly from your bruises or otherwise get very badly hurt. The lessons as set out here are not intended to reflect any order of priority.

1. *Leopards don't often change their spots.* The idiosyncrasies of headstrong entrepreneurs invariably become more pronounced over the years. Success confirms their habits and foibles; failure seems to do likewise. Don't assume that your venture capitalist cheque book or personal charms will fundamentally change any behavioural patterns or 'spots' of the CEO.

2. *High-profile shareholders/partners do not by themselves make a deal successful.* Prestigious and credible names on the share register may bring comfort to lenders or suppliers, but they often have their own agendas and their own core business pursuits that, over time, diverge from those of your investee company. This

divergence or lack of interest can spell big trouble for the investee company, especially in times when the going gets tough.

3. *A venture capitalist's financial returns are often not directly correlated to the distance between his office and the investee's head office.* This has been my experience with many of our most profitable investee companies situated far away from our Sydney offices—in Perth, Melbourne and San Francisco. And our worst investees have been as close as a block away in Sydney and as far away as Fiji. I decided to include this lesson in the list because the myth has grown up that venture capitalists only like to invest in companies within 45 minutes driving time.

4. *Beware of solutions looking for problems; the marketplace is more important than the science.* The challenge for early-stage investors in new technologies and processes is to be able to identify the strength and timing of actual commercial demand for the solutions that these new things purport to offer. It can be very expensive to be years ahead of the market.

5. *Have the courage to know when to stop flogging a dead horse.* I use the word 'courage' because it can be all too tempting to chase a failing deal with more bad money. It can be very hard for you to accept the investment for what it is, a failure. On the one hand, the venture capitalist should not give up on an investment merely because of temporary setbacks; but, on the other hand, he or she must learn to judge when enough is enough. Most people can only learn this on the job, not from reading books like this one.

6. *Never let a pathological optimist be the CEO.* The entrepreneur who genuinely deludes him or herself is ultimately more dangerous than the one who actually knows the truth but sets out to delude you.

7. *High-quality people get you high-quality outcomes*, especially if they have their own money on the line. Although this sounds trite, it is a recurring key lesson. If a high-quality and experienced management team is in place, be prepared to pay full price for the deal. If there's a low-quality and inexperienced team, chances are that no price will prove to be cheap.

8. *Critical analysis of the venture's core proposition is what distinguishes a sensible 'risk investment' from a 'punt'.* The time and effort you expend in really getting to grips with the fundamental business proposition, with working out whether the business really does have a sustainable competitive position, will be rewarded over time. You will still have the occasional failure, but generally you will produce excellent results for your investors.

9. Having said that, the good deals don't stay on the table for long in what has become a very competitive venture capital market. Ultimately, *timing is more important than analysis.* It would have been easy for us to develop analysis paralysis and never make an internet investment. But we did plunge in to the rapid and wildly flowing internet river. Here, as elsewhere, timing and luck played a very large part.

10. *Build future performance adjustments into your deal structures.* If you do this, your ultimate equity entitlement in a venture will depend on the venture's future performance, not on its past glories or on its wonderful forecasts.

11. *If the time comes when you need to fire the CEO (or some other key executive) of an investee company, don't procrastinate.* Every time I finally decided that a key executive was not right for the job, I took too long to make the change. Having made the change, I invariably looked back and asked, 'Why didn't we insist on that sooner?'

12. *An independent director usually makes a better chairperson than the entrepreneur CEO.* This lesson has been most pronounced in situations where the enterprise is not performing well. When the respective interests of external shareholders, employee shareholders and lenders diverge, the need for an independent chairperson becomes greatest.

13. *Prior to making an investment, be confident that you have no fewer than two alternative exit tracks.* As a venture capital investor you are usually a minority shareholder in an unlisted company, and without pre-agreed exit timetables and plans you can easily find yourself 'locked in' with nowhere to go.

14. *The opportunity for the venture capitalist to really add value is directly proportional to how poorly the investee company is performing.* Even when things are going to plan, the venture capitalist can usually still add value in the boardroom and elsewhere. A strong and organised management team can leverage off fresh ideas and inputs; but in the main such a team will achieve the business plan anyway. It is really when things go wrong that the venture capitalist has a big opportunity to help and to salvage value.

15. *Patience is still a virtue.* Here I'm actually referring essentially to the pre-investment period. Obviously, patience can prove a virtue *after* you have made an investment, too, although my experience is that a board and a management team that doesn't exhibit a constant sense of urgency is unlikely to produce above average results. But patience is crucial with respect to the discipline of *not* investing, of being able to say no, and of waiting for the right opportunities to come along.

16. *A well-structured shareholders' agreement never needs to come out of your desk.* A venture capitalist can do much to protect his or her minority status with a sensibly written shareholders' agreement. Such an agreement can also avoid unnecessary disputation and wasted energy for all parties if it deals with conflict resolution, exit timetables and procedure, hiring/firing of key executives, capital expenditure limits and other such key business issues.

17. *Don't be greedy!* You will never go broke leaving something on the table for the next guy; you will come a cropper one day if you try to catch the peak of the market every time you exit a deal. And if you try to price your companies' IPOs too high, the investors won't be there for the next one.

18. *Think globally, not parochially, when it comes to exit time.* Taking a company to an IPO offshore should not be regarded as un-Australian. By arranging access for the company to the most suitable capital markets, onshore or offshore, the venture capitalist will minimise the company's cost of capital while maximising shareholder values. Squandering or delaying the

commercial exploitation of Australian inventiveness is what must be avoided in the national interest.

19. *With acquisitions, one plus one sometimes equals less than two.* Assumptions about economies of scale, about the benefits from horizontal or vertical integration, about dividends from technology transfer, sometimes remain just that—assumptions. Frequently, I have seen the enthusiasm for growth by acquisition run ahead of thorough analysis. This results, more often than not, in damage to the offer or a diluting of the very strength of the core proposition that attracted you in the first place.

20. *Never make an investment without first having an explicit agreement with the investee company's owners about the exit process and timetable.* Getting out can be a lot harder than getting in. When the time is appropriate to sell, venture capitalists need to be able to move efficiently and in harmony with others involved. Entrepreneurs and founders often, and understandably, fall in love with their companies; their time horizons may shift and diverge significantly from those of the venture capitalists.

PART TWO:

Private equity, good and bad

It is late afternoon in May and Lea and I are relaxing as we chug through the Cape Cod Canal on Bob Stone's magnificent 68-foot racing ketch *Arcadia*, en route from Buzzards Bay in Massachusetts to Penobscot Bay in Maine.

Bob Stone, a much-loved uncle of Lea's, had been commodore of the New York Yacht Club (NYYC) at the time when the precocious America's Cup challenge by Alan Bond lifted the Auld Mug from its God-given place in NYYC's Manhattan quarters. Down to the last in a seven-race series it was a David and Goliath contest, a low-budget but high-technology challenge from those 'bloody Aussies' against the arrogance and might of the NYYC representing the United States of America.

Ben Lexcen, the mercurial designer of Australia's innovative winged-keel yacht, was angered by what he saw as 'spoilsport' behaviour by many in the NYYC camp. Half-way through the series, when asked what he would do with the cup were Australia to win it, Ben said he would run over it with his car and flatten it!

It was Commodore Bob Stone who personally decided to present Ben Lexcen with an old dented Plymouth hub cap during the award ceremony. In one amusing but gracious gesture, Bob almost single-handedly restored the great camaraderie between these two wonderful sailing teams. For this, Australian skipper John Bertrand was and remains a great fan of Bob.

Bob's crew for our passage up the coast tonight to Maine included his boat captain, Skip, and a couple of old sailing buddies, George and Johnny. Like Bob, these guys were in their mid- to late seventies. And like Bob, they loved their Mount Gay Rum and Coke. Indeed the yacht was fitted with a special hand pump which delivered rum from a below-decks tank directly into the cockpit, not something I had seen before or since.

By the time we were off Boston the cocktails were flowing. The night was clear and the sky was silvered by a completely full moon. With a full jib and both mainsails up, we had been making about 7 knots in a variable 15-knot breeze. I had been at the helm for some hours and retired down below for a kip, when at around 1 a.m. I was awakened by a violent lurch to starboard followed by a loud explosion. The boat had suffered an unintentional jibe, and Skip ordered me to take the helm while he attempted to disengage the hydraulic vang. The vang is a means of controlling the boom's position, laterally and vertically, relative to the deck. When *Arcadia* lurched suddenly during the accidental jibe, the vang was snapped by the force of the boom's weight.

The wind had strengthened to 25 or 30 knots and it seemed the Mount Gay had distracted the crew somewhat. Johnny, thrown clear across the cockpit, had suffered several broken ribs, but the only real discomfort for Bobby and George was they had both lost their mugs overboard. Skip jerry-rigged the vang and Lea assisted the wounded Johnny to his bunk.

We sailed on through the night and entered Penobscot Bay at first light in a gossamer mist. We were ghosting along in a mild breeze, dodging literally hundreds of brightly coloured lobster pots; one of these around a propeller or rudder would end this exciting outing so we were all very attentive. By 9 a.m. we had arrived at Bob's favourite Maine harbour, the quintessential lobster fisherman's Christmas Cove.

It was via the fax in the office of Christmas Cove's harbourside lobster restaurant that I sent my investment memo recommending CHAMP acquire a majority interest in Austar from John Malone's Liberty group. I was amazed to learn from the restauranteur that John Malone's holiday home was just up the road in Christmas Cove! Little did I know then that Malone's agreement to partner with CHAMP would lead to one of the most successful buy-outs in the history of Australian PE. This is described in Part Two.

Introduction

Since the publication of *Nothing Ventured, Nothing Gained* in 2000, private investing has been described in two broad categories: venture capital (VC) and private equity (PE). In both these areas of activity, investors are usually involved in unlisted equities. The VC investor is usually providing new risk equity capital at the start-up or early stage of development and expansion of a business enterprise. These are the subject of Part One of this book.

The PE investor is usually providing capital with which to acquire ownership of a reasonably mature business enterprise from current owners. Such a PE investor will often team up with the existing management team in the acquisition process, hence the term 'management buy-out' (MBO).

Risk equity capital 'ventured' by wealthy individual investors provided the early foundations of this exciting and growth-orientated sector. The strong returns achieved by these investors inevitably lead to the corporatising and institutionalising of the VC and PE business. Specialist managers emerged to raise and manage pooled funds provided by institutional investors, opening up the private equity markets to investors including pension funds, endowment funds, insurance and banking companies.

The specialist PE fund managers emerged in the United States during the 1960s. I was intrigued to study this innovation in capital markets while a student at the Harvard Business School from 1968 to 1970. Virtually all of the US venture capital and private equity managers were established as general partnerships (GPs), which managed funds provided by their investors, who were referred to as limited liability partners (LPs).

Since this GP/LP structure, with its 'see-through' tax structure, has never been part of the national taxation Acts of Australia, other corporate and unit trust structures have characterised the Australian PE management business. In 1970 I began Australia's first PE business, International Venture Corporation Pty Ltd, as a limited liability private company—that is, investors and the management were all in the same single limited liability structure. In those days, investments made and held for long-term gain (greater than twelve months was the guideline) enjoyed capital gains tax treatment.

Also starting in 1970 Joe Skrzynski was cutting his teeth in venture, expansion capital and buy out activities through Finance Facilities Pty Ltd. This was the non-real estate arm of the then high-profile Sydney property developer and entrepreneur Sir Paul Strasser. Joe's early experiences and successes included the very first business in licensed taverns, the expansion of a business that developed the first safety car seats for babies and a management buy-in through the public to private transaction of Ford Sherrington Ltd.

In 1987 Joe Skrzynski and I teamed up to form a VC and PE funds management company, Australian Mezzanine Investments Pty Ltd (AMIL), and raised Australia's first institutionally subscribed PE fund in a unit trust structure. The investors held their interest through units in the trust, and the manager was our separate private company that managed the trust.

It was not until 1998 that we believed a case existed for us to establish a dedicated buy-out fund in Australia. We would need to convince investors that the Australian capital markets were ready for such a product. We were able to describe the small buy-out transactions we had completed in the portfolios of our three prior funds, the AMIT Nos 1, 2, and 3 funds. We also referenced the efforts of the disbanded

Byvest Group which had completed a number of buy-outs during the earlier part of the 1990s. And of course we would be able to argue that a significantly successful buy-out market had already developed in the United States and the United Kingdom, so why not Australia.

Nonetheless it did require an article of faith on the part of Australian investors. We asked them to accept that if we could establish a supply—that is, hang up the shingle saying we have money for buy-outs—we could move the Australian market. We hypothesised that we could create a market demand once we demonstrated there was indeed a capital supply. Since the buy-out transactions would be considerably larger than the investments we had arranged for the AMIL funds, we needed to convince potential investors we had the requisite experience for such a step up. And there was still the question of whether the Australian banks would be prepared to provide the levels of debt funding necessary in the capital structures of MBO transactions.

CHAMP is born

The 'article of faith' to which I refer above, that establishing a supply of PE in Australia would indeed create a demand for MBOs, was a lot for us to ask of investors. And this time we knew we needed offshore investors in addition to our local institutions, since we would require a fund of not less than $500 million if our supply-side theory was to be credible in the marketplace.

We had begun to consider whether an alliance with a like-minded North American buy-out firm might strengthen our credibility with, and access to, offshore investors, when serendipity played its timely part. This arrived in the form of a call to me from Howard Morgan, then a young VP in the New York-based buy-out shop Castle Harlan, Inc. (CHI). Howard and Leonard Harlan had for some time been scouting out opportunities for expanding their buy-out business into Asia. Howard had been encouraged to talk to me through one of his younger CHI colleagues, Ben Sebel, an Australian recently graduated from the Harvard Business School. Prior to heading off for the business school, Ben had been 'drafted' by his then employer, Deloitte Tohmatsu, to serve as an executive assistant to the former premier of New South Wales, Nick Greiner, when he became chairman of

Deloitte's advisory board in Australia. Nick and I were close personal friends having both been economics students at the University of Sydney and MBAs in the same class of 1970 at the Harvard Business School.

In Part One I described the fearless and creative role played by Nick as chairman of one of our early 1990s investments in the education sector, Education and Training Australia (ETA). During those years, in his role as a young research assistant to Nick, Ben Sebel provided the analysis and research to make Nick look good when he turned up to chair the ETA board meetings. Ever courteous, smart, and eager to learn, Sebel had made a favourable impression on those of us working on the ETA deal.

And so it was I agreed to take a meeting with Howard Morgan, the stoutly structured, quintessentially positive, Republican American executive. His voice is one that can be heard across a crowded room; indeed my colleagues sometimes joke that Howard does not need any speakerphone when on our conference calls with New York. CHI was formed by John Castle and Leonard Harlan in 1987, the same year in which Joe and I had commenced AMIL. Castle was a pioneer in the VC sector of the United States and had risen through the rough and tumble of North American investment banking to become CEO of the NYC-based Donaldson, Lufkin and Jenrette (aka DLJ). John then became chairman of the Equitable Life Insurance Company when it acquired DLJ.

Harlan had also worked at DLJ when he and Castle first met. Now a very young 70-plus, he is a tireless and consummate networker. Nurturing an eclectic and wide network of friends and contacts around the globe, Leonard and his Harvard MBA wife Fleur maintain a travel schedule that would daunt even the most enthusiastic 20-year-old 'frequent flyer'.

Joe and I enjoyed many discussions with John, Leonard and Howard and concluded that partnering 50–50 with CHI in our PE management company would achieve at least four important benefits for the development of our business, and indeed the sector in Australia:

1. Accelerate our ability to attract offshore investors, especially existing LPs in CHI funds, to come to Australia. In spite of our successful investment record with our successive AMIL funds over more than ten years in Australia, we had been unable to convince North American investors to chance their arm in Australia. We were too far away, or too small scale, or in the wrong time zone, pioneering a buy-out concept that maybe Australia wasn't yet ready for, and so on.

   The partnership with CHI enabled us to break down these barriers and some of CHI's blue-chip limited partners became CHAMP I fund investors—for example, Verizon, MetLife, Getty and New England Life, among others.

2. Provide a platform for work experience exchange of our younger executives—that is, from Sydney to NYC and vice versa. This would lead to a transfer of intellectual property and experiences for the benefit of all concerned. It would assist us in recruiting, monitoring and keeping the best young talent.

   Indeed, in the twelve years since 2000, several of our Australian executives have completed exchange programs, varying from nine months to two years in length, in the New York office. And a number of CHI executives have also spent time in our Sydney office, including a two-year stint by Howard Morgan at the start of our partnership with CHI in 2000.

   This program has proved to be a resounding success, enabling us to offer members of our team a much richer and broader exposure to the world of PE. There has never been a gap in the 'waiting list' for this exchange program, probably good evidence for continuing it.

3. Provide the opportunity for a wider due diligence capability, observing precedents and differences in US and Australian business models and outcomes. Also we hoped that an occasional deal origination would occur—for example, early signalling by a US corporation of its intention to sell an Australian subsidiary.

4. Provide a cross-border set of opportunities and skills not available to our mid-market PE competitors. In this context I refer

you to the wonderfully successful portfolio company example of Austar in the CHAMP I fund, and United Malt Holdings and Study Group International in the CHAMP II fund. All three of these deals produced better than five times returns, and all of them involved assets, earnings and activities in Australia and the United States.

There were of course considerations, other than those four listed above, important to Joe and me, and important to Leonard Harlan and his founder partner John Castle. We shared 'owner-driver' cultures, we were seeking the internationalising of our firms, and we shared a passionate belief in the future for PE in Australasian markets. And so the CHAMP management company began as the successor company to AMIL. CHAMP would perform the GP management role for LP investors in the initial CHAMP buy-out fund.

Even with all of the above benefits in the partnership with CHI, we faced a daunting challenge. The offshore investors all wanted to see significant participation in the pioneering CHAMP I buy-out fund by Australian institutions. They did not want to be the 'bunnies'; any offshore commitments would be conditional on a demonstration of significant 'skin in the game' by Australians.

Interestingly, this became a two-way requirement. Several of our Australian supporters also wanted to see 'belief' in the management buy-out (MBO) investment model demonstrated by some experienced and sophisticated offshore MBO investors. But more about that later in the fundraising section.

Early support from the internationally leading fund of funds investor HabourVest proved to be something of a tipping point in this context. Indeed it can fairly be said that HarbourVest, guided by its senior partner in Hong Kong Philip Bilden, led the way for offshore investors into the Australian PE sector from 2000 onwards.

Now, ten or so years on from the publication of the first edition of *Nothing Ventured, Nothing Gained*, I often re-read the twenty lessons arising from my first 30 years in venture capital and small business investing. They all resonate to this day, and yet I have an additional fifteen lessons from a subsequent decade of private equity buy-out investing that I have summarised at the end of this part. Some of them overlap or at least reinforce the previous twenty, and I re-emphasise that these are lessons for me, some of which I hope will be of interest and relevance to you.

I have now been full time in the VC and PE business for close to 42 years. I have loved almost every minute of it and continue to do so. Why? Because it has involved me in an exciting diversity of industries and entrepreneurs. It has served up spills and thrills, to be sure, but net-net also an incredible set of growth stories in terms of new products and services, and increases in employees, earnings, export and taxes. It has also provided excellent returns for our investors. There is nothing else in the capital markets that comes close to the vitality, flexibility, efficacy, imagination and fun of the PE business. That's why!

More deals that went badly wrong

Sheridan Sheets

A bed linen manufacturer, Sheridan was a division of the publicly listed conglomerate Pacific Dunlop. Pacific Dunlop's activities ranged from batteries to food products, rubber, textiles and many others. Conglomerates had proven to be a viable business model in the 1960s and 1970s. Given a small market economy such as Australia, especially one so heavily protected against imports by tariffs, it made sense to aggregate diverse business operations where centralised management and administration might offer cost savings and other skills advantages.

As trade protection barriers began to be dismantled, this conglomerate business model was under pressure by the early 1980s. Pacific Dunlop withstood the onslaught of free markets longer than most; it was in many ways the last man standing in this proud and grand Melbourne-based business and political seat of postwar Australian society.

I was a great admirer of the Pacific Dunlop chairman, Sir Leslie Froggatt. I got to know him a little during my time as chairman of Austrade when Sir Leslie served pro bono on that board. Sir Leslie, 25 years my senior and considerably wiser and more experienced, was ever artful in convincing you that his bad idea, just ever so slightly modified, became your very good idea.

I attended one of Sir Leslie's last public-speaking events. It was a black tie affair and his after-dinner speech recounted one of the most enjoyable aspects of simultaneously being chairman of Pacific Dunlop Limited and the Argyle Diamond Mine company. He said this privilege provided him the opportunity to inform his lady friends that he always carried a condom in one pocket and a diamond in the other!

In 1986, the successful textile entrepreneurs Brender and Moss acquired the Sheridan business from Pacific Dunlop and the ACTIL sheets business from Entrade Corp, and merged all this with their company, Textile Industries of Australia. In 1993 these merged entities were subsequently sold to a US owner, Mr Brook Johnson.

Brook was a flamboyant American entrepreneur who had enjoyed some success in the east coast textiles industry of the United States where others had failed and more were soon to succumb. He had appointed one of his US executives, codenamed Manfred Moon, to run what had become his struggling Australian enterprise.

It was to be one of the first projects at CHAMP we investigated, and it was indeed the first investment completed by the CHAMP buy-out funds. We were among a small number of interested buyers invited by Brook Johnson to make an offer to acquire all of the Sheridan company.

By the year 2000 Sheridan still held the number-one brand recognition among Australian households for high-quality bed linen, the highest unaided brand recall in its category. Sheridan was a manufacturer selling into three segments: wholesale, retail and commercial. It sold its branded products—Sheridan, ACTIL and Carrington—at different price points in wholesale and retail. In the commercial segment it sold to end users in the hospitality, government and institutional markets under the ACTIL brand. The company also exported to the US, UK and Asian markets.

The bulk of the company's physical assets, operations and people were tied up in its substantial manufacturing facilities in Hobart and Adelaide. In Hobart, the company operated a fabric-printing plant. In Adelaide, the company had full line manufacturing, from weaving, to dyeing, printing, finishing, cutting and sewing. The business employed 1018 people in these operations.

But hey, why would you think you could make money out of such an old-line manufacturing model as this?

Well, our CORE PROPOSITION for this acquisition was as follows: 'An opportunity to acquire an iconic Australian brand company at a distressed price, to implement a radical change in its business model from a high-cost manufacturing one to that of a fast-moving consumer goods design and marketing one, sourcing its finished products offshore.'

The key entry and exit NUMBERS were as follows in Table 8.

As you can see, we lost all of our equity. So what went wrong?

It was on the KEY PEOPLE side where we made our first big mistake: we backed the incumbent CEO. Although he had presided over the manufacturing-driven model, we accepted that this had been a template delivered by his entrepreneur proprietor who had succeeded with niche textile manufacturing operations in the States. Manfred 'got it' that just because you had a strong brand didn't mean that the production manager could dictate to the sales team what product would be available, in which colours, and when. He 'got it' that production costs in Pakistan and China were less than 33 per cent those of Tasmania and South Australia. So he clearly understood that the business faced both a threat and an opportunity.

However, understanding and indeed articulating an intellectual construct is one thing; knowing how to act on it is another. Manfred was a Carolina mill manufacturer, 'dyed in the wool', as the expression goes. He was not able to be rewired for the urgent and difficult transition of the company. We simply backed the wrong guy!

To make matters worse, we could not understand the dysfunction in the sales and marketing team. It then came to light that Manfred had

Table 8: Sheridan Sheets entry and exit numbers

	Entry value (Nov 2000) ($m)		Exit value (Sept 2005) ($m)
Enterprise value	131.0	Enterprise value	60.0
Equity in	64.1	Equity out	0.0
Revenue at entry	189.4	Revenue at exit	168.8
EBITDA at entry	**20.2**	**EBITDA at exit**	**11.2**

over-promoted a young lady as head of sales with whom he was having an affair. Even in this company, 'between the sheets' behaviour at the top was unlikely to promote best-practice benchmarks.

Our second big mistake was a miscalculation of how much time we had to transition the business to a new model. We thought we had at least five years within which to complete an orderly shift from Australian manufacturing to offshore supply. As it emerged, and with the benefits of hindsight, we probably had less than twelve months.

China had been exporting bed linen into Australia since the early 1990s, but the products were of low quality for the most part. China's principal focus had been on high-volume, low-price products for the massive North American market. Sheridan was all about high-quality, high-margin products; although we knew China would ultimately be able to supply such quality, we underestimated just how soon it could and would. And we reckoned that even when China did move into smaller run, higher quality supply, it would require some time to convince Australian customers to sleep between Chinese sheets rather than Australian ones. Indeed, one of the reasons for our hope that we had five years to transition was our fear that it would be a difficult education/marketing exercise to convince our customers to accept Sheridan sheets, made in China.

Another fashion nuance coincided with this onslaught from China. At the very time CHAMP acquired Sheridan, the fashion began to move away from printed sheets, where we were a clear number-one, to more simple patterns and textured sheets. Our asset base was geared to printed sheets and we had basically missed this fashion shift in our due diligence.

Sheridan needed to become a Nike with a comprehensive outsourcing production model and an in-house commitment to first-in-class marketing. Its major asset was its name and its customer base, not its high-cost manufacturing plant and equipment. And the customer demands for fashion and quality at a price were moving so rapidly that the company had months, not years, to re-invent itself.

To be fair, we did move with alacrity and high energy once we understood the urgency of the situation. The closure of the facilities in Hobart and Adelaide was a difficult and agonising task for senior management of Sheridan and CHAMP. It was worse for the employees and their unions, men and women who grew up in the textiles manufacturing sector and whose families depended on its viability. Through no real fault of their own, these Australian plants could no longer compete. We had initially assumed a five-year phase-down period during which redundancies and outplacement of employees could be achieved in a more orderly manner. This was not to be, but at least the sale of real estate assets funded the full redundancy obligations to all employees.

The closing of facilities had to be synchronised with the run-down of inventories and the sourcing of alternative supplies from sixteen offshore mills in Pakistan and China. As Joe Skrzynski said to me one day, 'If you say it quickly and wave your arms around, it all looks pretty simple, really.' Of course it was a very complex logistics exercise: time and distance from market, language and culture were just a few of the challenges for quality control in these new supply lines. Let me give you one ripper of an example.

Our purchasing agent, Li and Fung in Hong Kong, achieved high standards of quality control on thread count, colour, sizing and so on. One basic check on volumes was measuring the weight of containers. It took us several months of failed reconciliations from one Pakistan mill before we discovered fake bottoms in their containers that were filled with gravel! The quality was right, and so was the aggregate weight . . .

An interesting postscript on this offshore sourcing was the almost instant acceptance of the 'made in China' label by the end customers of Sheridan.

All of this took more time and money. We had to inject an additional $16 million of equity to placate the banks. We parted company with Manfred and invited old hand and good friend of CHAMP Ken Terry to step in as executive chair while we searched for a new CEO. Ken had diverse commercial experience, most notably as the successful CEO of Carrier air conditioning in this part of the world. He steadied things until we appointed Peter Sitch as the new CEO. Peter had the sales and marketing background appropriate for the new Sheridan business model, having previously run the marketing side for a similar business that supplied pillows and pillowslips to the same customer channels. Peter made a fair fist of a tough job but in a three-year period was unable to achieve a turnaround. The company continued to trip its banking covenants, so while the banking syndicate recognised CHAMP's efforts to re-invent the company it agreed with us that it was time to find a new owner.

The exit
We did not have a long list of possible buyers for the business, but there was one 'natural owner' in the form of Pacific Brands. This company had itself just been through a very successful phase of ownership by another private equity group. CVC had purchased the business when it was a division of the struggling publicly listed company Pacific Dunlop (also the former owner of Sheridan). After a period of refocusing on its core strength of branded products retailing, the business completed a successful IPO in 2004 as Pacific Brands.

The company distributed a broad range of iconic Australian consumer brands such as King Gee work clothes and Bonds singlets and underwear. Sheridan sheets was a wonderful fit: a brand leader sold into the same retail channels, it offered immediate and obvious synergies and economies of scale for Pacific Brands.

To cut a long and tough story short, we sold the Sheridan business for half what we paid for it. But in doing so we were able to ensure that all of the trade suppliers and employees came out whole, which was not only reputationally important for CHAMP but also emotionally so. This was also an outcome only possible because of the constructive engagement by the banking syndicate, headed by Westpac.

Lesson one: *The strength and good sense of the core proposition may lure you into underestimating and even rationalising how much time you have*, especially when it is all about changing the fundamental operations of the company.

Lesson two: *Many executives can accept the need for fundamental and paradigmal change, but few have the courage, passion and tenacity needed* *to implement such change in a timely manner.* In this case CHAMP's assessment of senior managers' ability to make fundamental change was naïve. And our expectations of the incumbent CEO may have even been unreasonable. To expect a 'dyed in the wool' manufacturer to implement a product outsourcing/marketing-driven turnaround, in rapid fire time, was at best naïve and perhaps unfair.

Australian Discount Retail

Australian Discount Retail (ADR) was the name of the holding company formed by CHAMP and Catalyst Private Equity to acquire and merge two competing discount store businesses. One of these was part of the Millers Retail group, a division comprising several hundred Go-Lo, Crazy Clark's, and Chickenfeed stores; the other was a New Zealand discounter called The Warehouse.

We chose to partner with our friends at Catalyst as they had previous retail successes under their belt, including the Just Jeans retail business. The chairman of Just Jeans, Jonathan Pinshaw, agreed to become chairman of ADR, bringing his history of successful experience with retailers such as OPSM and Freedom Furniture. Catalyst partner Trent Peterson was known and liked by us, and he joined the ADR board alongside CHAMP project director David Jones.

Prior to this consolidation by CHAMP and Catalyst, the separate discount businesses were fierce competitors and by 2004 were all struggling to stay afloat.

So why did we think there was a good opportunity here? What was the CORE PROPOSITION? We examined the success experienced by the leading operations in this discount retail sector in the United States, often referred to as the dollar-store business. There the sector had established steady growth and resilience through economic cycles; to some extent these dollar-store operators benefited in tougher economic times as consumers focused on low price.

One of CHAMP's senior executives, David Jones, had seen up close the success of another discount store operator, The Reject Shop (TRS).

Indeed, during his earlier days in the private equity section of Macquarie Bank, David had championed Macquarie's investment in TRS in 1994 and was point man on that company's board. David had witnessed the key operating metrics for success in this business: sales margin per square metre of shelf space, inventory turns, and average dollar basket purchase per customer. This was a dollar and cents business requiring real-time merchandising skills for sustained market share.

So our CORE PROPOSITION was: 'This was an opportunity to acquire currently cutthroat competing businesses at distressed values where an immediate uplift in value would be derived from (a) the reduction in competition and (b) the synergies from joint purchasing, IT warehousing, and management.' Seven warehouses would be reduced to three, two merchandising teams to one and two finance teams to one.

In the medium term, we would re-offer a cleaned up business of greater scale and appeal to IPO markets, with revenues greater than $1 billion and EBITDA of not less than $75 million.

As always, the KEY PEOPLE were important to the deal. The CEO of the merged group was a no-nonsense, crusty personality, Ian Tsicalas. Phase one of our ownership was going to be all about harvesting what we saw as the low-hanging fruit, the produce of bringing the businesses together. Ian was the right man for this part of the job, but we were unsure whether he would prove to be the right man to lead phase two of the project, namely lifting like-for-like store performance. Prior to running the Warehouse business in Australia, Ian had managed the Commander telecoms business and BBC Hardware. As CEO of The Warehouse, Ian established an organisation structure of command and control; in addition to being CEO he was the de facto head of merchandising to whom a large number of product managers directly reported. Whether this would succeed in phase two we were doubtful. Meantime, Ian energetically engaged in delivering the phase one cost savings and cash generation targets.

Ian was able to shut down surplus warehouses, consolidating from seven owned or leased facilities around the country into three. This also significantly reduced the headcount in the back office functions of purchasing, IT and finance. At the same time, old and surplus inventories were discounted out and the business built cash balances to a tidy $120 million within fifteen months of our ownership.

The success of this phase one enabled us to return all of our $70 million investment. This, of course, required our banks' approval. Given the on-budget performance of ADR's small stores, the satisfactory but still challenging performance of the large retail format stores (aka big box stores), and the greater than budgeted synergies already achieved, and given management's confidence in the phase two growth to come, the approval was readily forthcoming.

One year later we realised that phase two was not yet going to plan. Like-for-like sales in the smaller stores were still holding, but the big box Warehouse store sales were sagging. While our CEO had done a great job in phase one, we were now confirmed in the view that he lacked the merchandising skills needed for a performance turnaround in the newly combined discount store formats.

The ADR board appointed a new CEO, Peter Wilkinson, and a new head of merchandising, Richard Brough. Peter had a long background in retail, having run both Myer and David Jones, while Richard came with Woolworths buyer experience. The combined skills of these two experienced executives was judged to be what ADR needed.

However the turnaround never came! The big box format never did fit well with the smaller store model. What worked in a small Crazy Clark's or Chickenfeed store did not necessarily work in a large Warehouse big box store. Differences in product ranging, management cultures and IT systems were a few of the problems the company deemed unable to solve. Sales and profits headed south and the shareholders, CHAMP and Catalyst, each injected $10 million of new equity, (a) to enable the company to renegotiate its banking covenants, and (b) to provide the new management team more time to effect a turnaround.

Like many retail businesses, the discount retail sales are heavily skewed to the two or three weeks of Christmas trading. For ADR, close to 90 per cent of its annual budgeted profits had to be delivered in the single month of December. Apart from Easter, buoyed by sales of chocolate eggs, the rest of the year delivered operating losses. Hundreds of millions of dollars of purchase orders would be placed nine months earlier, primarily with Chinese manufacturers, and you held your breath hoping the merchandising team got it right. Of course the merchandise had to be advertised, displayed and sold well, but the essential bets were laid nine months before the customers entered your stores.

To cut this difficult story short, the business did not get enough of these decisions right. Following another disappointing Christmas trading performance in December 2008, banking covenants were breached and ADR was placed in voluntary administration (VA).

The key NUMBERS showing the big decline in the enterprise value between when we acquired the business in 2005 and when we sold in 2009 are included in Table 9 below.

The exit

Prior to the banks' decision to move the company into VA, the shareholders, CHAMP and Catalyst, each agreed to invest an additional $10 million conditional upon further covenant revisions necessary to enable ADR to soldier on. We were willing to pursue a turnaround, especially now that the new IT systems had finally been debugged and were providing reliable data for management. The banks, however, insisted on larger debt paydown and, in our investors' interest, we had to make that age-old judgement call: were we really prepared to put more good money after bad? When do you stop flogging a dead horse? (See Lesson 5 in Part One.) In this case, when might a new owner do a better job with fresh ideas and fresh capital? And so it was the business

Table 9: ADR entry and exit numbers

	Entry value Dec 2005 ($m)		Exit value Jan 2009 ($m)
Enterprise value	200.0	Enterprise value	49.9
Equity in	70.0	Equity out	60.5
Revenue at entry	1037.6	Revenue at exit	916.7
EBITDA at entry	**27.5**	**EBITDA at exit**	**10.0**

was sold in January 2009 to the successful retail entrepreneur Jan Cameron (of Kathmandu retail fame).

The banks got out clean and we all hope Jan will make a better fist of the business than we did!

Lesson one: *Don't go into a turnaround deal unless you already have the turnaround CEO who you know can do the job.* In this case, our well-founded confidence in the immediately available harvest of low-hanging synergy fruits duped us into insufficient analysis of the turnaround task that was really required for a sustainable investment success.

Lesson two: *Have the courage to know when to stop flogging a dead horse.* This is a repeat of Lesson 5 in Part One, learned in the Rumentek experience. As disappointed as we were with the outcome of the ADR deal, we did at least limit our loss to just 10 per cent of our investment.

Lesson three: *If you mix a bucket of clear water with a bucket of muddy water, you finish up with a bigger bucket of muddy water!* I first mention this old Dutch proverb when discussing Specialty Jewellery Australia in Part One, and it certainly applies to the ADR experience. Mixing a profitable small-store format business with a loss-making big box format retailer was a dumb idea. Each format needed different store management, different merchandising skills, different customers. They were, and always will be, different businesses requiring different things for success.

Other deals that went wonderfully right

Austar

Austar is a publicly listed pay-TV company, operating what is effectively a monopoly subscription business in regional Australia. It of course competes with free-to-air TV and co-exists with Foxtel, which supplies pay-TV to metropolitan Australia.

Our GP company, formally called AMIL, had acted as a consultant to the ABC to examine the possible development opportunities for pay TV in Australia. Joe Skrzynski previously served as chair of the Broadcasting Council of Australia and his good friend Kim Williams was the CEO of the ABC. At this time one of my ex-roommates from the Harvard Business School, Jim Robbins, had become president of the Cox Cable Co. in the States. We introduced Jim to the ABC and Joe assisted negotiations with Cox, Nickelodeon, CNN, News Corp and Australis, the early stage Sydney-based pay TV aspirant.

These experienced media groups had come together to explore the prospects for establishing a pay TV business in Australia. Could this consortium of local and offshore media players provide the program content and operational skills necessary for a viable business? Viability depended on having at least a 30 per cent penetration of households in a market that was already saturated with well-established 'free' television—that is, television funded by advertising revenues not consumer subscriptions.

The numbers simply did not add up and the consortium never proceeded. Australis struggled on alone, endeavouring to provide a pay TV service utilising microwave technology. The company was unable to meaningfully penetrate the market and sold off a number of its franchises to Austar. A subsidiary of one of the pioneer cable TV companies in the United States, United International Holdings, Austar would become the successful pioneering entrant in the Australian pay TV sector. Following the demise of the Australis microwave offering, Austar benefited from the arrival of digital satellite technology. This technology enabled the company to offer a higher quality delivery at lower cost to households in regional Australia.

I first met the Austar CEO, John Porter, at new-media conferences in 2000 and 2001 where he confidently predicted the rise and rise of pay TV in Australia. It wasn't until early 2002 when the Austar share price collapsed from a high of $9 per share down to about 10 cents that we renewed our acquaintance with John Porter.

Howard Morgan was on secondment to CHAMP from our NYC partners, Castle Harlan, Inc. At his Sunday church group in Sydney, Howard met the recently resigned CFO of Austar, Jonathan Morphett. Jonathan mentioned his interest in exploring a career in private equity and so Howard arranged for him to meet with me at CHAMP.

Jonathan impressed me with his openness and quiet professionalism so I made the suggestion that he might care to demonstrate his analytical skills by preparing the case for a buy-out and privatisation of Austar. His work impressed us and Jonathan became a key consultant to CHAMP to help progress a deal.

Our CORE PROPOSITION for this Austar deal was rooted in the belief that everyone else had prematurely given up on what must surely become a highly valuable regional monopoly. We believed that were we to provide fresh equity capital for growth, conditional upon fundamental debt reduction and restructuring, the highly motivated and underrated management team would significantly increase the company's low (by the rest of the world's standards) market penetration in its monopoly franchise in regional Australia.

The KEY PEOPLE were the CEO, John Porter, and his senior management team, all critical to the operations. Key to any transaction would also be John Porter's chairman and immediate boss, Mike Fries, and his colleagues in Colorado, Gene Schneider and John Malone.

John Porter was a bear of a man from Minneapolis who had worked in the US cable TV business for many years, most recently with the United Global Company (UGC) head office in Denver, Colorado. UGC was in turn majority owned and controlled by John Malone's company, Liberty Global.

Married with three boys, John Porter was an enigma to us at first. Always courteous, open and good fun, he had a laid-back style that initially had me worrying about just how serious and committed he really was. And remember the context: his company's market equity had just been trashed from a high of $3.5 billion to just $350 million in only a little over twelve months. Rumours were strong that Austar's fifteen-member banking syndicate was about to move in, and the company's public shareholders, brokers and analysts were already up in arms. Yet John continued to impress us with his command of the day to day operating numbers on the one hand, and his steadfast and articulate belief in the strategic imperative for his business on the other. More on this soon.

Furthermore, our meetings with John's senior management team impressed us even more. And yet it seemed the market had given up on this management team, with everyone heading for the nearest exit sign.

Dana Strong, who had responsibility for the company's large call centre and customer service, was effectively chief operating officer reporting to John. Also US-born, Dana is the most charming, phlegmatic, clear-thinking and effective COO I have yet encountered. She also has the best collection of shoes known to humankind.

Deanne Weir, internal counsel and HR boss, carried the stress and strain of the array of legal and commercial issues facing the enterprise. Reporting directly to John, Deanne gave very wise counsel on all of these matters, always acting patiently and tenaciously.

Nikki Warburton was chief marketing executive, again reporting to John. Vivacious and energetic, Nikki was committed to the challenge of lifting Austar's household penetration from its then 20 per cent to 30 per cent and beyond.

Philip Knox was the CFO. He had his hands full with public company filings and stock exchange time lines, not to mention the demands of a fifteen-member banking syndicate whose covenants were now in breach. Again, we were well enough impressed with this CFO's ability to be all over the critical cash flow and earnings information.

Frankly, we concluded that the team looked very fit for purpose, in spite of the mess the company had got itself into. And it was a team staunchly loyal to their CEO, a man who seemed well prepared and committed to take his company forward, if only someone like CHAMP could help him solve the company's serious balance sheet problems immediately.

The KEY NUMBERS going in and out for this investment are shown in Table 10.

The negotiations turned out to be longer and more complex than we had imagined. John Porter arranged for me to speak with his chairman in Colorado, Mike Fries. Howard Morgan accompanied me on this visit and we both liked him from the get-go; he was the quintessential no-nonsense, tough, quick-thinking American executive. The upfront issue for Mike was to understand how we proposed to solve the Austar balance sheet problem, a euphemism for the company's massive debt overload. In particular, how could CHAMP take care of

Table 10: Austar entry and exit numbers

	Entry value		Exit value Dec 2005
	($m)		($m)
Enterprise value	544.0	Enterprise value	1256.3
Equity in	81.6	Equity out	556.8
Revenue at entry	321.0	Revenue at exit	502.8
EBITDA at entry	22.0	EBITDA at exit	125.0
		IRR	107%
		Times money	6.8x

the $700 million of junk bonds that had been issued to hedge funds in the US market, secured by mortgage on the 51 per cent majority shareholding in Austar then owned by US cable TV company, UGC. UGC was controlled by the legendary media entrepreneur John Malone, whose company Liberty Global was the majority shareholder in UGC.

And all of this $700 million junk-bond debt was buried beneath, and deeply subordinated to, the $400 million plus senior loan facility provided by the fifteen banks from around the world! If we could sort all of this mess out, we could let management get on with building a first-class pay TV business.

From our inquiries, we knew that the junk-bondholders were furious with Colorado company UGC, which had promoted the issue. The bonds were collateralised by UGC's majority stock holding in Austar, now worth a mere fraction of the bonds' face value.

Mike Fries, UGC's president, explained to us that relationships between UGC and the bondholders had soured to a point where dialogue was impossible. This became our opportunity; to approach the bondholders with a 'clean hands' offer and take control of the majority stock in Austar, subject to a shareholders' agreement with UGC.

Credit Suisse First Boston (CSFB) had managed the original bond offer and, with the help of its Denver-based partner David Poznack, Paul Wilson and I contacted the major hedge funds holding the bonds (Golden Tree, Mackay Shields and others). Between August and November 2002 we had successfully negotiated to purchase their bonds at 7 cents in the face dollar value. This offer was still conditional upon a triple pike with half twist:

1. securing 100 per cent acceptance from all bondholders via a Chapter 11 process in the NYC Bankruptcy Court
2. completing a shareholders' agreement with UGC regarding the future management and control of Austar
3. obtaining a special waiver from the Australian Stock Exchange enabling us to acquire effective control of Austar other than by way of an offer to all shareholders.

To paraphrase Joe Skrzynski, say it all quickly and throw your arms around and it looks easy!

Each pike in this triple needed to be co-dependent and coordinated. Our NY partners, Castle Harlan, Inc., helped to guide us through the thickets of the New York Bankruptcy Court where we eventually did achieve the mandatory 100 per cent approval of the bondholders. And as matters transpired, the US court process provided the solution to the ASX waiver we required, a waiver that would otherwise never have eventuated.

The 7 cents in the face dollar value of the bonds placed a 'see-through' or equivalent price of 16 cents per underlying Austar share. Even though CHAMP was proposing to extend an offer to all other shareholders at 16 cents and to underwrite a rights issue at this price, such actions would not cure the breach—that is, any acquisition or agreement to acquire greater than 19.9 per cent of the shares via a deal with the bondholders would be unlawful.

This riddle seemed insoluble to all of our advisers but one. Joe Skrzynski invited John Atanaskovic, senior partner of the Atanaskovic Hartnell law firm based in Sydney, to find a way. Atanaskovic, often seen as an 'enfant terrible' in the litigation world, had a well-earned reputation for innovative thought and tenacity. He had long been a key adviser to News Corp and relished the challenge we presented to him. His solution was to argue the principle of 'international comity', which establishes that if a public court process in a recognised jurisdiction, such as New York, were to approve the bondholders' transfer, then the ASX would respect the decision. This proved to be the case and was the first time the ASX had ever approved such an exemption.

Prior to lodging our offer in the New York court we had completed our negotiations with UGC in Denver. These were the negotiations for the future management and governance of Austar. A number of us were involved in the rough-and-tumble discussions with UGC, principally Howard Morgan, David Jones and myself. Matters of structure, UGC reps and warranties, fees, public rights issue, the proposed approach to the bank syndicate, pre-emptive clauses, management incentives and much more all required sustained attention to detail.

Mike Fries conveyed UGC's final approval by telephone on Christmas Day 2002. From Christmas Cove in Penobscot Bay, Maine in July (see Introduction, Part Two) to Christmas Day in Sydney, 2002!

So the triple pike with half twist was done but, to mix my athletic metaphors, just one more hurdle had to be jumped. Unless we could persuade Austar's fifteen-bank 'underwater' syndicate to waive its existing breaches of loan covenants and to renegotiate improved terms and covenants there would be no deal. This herculean task fell primarily on the shoulders of David Jones, assisted by Fiona Lock.

The $400 million senior debt was a syndicated facility provided by fifteen banks with no clear lead bank syndicate manager. An 80 per cent approval by value was required for any reset of covenants.

Austar's 2002 December year EBITDA was only a shade over $20 million, so the senior debt was close to twenty times EBITDA. Most of these banks had tossed the problem into their work-out divisions, and this was where we walked in at the close of 2002. Without a major reset of covenants, we made it quite clear CHAMP would not proceed with its proposed Austar deal, including an underwritten rights issue of $75 million. This issue would be used to paydown some of the debt and to fund capital expenditure needs of the company. The informal lead role for the banks rested with JP Morgan executive Steve Brimo.

Steve shared our frustrations and would repeatedly advise David Jones and me that 'it was a process' and that we needed more patience. With our triple pike of approvals achieved, we were now suspended in this 'process' that was to drag on for four more months before we finally got a satisfactory solution with the banks.

The recap of Austar's balance sheet was subsequently further enhanced by the company's issuance of a $100 million hybrid corporate bond, listed as 'STARS' on the ASX. Fiona Lock, now a director of CHAMP (and arguably the most senior level female executive in the Australian PE sector today), worked with Austar's CFO Philip Knox and internal counsel Deanne Weir to pull off this very successful and oversubscribed corporate bond issue.

This successful reset of the banks' debt enabled Porter and his management team to tenaciously improve operating performance. His team relentlessly pursued new subscribers, increased average revenue per user (ARPU), lowered customer churn rates, improved call-centre performance, speeded up truck rolls for connections, sold surplus and non-core assets, introduced new program and product development, and more. This they did with our encouragement and agreement regarding the daily and weekly key performance indicators. They beat their own targets every year and grew EBITDA from $22 million in 2002 to $125 million in 2005 and then to $140 million in 2006. They were a magnificent operating team.

The exit

The exit would prove to be as exciting as the entry.

Simon Mordant, a founding partner of the highly successful boutique investment house Caliburn Partners (renamed Greenhill in October 2012), accompanied me on a visit to Mike Fries at UGC headquarters in Denver, Colorado. Mordant, as round as he is tall, is a wise advisor and talented investment banker. An original thinker, he is a passionate benefactor and collector of contemporary art in Australia, and chairman of the recently expanded Museum of Contemporary Art on the edge of Sydney Harbour's Circular Quay.

Our purpose in Denver was to determine whether Mike Fries was a buyer or a seller and, in either case, at what price. We certainly did not come away with any deal; it was very clear that UGC would not be well disposed to buy back shares at more than $1 when they had sold to us at 16 cents less than three years before.

Simon believed we would be able to realise a higher price from an institutional selldown. Normally this would involve a prospectus process, rumour and distraction with an extended book build conducted by brokers, and all the risks that come with delay. Simon convinced us he could achieve what we wanted without any of these problems.

We reached agreement with UGC that we would agree to sell 224 million of our shares to them, sufficient to give UGC 51 per cent voting control of Austar. These would be sold at $1 per share, conditional on our sale of the balance of 298 million shares. These would be sold by a 'blind-date' auction process pioneered and conducted by Simon's firm in December 2005.

Caliburn alerted a number of competitor investment banks of a planned selldown by an unidentified investor in an unidentified listed company. These banks would be invited to bid between close of market and opening time the following morning. In other words, each bidder would be advised after close of trading the name of the seller, CHAMP, and the name of the company, Austar. Each bidder would then have twelve hours until opening time of market the following morning in which to confirm its unconditional cash bid. No prospectus, no management presentations, no reps and warranties (other than as to ownership), no delays.

The winner in this process was Goldman Sachs at $1.15 per share in April 2003. This selldown, combined with our sellback to UGC, produced a profit for CHAMP of $475 million or 6.8 times its original investment.

Lesson one: *Look for that special angle you can bring the deal.* In the case of Austar, there were two: bringing 'clean hands' to the vendor, enabling us to solve a problem (namely, a compromise of the junk bondholders position), and discovery of the pioneering concept of 'international comity', which enabled a transaction otherwise impossible.

Lesson two: *When talented operating executives keep beating their own stretch targets, as the Austar team did, don't get in their way.*

Lesson three: *The 'blind date' institutional selldown process can provide an outstanding exit outcome.*

Study Group International

I ask you not to begin this story without first reading the Education and Training Australia (ETA) case in Part One. Our nerve-racking experience and ultimate success with the earlier ETA investment gave us the 'special angle' we always like to have when considering any new investment opportunity.

What is a 'special angle'? In private equity, compared to public equity, you are often dealing in imperfect information marketplaces free from the continuous disclosure requirements of stock exchange regulators. Nor does the seller necessarily take the highest cash price he is offered since there may by other benefits important to him, such as the likely impact on family members and employees, customers, intellectual property and reputation.

In this instance, we already knew the nucleus of Study Group International's embryonic cells, ETA. And we knew and highly regarded the man we found to run ETA, Arvid Petersen. Arvid had continued to successfully build ETA after we sold out to the London Daily Mail Group (LDMG). Predictably, Arvid continued to expand the rebadged Study Group International (SGI) business into Europe and the United States. He did a great job for the publicly listed LDMG and they in turn were very constructive and expansion-oriented owners. Nonetheless, SGI was never really a core part of the LDMG enterprise, and we always thought it might one day come back on the market. Arvid thought so too!

Arvid had stepped out of the CEO role at SGI and later resigned from the board so that he could join CHAMP when the SGI business came up for sale in late 2006. Arvid was our 'special angle' in the bid process; with his knowledge and with our confidence in his judgement we were positioned to move speedily and aggressively. We were able to convince the vendor that we could and would complete a transaction efficiently. We were not the highest bidder but we were the best and most knowledgeable one.

Our CORE PROPOSITION was straightforward. This was a business and a sector we knew. SGI enjoyed a leading presence in the three English-language countries most attractive to students from the developing nations of China, India, Indonesia and others. SGI's teaching facilities in the United Kingdom, Australia and the United States positioned it to offer offshore students a choice of foundation courses as gateways into university degree courses in the most sought after Anglophile destinations in the world. We believed the demand for higher margin products could in fact prove almost insatiable, and we were confident this private education business would prove to be a hotly contested sector for investors.

Next, the KEY PEOPLE. Ben Sebel, now a shareholder and a managing director in CHAMP, was our project director for the SGI deal. Back in the early nineties, Ben had been seconded by his then employer, Deloitte Tohmatsu, to work as an analyst assistant to Nick Greiner, former premier of New South Wales and then chairman of ETA. In that role Ben became intimately familiar with the ETA company. Ben subsequently completed his MBA at Harvard and joined Goldman Sachs in New York. When Castle Harlan, Inc. (CHI) co-founder Leonard Harlan was seeking a partner for his firm's ambitions in Australia, he contacted his former Australian classmate from Harvard Business School Roger Sebel. Roger introduced Leonard to his son Ben, who in turn introduced Leonard and Howard Morgan to Nick Greiner and to me . . . and, as described previously, these introductions led to the formation of the AMIL successor company CHAMP.

Ben is a quiet achiever: unflappable, calm, conservative and thoughtful. He's rather similar to Arvid in these attributes, although Arvid also exudes his own special charisma, attracting those around him to want to be on his team. The karma of these two unflappable cool cats was to be tested on day one of our ownership of SGI. I was on hand in London for the handover. I was well aware that the incumbent CEO was at once unconvinced about our plans for the business but equally convinced that his own salary package and incentive program needed to be mightily enhanced. It was palpably clear that he was not the man for us; Arvid and Ben calmly but firmly terminated this CEO's appointment during day one! Arvid was appointed as CEO that same day.

The man who had greatly impressed all of us during the due diligence and transaction process was the CFO, Andrew Mills. Based in the London head office, Andrew was all over the numbers, not just for the UK campuses but also for those in the United States and Australia, and for the sales and marketing offices in Europe, China and elsewhere. He was more than just a good accounting numbers CFO— he also understood the key drivers for the business and could talk to the metrics important for performance measurement. When Arvid moved the head office to Sydney a few months later, Andrew agreed to move his family to Australia and continue as group CFO.

It was to be another eight months before Arvid recruited a new CEO, Heith Mackay-Cruise, enabling him to step back into an executive chair role. Heath was not from the education sector, most recently being managing director of the Packer-owned media business Publishing and Broadcasting Limited (PBL) in New Zealand. At just 36 years of age, Heith was a young, energetic and confident executive.

With more than 35 000 students attending a variety of English-language courses, vocational colleges and foundation courses articulating into major universities in the United Kingdom, Australia, and the United States each year, there were lots of moving parts to be oiled and maintained. All of this was supported by approximately 3000 commission-based independent agents worldwide. Heith was tasked with improving the efficiency of these operations, enabling Arvid to devote more of his time to capturing some of the strategic opportunities available to SGI.

To assist in this strategic thinking we invited my longtime friend Phil Handy to join the SGI board. Phil is another HBS classmate of mine who has been a repeat affiliate investor in all of our AMIT and CHAMP funds over the past 25 years. A resident of Winterpark, Florida and Sun Valley, Idaho, Phil is a staunch Republican. He served as chair of the Federal Education Advisory Board in the George Bush administration and was well positioned to assist Study Group ambitions in the US private education market. Rarely early, occasionally AWOL, Phil loves the big ideas and is wired to think outside the box.

So how did the SGI NUMBERS pan out? The numbers were as shown in Table 11.

Table 11: SGI entry and exit numbers

	Entry value Sep 2006 ($m)		Exit value Jul 2010 ($m)
Enterprise value	180.0	Enterprise value	660.0
Equity in	81.8	Equity out	431.6
Revenue at entry	272.3	Revenue at exit	447.4
EBITDA at entry	23.6	EBITDA at exit	60.2
		IRR	56%
		Times money	5.3x

The key strategic initiative was the development of what we called International Study Centres (ISCs), partnerships with universities in the United States, the United Kingdom and Australia where the revenue margins were double those of other products such as English-language training. In the time of our ownership, seventeen such centres were successfully established. Other expansion was achieved via the establishment of additional regional marketing and sales support offices in China, India and Canada. In the final year of ownership, fiscal year 2010, our total student base of 50 000 was derived from the countries shown in Figure 1.

And one of the significant value contributions from CHAMP came in the form of two bolt-on acquisitions in the vocational education segment. These were championed by Darren Smorgon, a key member of the SGI project team in CHAMP, who had developed a relationship with a young entrepreneur named Warren Jacobson. Jacobson had two businesses under contract, one a physical fitness trainers' college and the other a health and wellness college, with combined EBITDAs of approximately $8 million.

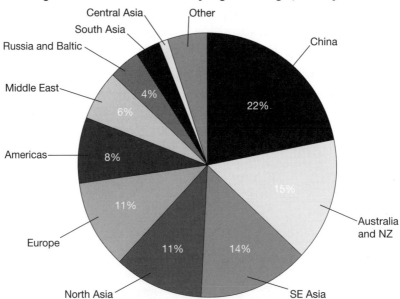

Figure 1: SGI student weeks by region of origin, fiscal year 2010

Darren convinced Jacobson in the wisdom of selling these into a newly formed division of SGI, Careers Education Australia. SGI acquired the business for just under five times EBITDA, which provided a healthy upside upon our subsequent sale of all of SGI to Providence Equity for eleven times EBITDA.

The exit

Education had indeed become a hot sector for investors. Although a high-growth segment of the world economy, most of the sector in Australia is still government owned and run. As a result, investors have difficulty investing funds in what might otherwise warrant a sizable allocation in any portfolio.

SGI had performed superbly and still had very strong growth prospects. Well managed with sophisticated reporting and governance protocols, in CHAMP's view it was ready for an IPO. We have always held the view that we should only ever sell by way of IPO if we are highly confident in the company's future and that the strike price will never fall below the listing price. We might be criticised by some for 'leaving too much on the table'; I would *never* trade that for the opposite reputation. Indeed, of the eleven (including Austar) IPOs completed by the CHAMP group since 1998 (Cuppa Cup was the first), only one (LookSmart) was below its IPO listing price 24 months after listing and none was below their IPO price twelve months after listing. Contrary to the popular press portrayal of greedy public float prices, CHAMP's IPOs have outperformed the public equity indices by a comfortable margin— for example, Figure 2 shows the performance of CHAMP's buy-out IPOs versus the All Ords.

And as a direct result, when we do bring our portfolio companies to market, the investment bankers and brokers are able to emphasise our track record in this regard to their clients. We are proud of this record and it is very important to us that we leave our portfolio companies in better shape than we found them.

In January 2010 we appointed Credit Suisse and Deutsche Bank to run a dual track process for the sale of SGI—that is, to prepare for an IPO and also to attract trade buyer and financial buyer interest. Some

Figure 2: Annual stock market returns of CHAMP Group buy-out IPOs vs All Ords

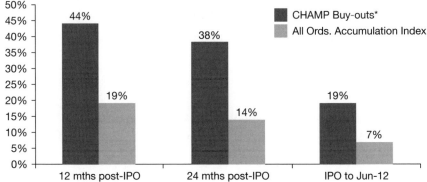

Source: IRESS, Capital IQ, CHAMP

*Australia (1999), Austar (2005), Bradken (2004), Cuppa Cup (1998), Dexion (2005), Mastermyne (2010), MIA (2000)

of SGI's competitors such as Navitas, the Apollo Group and Kaplan (owned by the *Washington Post*) actively engaged. So too did several of the larger international private equity groups, including Carlyle, Bain & Company, and Providence Equity Partners.

One of the frontrunners, Kaplan, pulled a stunt within 48 hours of the agreed final bid date, demanding another two weeks for more due diligence or it would otherwise withdraw. We were unimpressed by this last-minute tactic; we rejected their demand but invited them and one other well-advanced and credible party to submit a non-binding offer to us within 48 hours. Providence Private Equity did so with an offer superior to others and finalised a binding offer letter within two days of the agreed 48-hour deadline after conducting a very professional due diligence process assisted by their own experience and success in the education sector in the United States and elsewhere.

As it transpired, our timing for this more than eleven times EBITDA exit was better than we knew. Within months of our sale, a number of physical attacks on Indian students in Melbourne gained front-page publicity here and offshore. This in turn led to considerable press coverage of inadequacies in security, accommodation and pastoral care of foreign students by some of the more marginal agents and school operators.

Many years of hard-earned reputation in offshore markets were to be sorely tested as students began to turn away from Australia.

For the record, no abuse of or attacks on Indian students occurred on SGI campuses in Australia or anywhere else. And SGI, under Providence ownership, is on track for continued growth.

Lesson one: *If you hope to make exceptional returns for your investors, like six times your money as in SGI, then you better have a special angle.* This can be a special person with insider knowledge, a bolt-on acquisition target and/or new products and services that can step change the company's margins. Here we had the successful ex-CEO in our team and we developed the ISCs as a new product with dramatically higher growth at greater margins.

Lesson two: *A well-executed sale process begins on day one of your ownership.* The online data room provided to us when we acquired SGI was constantly updated thereafter by the CFO. Projections then provided by SGI's management team were sensibly conservative so that no disappointments were experienced by bidders during the due diligence and sale process. The well-prepared and maintained data room enabled management to stay focused on operations rather than scrambling to find information to satisfy bidders' questions. (Note that 710 separate questions were tabled by the bidders permitted to access the data room.)

Manassen Foods Australia

Way back in 1975 I became the inaugural director of the Young Presidents' Organization (YPO) in Sydney. Established in the 1950s in the United States by Ray Hickock (of Hickock fame), YPO was and is a not-for-profit organisation for young CEOs and their spouses, dedicated to education via idea exchange of its members. Now a worldwide phenomenon, its members number several thousands of CEOs, a mix of self-made entrepreneurs and big corporate professional executives.

The annual aggregate sales of whose member companies approximate the GDP of the United States.

I first met Arvid Petersen through YPO. Arvid had joined when he was CEO of Pepsi-Cola in Australia, prior to my invitation for him to become the CEO of Education and Training Australia Pty Ltd, our portfolio company in the private education sector (see Part One). And it was through YPO that I also first met Roy Manassen.

Roy had built a food importing and distribution business, Manassen Foods Australia (MFA). Selling primarily to the big supermarket chains, Manassen Foods was more than just a traditional third-party distributor. In most cases, MFA owned the Australian and New Zealand brand rights for the products it agreed to distribute for its offshore suppliers. And, in most cases, MFA concentrated on niche categories where it could be number one or two in terms of shelf space power. So, for example, products like King Oscar sardines from Norway, Carr's water crackers and McVitie's digestive biscuits occupy the number-one position in their respective niche markets.

The giant and oligopolistic supermarket chains of Coles and Woolworths in Australia now dominate between 25 and 50 per cent of many product categories with their own brands. This has enabled the chains to squeeze down prices and margins, all ostensibly in the best interests of Australian consumers. While those consumer benefits are in part true, they should be balanced by the resulting reduction in incentive and capability for smaller suppliers to innovate, develop and promote their own products. In the small market economy of Australia, there should ideally be some checks and balances on the power of the giant food retailers. Do you really want the majority of food and beverage offerings to be Coles and Woolworths labels? Do you really want to witness the demise of so many diverse suppliers and retailers? Or would you favour a public policy intervention—say, a cap of 20 per cent on own-label share of any food or beverage category? Admittedly this is an intrusive market intervention, but one I believe is warranted.

CHAMP had been searching for an appropriate investment in the food and beverage sector, believing it to be a desirable inclusion in the portfolio mix of the CHAMP II buy-out fund. I had therefore approached

Roy to seek his advice and, in particular, to explore whether he might be interested in allowing CHAMP to become his partner for expansion.

The CORE PROPOSITION we presented to Roy was this: Manassen's established distribution infrastructure and experienced management team would enable a rapid scaling up via selected bolt-on acquisitions and additional brand distribution agreements. Provided MFA-owned brands occupied number one, two or three position in niche markets, the company could withstand what we feared would be a continuing trend by Coles and Woolworths to aggressively build their own private label businesses. A final component of the core proposition was the belief that MFA would accelerate its penetration of the food services channel (cafes, hotels and clubs, and so on) over the next five years, so further reducing its dependency on the supermarkets.

If all of this could be achieved, the company could double its sales and profits within five years. With sales greater than $500 million and EBITDA at above $50 million, the company would then be an attractive IPO as an independent food company, owning its own brands in a steadily growing food and beverages sector of the Australian and New Zealand economies.

Roy Manassen was enthusiastic about this proposition but challenged us about CHAMP's ability to really deliver on these growth ideas. He would only agree to the sale of a controlling interest in his company once CHAMP could actually bring viable acquisition opportunities to the table. In other words, Roy was prepared to own a smaller slice of an expanding pie.

CHAMP's finance director, Barry Zuckerman, had recently met the immediate past general manager of MFA, Gary Berger. When Barry arranged for us to seek his ideas and advice, we found Gary to be a very entrepreneurial, enthusiastic, 'glass three quarters full' style of executive, still in his early thirties. He had recently left his job at MFA to find private equity opportunities, and so he was pleased to meet with us and keen to help. We decided to provide him a desk and resources at CHAMP with the specific mission of finding acquisition opportunities suitable for MFA. Given Gary's continuing strong friendship with Roy, this plan had Roy's full support.

Gary's direct and fearlessly disarming style enabled him to quickly visit with a very large number of smaller food company prospects. These were qualified by his own knowledge of what could sensibly fit with MFA's existing product portfolio. Working with Cameron Buchanan and Fiona Lock at CHAMP, Gary negotiated commitments to acquire two businesses with strong synergies with MFA. While the combined EBITDAs of these potential add-ons were a modest $5 million, they offered strong and sensible growth prospects for MFA. Most importantly, our unearthing of these opportunities convinced Roy that CHAMP was indeed the right value-add partner for his company. And so it was that we completed simultaneous closings with MFA and the bolt-ons, resulting in the numbers at entry shown in Table 12.

In terms of the KEY PEOPLE, Roy Manassen was the main player. As founder and executive chairman, he had been the key driver in the development of the business over the previous fifteen years. He led from the front, with a high-energy personality and relentless attention to detail.

I have a wonderful anecdote which helps illustrate Roy's intensity and focus. At the end of a long and at times frustrating process in the negotiations for the later sale of MFA to China's Bright Food, there came a vital day in September 2011, the 'take it or leave it' day on price and terms. Roy, arriving downtown in his BMW, too late to get to a parking station, parked in busy George Street, Sydney, and ran into the all-important meeting. The meeting went for six hours and culminated in a definitive agreement. Roy walked back to his car afterwards

Table 12: Manassen entry and exit numbers

	Entry value Apr 2006 ($m)		Exit value Nov 2011 ($m)
Enterprise value	154.6	Enterprise value	532.0
Equity in	86.7	Equity out	232.4
Revenue at entry	209.1	Revenue at exit	594.5
EBITDA at entry	21.5	EBITDA at exit	69.0
		IRR	20%
		Times money	2.6x

but was unable to find his keys. Frustrated, he leaned back on the car and realised it was actually running. He had leapt out of the car that morning, leaving the key in the ignition and the motor idling all day—somewhat focused on the meeting agenda, you might say!

Three years prior to our involvement, Roy had begun a pullback from a full-time CEO role to one of active chair role. He had been ably supported by other shareholder executives in the business, and his pullback was further facilitated by the appointment of Gary Berger to the general manager role. After Gary moved on from MFA in search of a career in private equity (he subsequently joined the Ironbridge PE shop), it would fall to Roy and CHAMP to recruit a new CEO to lead the next growth phase for MFA.

The Melbourne-based partner in the business, Phil Jones, was and is a very experienced and effusive business development executive. Phil was the point person for key product suppliers' relationships and arrangements. Maybe even better than Roy, Phil knew what MFA's big customers needed and how best to motivate his suppliers to satisfy those needs at the right price. Basic, you might say, but in fact requiring relentless attention to detail, packaging, promotional tactics, personal relationships, new product development, logistics and customer service.

As in all of our successful portfolio companies, the CFO position was filled by an analytically strong and clear-thinking executive. Wayne McIntosh provided essential knowledge and glue in this business comprised of so many hundreds of SKUs, differentiated inventory fill rates and currency exposures. Wayne's somewhat dour and no-nonsense approach could lead the uninitiated to underestimate the breadth of his talents, but these skills were ably demonstrated when he stepped up to the plate as interim CEO between the time of our first CEO, Michael Bracka, and his successor, Geoff Erby.

Prior to his appointment at the helm of MFA, Michael Bracka had served as CEO for Kelloggs in Australia; he brought a wealth of FMCG experience and enthusiasm with him.

Geoff Erby was subsequently recruited to take over from Michael in 2010 to continue the growth and lead MFA towards an exit event. Geoff had been a senior executive in the Goodman Fielder food group, where he had performed extremely well in challenging consumer retail markets. A quietly competent and effective CEO, thoroughly versed in the dos and don'ts of the FMCG sector in Australia, Geoff was a stand-out choice for the leader who could accelerate MFA's trajectory. Geoff's performance in the job underscores Lesson 11 in Part One, namely when it comes time to make a change at the top, don't procrastinate.

Cameron Buchanan, a managing director in CHAMP, was our project leader for this MFA investment. As chairman of the MFA board, Cameron very quickly forged a strong and productive relationship with Roy Manassen, something that was essential to the growth of the company and for the exit. In many respects, Cameron has much in common with Roy: tell it like it is, don't beat around the bush, call a spade a spade, never blink but know when to fold, be brutally honest and fair . . . Cameron and Roy are like two sides of the same page on these things, and these attributes turned out to be critical to the outcome of the exit process.

Now to the NUMBERS. At the time we completed the acquisition of approximately a 70 per cent interest in MFA (including the initial bolt-ons), Roy and his executive partners held the other 30 per cent. Sales were $250 million per annum, with an EBITDA of approximately $24 million per annum. Our plan was to grow this to greater than $500 million in revenues and $50 million in EBITDA via acquisitions and organic growth.

At the outset, Cameron pushed for a robust review of the relevance and profitability of MFA's existing 500 product lines and brands. Assisted by the HUB consulting group (now renamed Value Line), this proved to be a most valuable exercise. The study identified over 100 SKUs to be phased out, releasing funds from inventory for more profitable brands. Importantly, it also provided an invaluable roadmap for where MFA should be seeking to grow.

During the ensuing five years, the company completed nine separate brand and company acquisitions. These averaged four times EBITDA purchase price, so providing handsome arbitrage for the overall enterprise valuation. Importantly, they were also all additional 'owned brands' for MFA in growth niche segments of the Australian food sector.

MFA also completed one major acquisition, namely the Sunbeam fruit, nuts and juice business. This was a further demonstration of CHAMP's 'value add' because the opportunity came to CHAMP via a past relationship with the controlling shareholders in the unlisted public Sunbeam company. With sales of $200 million and a number-one shelf position in the major retailers, Sunbeam was a wonderful fold into Manassen's distribution and sales infrastructure and culture. We were never going to 'steal' this business, especially given some of the wiliest entrepreneurs on the east coast (including Peter Younghans from Melbourne, and Sam Gazal and Charles Gullotta from Sydney) were big shareholders in Sunbeam. They had done a very able job of moving Sunbeam from its legacy cooperative growers culture into a modern corporate marketing one, in the process creating value for themselves and the other almost 2000 shareholders. MFA successfully completed a scheme of arrangement (75 per cent shareholder approval) takeover of Sunbeam, almost doubling the size of the Manassen group in the process.

By fiscal year end 2011, MFA had revenues of $560 million and EBITDA of approximately $60 million; we agreed with the MFA board that it was now appropriate to seek an exit. While the markets were not propitious for an IPO, we always believed that MFA's portfolio of brands and national distribution strength would prove attractive to trade buyers. Indeed, Bright Food from China had already expressed its interest in the company.

The exit
The approach by Bright Food was somewhat sceptically received by both Cameron and Roy. Like all of us, they had witnessed a number of false starts and failed acquisition attempts by Bright in recent times, such as their approach to United Biscuits in the United Kingdom, the CSR company in Australia and several other prominent forays around the world. Bright Food, a Chinese state-owned food and beverages conglomerate, was nonetheless genuinely keen to do business in and with Australia. With Bright advised by Nomura/Jafco and MFA by UBS and Merrill Lynch, both sides entered an extended period of discussions and due diligence.

Without considerable patience and tenacity over many months, no deal could ever have been reached. Very early in the discussions, Roy and Cameron established a clear in-principle position with their Bright counterparts regarding a multiple of earnings price expectation. They ruled a line in the sand about this and never blinked in spite of a number of attempts by the purchaser to argue a lower valuation.

No vendor wants to be unnecessarily exposed to a broken sale process. The costs and distraction to management is one thing, but the potential impact on employees, suppliers and customers is even more concerning. So, given Bright's 'false start' reputation, what was the best way to manage these dangerous exposures?

First, stay out of the amazingly porous Australian business gossip columns, like *AFR*'s 'Street Talk' and the *Sydney Morning Herald*'s 'CBD', for as long as possible.

Secondly, be resolute from the outset about the 'rules of engagement'; these were set early by Cameron and Roy. It helps to have an already very wealthy partner like Roy, passionate about his business and focused on a successful outcome, yet genuinely indifferent about whether the business is sold or not—if the price is sensible, great, otherwise don't bother.

Third, complete a very detailed terms sheet negotiation, including draft shareholders' agreement documentation, prior to the final due diligence phase. This terms sheet included a break fee in excess of $20 million dollars, designed to act as a disincentive for any arbitrary or capricious change of mind by the vendor. The break fee was bank guaranteed and, although still a poor and unsatisfactory second prize, it did nonetheless provide all of us with comfort that Bright were indeed of genuine intent. There was no MAC (material adverse consequence) out, only Australian Foreign Investment Review Board approval and Chinese Government approval. We were not prepared to grant the purchaser a free option. In other words, if the Chinese Government approval was not forthcoming, we would at least collect a substantial break fee.

Bright's internal due diligence team was fifteen in number, forensic and professional. Led by the Shanghai chairman of Bright Food

& Beverage Company, Mr Ge, the Bright team was very keen to uti-
lise MFA as its platform for further activities in Australia. They also
seemed fully committed to delivering some of MFA's products via
their several thousand supermarkets throughout mainland China. On
30 August 2011, Mr Ge was quoted on the front page of the Australian
Financial Review: 'What we do at Bright Food is try to enable every
citizen in China to take a bite of Australian wine and taste confection-
ary from Australia and this is of enormous influence.'

In November 2011, we completed the sale of 75 per cent of the shares
in MFA to Bright, with CHAMP retaining a 10 per cent shareholding
and Roy and his management team 15 per cent. It was important for
Bright to ensure that Roy, and less importantly CHAMP, still had 'skin
in the game' and reasons to continue to support MFA.

We view the Bright relationship as an important opportunity for MFA
and CHAMP well beyond the successful MFA exit itself. Indeed Bright's
plans for a HK listing of the Manassen company was an important moti-
vation for CHAMP to retain a 10 per cent shareholding in the company.

Lesson one: *Do not embark on a bolt-on or roll-up acquisition strategy
unless you already have a strong core platform in place.* Only a proven
operating executive team, with scalable IT and governance systems
in place, can extract the potential benefits that roll-ups promise. We
enabled Manassen Foods to complete eleven successful bolt-ons,
delivering both purchase price arbitrage as well as building the scale
necessary for sustainable success in an oligopolistic marketplace.

Lesson two: *Be wary of companies where their biggest customers are also
their toughest competitors.* The growth of private-label marketing by
Coles and Woolworths has dramatically damaged the profitability and
prospects of small manufacturing enterprises in the food and beverages
sector of Australia.

Manassen's portfolio of its own brand of niche products such as
King Oscar sardines, S&W mayonnaise, McVitie's digestive biscuits,
has minimised, but by no means eliminated, the threat of home label
competition.

United Malt Holdings

Why would you want to invest in an agriculturally based commodity product like malt? Maybe because nobody else wanted to at the time, although it's preferable to come up with a few more reasons than that . . .

In 2006, John Haddock was enjoying his time in New York as an exchange executive in the offices of CHAMP's US affiliate, CHI. With David Pittaway, a CHI managing director, John had spent several months on a prospective deal with United Malt Holdings (UMH). He had become intrigued with this globally entrenched maltster, a company processing and supplying the major beer companies with the malt they needed in the manufacture of man's favourite amber liquid.

John was in those days a young man easy to underestimate—not any more. His style of somehow encouraging you to have a laugh at his expense presents a warmth of personality that disguises a steely and tenacious patience and resolve within. These qualities have enabled him to get deals across the line when others might have long given up the chase.

During the eighteen-month period between when this deal was first presented and when it was completed by CHI and CHAMP, there continued to be heightened scepticism within our executive teams. Why take on what seemed to be a cyclically exposed commodities business, whose forecast EBITDA had been downgraded from $50 million to $29 million in this eighteen-month period of due diligence?

The business was bought to the attention of CHI by a 'friend of the firm' who understood that UMH was unloved and non-core to both of the current 50 per cent owners. These two large agribusiness shareholders, ConAgra Foods, United States, and Tiger Brands, South Africa, were motivated to sell UMH and concentrate on other priorities.

At the time of the purchase by CHI and CHAMP, UMH was the fourth largest and most diversified malt producer in the world. It had annual production of approximately one million tonnes and operated from fourteen plants worldwide in Australia (Barrett Burston Malting), United Kingdom (Bairds Malt), Canada (Canada Malting Company) and the United States (Great Western Malting). UMH's core customers were the large brewers and whisky distillers who use malt in their production process. Key customers included Foster's, SAB Miller, Heineken, AB-Inbev and Diageo.

In September 2006, the CHAMP II and CHI IV Fund acquired UMH for approximately $155 million. At the time of acquisition the business had revenue of approximately $300 million and EBITDA of $25 million.

The CORE PROPOSITION for the UMH deal was this: The company was being sold by two owners for whom UMH was no longer of core interest. This sale was taking place at the bottom of the market, while demand for malt would soon begin to outstrip supply. There would soon be a shortage of malting manufacturing capacity around the globe, exacerbated by the emerging demand for oil from crops. This would shift UMH from being a price taker to a price maker. We would be purchasing the enterprise for US$150 million (down from the asking price of $280 million just eighteen months earlier), well below the replacement value of the plant and equipment.

Our confidence in this core proposition was bolstered by the credible plans of the senior management team for 'de-risking' the business by moving customers to a toll manufacturing basis, so transferring the exposure to volatility in the price of the raw material, malt barley, from the malt manufacturer to the brewers and distillers.

The investment NUMBERS for this deal were as shown in the following Table 13.

Table 13: UMH entry and exit numbers

	Entry value Sep 2006 (US$m)		Exit value Nov 2009 (US$m)
Enterprise value	154.0	Enterprise value	664.3
Equity in	29.4	Equity out	181.3
Revenue at entry	298.6	Revenue at exit	614.6
EBITDA at entry	25.1	EBITDA at exit	113.2
		Times money	6.2x
		IRR	89.6%

Looking at the KEY PEOPLE, CHAMP and CHI were able to bring their cross-border capabilities to great use in this transaction. Led by David Pittaway for CHI and John Haddock (ably supported at the senior level by Ben Sebel) for CHAMP, the combined efforts in due diligence, deal execution and project management through the exit arguably could not be matched by any other mid-market GP in the private equity business.

This was very similar to the Austar deal, where execution required the combination of the North American and Australian resources of CHI and CHAMP respectively. Indeed, both these cross-border deals achieved better than six times investment cost for our investors, and both deals earned AVCAL's 'best buy-out' industry awards.

Foster's was a most important end customer for UMH in Australia. Indeed, close to a third of UMH's EBITDA would be derived from Australian domestic sales and exports from Australia into Asia. So having PE project management in both North America and Australia was of fundamental importance.

The most important individual in the whole mix was the CEO of UMH, Jim Anderson. Based in Omaha, Nebraska, Jim proved to be a remarkably successful CEO in driving earnings from $29 million in 2006 to over $120 million at the time of our exit three and a half years later. Jim is a plain-speaking, charismatic and hard-driving CEO. Physically very fit, he had played as a quarterback and a linebacker at a high competition level in his university days. He demanded the highest performance from his four divisional general managers and handsomely rewarded them for their efforts.

Jim was convinced he could grow earnings and simultaneously reduce the inherent risk profile of this raw material processing company. He, and we, embarked on a path that would convert customers' supply arrangements from short-term to long-term tolling contracts. Within our ownership period, long-term contracts moved from 20 to 80 per cent of total production. The top ten customers' share of supply was reduced from two thirds to less than half as the company successfully rode the wave of microbrewers' expanding popularity.

Jim and his team were also focused on optimising net margin by customer. There are many different malt compositions; while rarely more than 6 per cent of any brewer's total cost of goods, the impact of malt on colour and taste is of great importance. These product features provided UMH the opportunity to achieve other than just commodity margins. Jim would work with a customer's chemists and plant engineers to provide specially customised malts that would meet particular taste and colour specifications, always with a consistency of quality and delivery. Nowhere was this more evident than when doing business with the whisky distillers. Jim and his UK team were highly successful in expanding their business with the leading distillers, where the gross margin per tonne of malt was often seven times higher than that achievable with the big beer brewers such as Millers and Foster's.

So, through better utilisation of the assets we had acquired from Conagra and Tiger, through forensic focus on margin by customers and offering higher-margin customised malt solutions, 90 per cent of the impressive earnings improvement was derived from organic growth. The low point in monthly earnings was reached in September 2006, the month when we acquired the company. Every month thereafter earnings increased—timing was good and the operational improvements were great.

Jim was articulate in convincing CHAMP and CHI to undertake a $100 million capital expenditure program that would deliver the next stage of growth. We committed to build a greenfield plant near Brisbane, underpinned by a twenty-year contract from Foster's, and a brownfield expansion of existing capacity in Scotland, underpinned by several long-term contracts with the Scottish distillers. These commitments would lock in future growth and also benefit the next owners.

The exit

In November 2009, CHI and CHAMP sold the business to listed Australian agribusiness Graincorp for $655 million. At the time of sale, the business had revenue of $700 million and EBITDA of $116 million. The CHAMP funds returned 6.2 times their money at an IRR of 90 per cent from the equity they invested into the business. Not too shabby for what most people superficially viewed as a boring agricultural commodities business!

In spite of the wobbly state of the equity markets worldwide, we had developed the view that the Australian public equities market could provide an attractive IPO exit opportunity for UMH at the right time. After all, Australia was a significant producer and exporter of a wide range of grains and food products. In meat and livestock, wool, wheat, wine and many other agribusiness products, Australia was a scale player in world markets. So an IPO for UMH in Australia should be a credible option.

During our time of ownership, John Haddock had made it his business to get to know some of the larger agribusiness companies in Australia and abroad. John focused on those companies for which UMH might prove an attractive fit in terms of logistic infrastructures and key customers. One such company was the Graincorp group, publicly listed in Australia.

In the first half of 2009 we commenced a dual-track process, seeking trade buyer interest while preparing for an IPO alternative. In June 2009 the Graincorp CEO convinced us of his desire to acquire UMH. By this time we had evidence that an IPO would be strongly supported by institutional investors, and so we were not prepared to suspend float plans. While we were confident that Graincorp would be a great home for UMH and would assist UMH's next expansion phase, we nonetheless did not want to fall between the two exit 'stools', the potential IPO and the possible trade sale.

Given that UMH would roughly double the size of Graincorp, it was clear that such an acquisition was a 'game changer', and quite a major decision for the Graincorp board. We needed to be sure that the proposed transaction had full board knowledge and support, and this was essential before we would consider Graincorp as a viable alternative to an IPO. It was agreed that I should explain this position clearly and directly to the Graincorp chair, Don Taylor. Fortunately, Don understood and was agreeable to organising his full board to attend a detailed presentation from the UMH management team.

Don is a hands-on style of chairman who had been involved with Graincorp since its early grower co-op days, well before its public company status. During one meal-time break in the management presentation day, I asked Don what he would do if his CEO ever moved on. His immediate answer was, 'I would take over as CEO the same day—no problem.'

We continued the IPO process right up to the day when the sale documentation was executed by Graincorp, so maintaining a sensible tension for price and terms.

Lesson one: *Sometimes it is well worth 'staying around the hoop' because you may be the only player left on the court when the ball just bounces your way, if you are patient enough.* In the UMH case, we worked and waited eighteen months as the markets declined and the vendor's price expectations were realistically recalibrated.

Lesson two: *Look for whether you can turn a price-taker business into a price-maker by differentiating service and/or customising product specification.* If you can, you will probably be able to buy low and sell high. The UMH management team delivered on both service and product differentiation, so enabling rapid earnings growth with existing and new customers.

Lesson three: *Be prepared to embrace cross-border complexity in the deal, not shy away from it.* Cultural, time zone, currency, tax and other such challenges do reduce the field of credible buyers. With the combined offices and resources of CHAMP and CHI in Sydney, Brisbane, Singapore and New York, we were well suited to the UMH geographies and prospects. Few other GPs could compete, and the trade buyers seemed to be preoccupied with their industry doldrums at that time. This was also true with our Austar transaction, as described earlier.

Accolade Wines

This deal fits the 'straw hats in winter' description: why buy a wine company when the world seems to have too much wine and not enough buyers? When wine companies are going broke, when Australian exporters are squeezed for margin by the rapidly escalating Aussie dollar, and when the oligopoly of Australia's grocery chains are hell-bent on expanding their own house-brand wines in preference to the brands of their long-term wine company suppliers? You must be kidding!

So what was CHAMP thinking in January 2011 when it completed the acquisition of Constellation Wines Australia (CWA) now renamed Accolade Wines?

Accolade Wines is the largest producer in Australia and the largest marketer of Australian wines in the United Kingdom. Its main brands include the famous pioneering Hardys (established in the 1850s in South Australia), Houghton (which celebrated its 175th anniversary in Perth in 2011), Brookland Valley, Banrock Station, Bay of Fires, Leasingham, Tintara, Reynella, Stanley, Omni and many more.

The company also owns vineyards and brands in South Africa, including Kumala, Flagstone and Fish Hoek. It owns the Californian brand Echo Falls, now the second largest volume wine sold into the UK market. In the United Kingdom, Accolade owns and operates the largest and most modern bottling facility at Accolade Park in Bristol, bottling 400 bottles each minute, 24 by 7 every week of every year. The company also owns the very successful Matthew Clark distribution company fifty–fifty with the Punch Taverns group.

With a 250 000-tonne grape crush in its Australian wineries, 1600 employees, worldwide volume of approximately 40 million case equivalent (so that's approximately 480 million wine bottles), and sales of close to $900 million per annum, CWA was in fact struggling to make a profit in Australia and Europe when the business was first brought to our attention by CHAMP deputy chairman Nick Greiner in 2010. Nick has long been interested in the wine sector; more than just a voyeur and consumer, he had once owned a small vineyard in the Hunter Valley. Nick had also served several years on the board of McGuigan Wines together with David Clarke, the successful Macquarie Bank chairman and proprietor of Pooles Rock wines company, Ian Ferrier, the celebrated insolvency fix-it man, and veteran wine impresario Brian McGuigan.

Like so many others, McGuigan Wines had struggled to produce any returns for its shareholders in the ever-toughening wine markets. Renamed Australian Vintage Limited (AVL), the company had examined the merits of a merger with the Australian business of the world's largest wine company, Constellation Wines Inc., listed on the New York stock exchange. Prima facie, there appeared to be some $50 million of savings to be extracted were the production and logistic activities of the two enterprises sensibly merged. However, Constellation wished to also take some cash off the table as part of the exercise, and this proved a stumbling block for AVL, and the merger never happened. Thus came an opportunity for CHAMP.

One of Nick Greiner's many 'hats' was worn as chairman of Citigroup's local advisory board in Australia. Following his short but entrepreneurially effective period as premier of New South Wales, Nick became a most sought after adviser and company director in the country, and for good reason. Commercially savvy, not hung up on the opacity of political correctness and factional obligations, Greiner boldly wrought overdue market reforms as premier. This success earned him bipartisan respect that has survived the decades since his loss of office.

Of his many directorships of recent years, including Citigroup, Coles, QBE, AVL, Bradken, Nuance and Rothschild, the CHAMP board is, of course, his most satisfying and famous one. I say that tongue in cheek, but as chairman of CHAMP I have been amazed by the extraordinary range of Nick's contacts and friends, a network enabling him to gain access and knowledge about almost any project in whatever sector we may be considering. Nick has been a long and strong friend and a most effective non-executive director.

Citigroup, as advisors to Constellation Wines, were introduced to CHAMP as a potential solution to their client's underperforming offshore subsidiary. After all, CHAMP had experienced a very successful involvement in the wine sector with its ownership of the Cuppa

Cup Vineyards business in the 1990s (see Part One). This Australian, French and UK wine company was ultimately sold to the Southcorp group in 1999 with a 2.5-times return on our capital. Since then we had been hoping to find another investment in the sector, but were stumped by the capital intensity always characterising these wine companies. Not only capital tied up in vineyards, wineries and bottling facilities, but also in the inventories of finished wines. Most businesses nowadays measure their inventories in terms of days and weeks; not so in the wine industry where red wine can be measured in multiple vintage years, and even white wine is stored nine to twelve months or more.

The CORE PROPOSITION for the Accolade investment was described to CHAMP's investment committee as an opportunity for CHAMP to acquire a major global wine company at a significant discount to net asset value and at a low point in the wine sector's cyclical economics. Constellation had over-capitalised the company's vineyard and winery assets for an extended period of time, while simultaneously under-investing in basic sales and operating processes. Cost reduction initiatives and a refocusing of the sales and marketing function of the company could enhance the upside, while the downside risk to CHAMP could be minimised through attractive transaction pricing, asset protection and structuring.

The circumstances framing this core proposition were that CHAMP could:

- buy well-developed and high-quality fixed assets (vineyards, wineries, warehouses and state-of-the-art packaging facilities) and net working capital with a total book value of approximately A$900 million for A$310 million
- implement identified business improvement initiatives by reducing complexity and redundant activities
- continue to facilitate the company's transition from its legacy position as a winemaker-led model to an actively managed FMCG customer-focused business model
- de-risk the investment via a transaction structure that provided mortgage security for its initial investment.

This opportunity offered CHAMP an unusually attractive entry into the wine sector, while avoiding the capital intensity that has historically characterised the industry. Given the recent years of over-investment in fixed assets and inventory by Constellation, the forward-looking capital expenditure profile was modest and free cash flow generation was strong.

The key numbers at the start of this deal are set out in Table 14 . . . the exit numbers will hopefully excite us all in the next edition of this book!

And what about the KEY PEOPLE? John Haddock, a CHAMP managing director, had become intrigued by the Constellation situation. With his recent successful experience as CHAMP's key project director of another agribusiness, United Malt Holdings, John could sniff another counter cyclical opportunity with Accolade.

John and I were introduced by Citigroup's James Douglas to Paul Hetterich, the Constellation executive in charge of their non-US businesses.

Paul was based in Rochester, New Jersey, the head office of the NYSE listed Constellation Wines. Tall, lean, rapid-fire talking, open yet wily, Paul knew the business inside out. He was refreshingly frank about the errors that had been made in their Australian acquisitions and rollout, the overpayments, the brand portfolio inconsistencies. He also pointed to the opportunities now possible, including the likely removal of the supply glut as demand and supply curves gradually adjusted, and the benefits of scale when dealing with the major grocery customers.

Table 14: Accolade entry numbers

	Entry value Jan 2011
	($m)
Enterprise value	288.0
Equity in	250.0*
Revenue at entry	931.0
EBITDA at entry	35.8

Note: Of the $250 million provided by CHAMP, $100 million has since been returned pursuant to a long-term facility provided to Accolade by GE Finance.

We hosted Paul and two of his colleagues on board *Archina* for a twilight supper sail on Sydney Harbour. After sampling a number of the company's higher premium wines, we settled into a 'what sort of a deal are you really after' discussion on the aft deck. This discussion led John and me to believe we might well find an acceptable way back into the wine business with a deal structure avoiding the capital intensity normally intimidating PE involvement in the wine industry issue, and also enabling the downside to be virtually eliminated.

We landed on an in-principle understanding with Paul whereby CHAMP would provide $250 million in cash, secured against approximately $900 million in assets. This would see CHAMP acquiring an 80 per cent shareholding, and Constellation taking $200 million cash back to the United States while retaining a 20 per cent shareholding and upside in the future of the business.

Paul was confident that he could 'sell' this deal structure to his colleagues and encouraged me to meet with his boss, Bob Sands, the president and co-founder of Constellation Wines.

Just a few weeks later it was arranged that Paul would introduce me to Bob for a discussion over dinner at the upmarket Sorellina restaurant in downtown Boston. Paul waved me over to the sommelier's bar where Bob already had three bottles of Constellation's premium reds decanted. Bob was every inch the self-made billionaire: confident, exuberant with a dash of brashness, no ice and never shaken. There was no small talk, just an immediate barrage of questions about the size of CHAMP, what I knew about the wine business, why I would place a $250 million bet on the turnaround in Australia, whether we would be able to meet their deadlines, and so on.

Only after these delicious reds had accompanied a splendid meal did any non-deal conversation emerge. I asked Bob how it felt to be a billionaire. He allowed that the money hadn't changed his life too much, although having his own jet was certainly saving a lot of time at the airports nowadays. Bob described to me how his father had established a small wine business at the end of World War II. Mr Sands senior had purchased volumes of fortified wine that he made into sacrament wines for the church. He was able to capture a healthy share of this blessed niche during the postwar decades, and it was this small business that then became the basis of the table wine business developed by Bob and his brother, Bill. Now listed on the NYSE, Constellation boasts a market capitalisation of approximately US$4.2 billion. The two brothers had completed a string of acquisitions, assembling a range of premium, high-margin wine brands, such as Robert Mondavi and Ravenswood.

Bob was a deal-maker through and through; it was clear to me that he was fed up with his thwarted efforts to expand in Australia. In short, he and his team had been unable to replicate the high premium US business model in Australia and the United Kingdom. He was ready to cut and run, the billionaire sensibly moving back to what he knew and did best in his own premium wines backyard of North America.

The key operating executive recently anointed by Constellation as the CEO for their non-US business was and is Troy Christensen. Troy already had more than ten years with Constellation in the United States prior to being asked to move to London and 'sort out' the UK business. He is now the CEO of Accolade Wines, the new name recommended by Troy and embraced by CHAMP as a suitably aspirational one for the company now under our control. With a CPA qualification from Northern Illinois University and a master's in management from Kellogg Graduate School, Troy has held senior accountancy, controller and CFO roles prior to his present responsibility. By nature and training he is a fastidiously analytical CEO. Options are flushed out and deeply studied, weightings assessed and spreadsheets run to ground prior to any final recommendation being championed. A team-oriented leader working for consensus-based decisions as opposed to top-down commands, Troy is likely to avoid ill-considered or resented directives. While this style can be prone to missing the occasional opportunity available to a more intuitive personality, in this multi-product, multi-geography and complex enterprise, Troy's 'better safe than sorry' style is likely to be appropriate.

Next steps
Our business plan contemplates steady improvement in the two high-volume but low-margin core markets of Australia and the United

Kingdom. We have lifted EBITDA from a $30 million run rate to $60 million in the 2012 financial year. This has involved rationalisation of the product range and brands, with a reduction of SKUs from 450 to 250, together with some cost savings throughout the group. To some extent, this was always the 'low-hanging fruit'. The real challenge for the next few years is how to re-establish a profitable presence for our major brands like Hardys and Houghton in the US market, and how to ensure our fair share in the rapidly expanding and healthy margin Chinese market. And then there's the matter of how we best cope with the ever-expanding dominance of the grocery chains: Tesco and Sainsbury's in the United Kingdom, Coles and Woolworths in Australia. Can we make better use of our scale in production, logistics and marketing to maintain reasonable profit margins in our key brands, while also participating as a supplier of house label wines for these guerrilla grocers?

These are just a few of the questions and challenges for us in delivering on the core proposition we posited for this exciting investment.

Lessons learned: Like me, you will only know the outcome for this bold investment in a few years' time! No doubt there will be important lessons from this wine venture, but they will be for another day when I can share them with you under the dazzling lights of hindsight—and perhaps over a glass of Eileen Hardy vintage shiraz.

Another thirteen lessons
for me

The following thirteen lessons from my past decade of buy-out experience complement the twenty lessons listed in Part One. They hold indelible instruction for me and I hope may be of relevance to you.

1. *Beware the strength and good sense of the core proposition does not lure you into underestimating how much time you have,* especially when it is all about changing the fundamental operations of a company, like Sheridan.

    Given the speed with which the pressure from imports crushed Sheridan's margins, we badly underestimated how long we had to restructure the company's operations. Not only did we pay too much for the business, we also over-leveraged the capital structure with bank debt. I compare this with the more recent Accolade deal in which we have similar challenges for re-engineering the company's business model but where we have only modest debt on the balance sheet. We have built in a more realistic time frame and capital structure with which to achieve the changes necessary for success.

2. *Don't go into a turnaround deal unless you already have the turn-around CEO who you know can do the job.* In the case of Australian Discount Retail (ADR), our well-founded confidence in the immediate harvest of low-hanging fruits duped us into insufficiently analysing of the fundamental turnaround task ultimately required for transformation of the business model.

   This experience helped us focus on the fundamental challenges in the Accolade company which await us after the upfront harvest from rationalising product SKUs, sale of excess inventories and non-core assets. While attracted to the low hanging fruit,we have focused on the re-engineering tasks from day one.

3. *Many executives can intellectually grasp the need for fundamental and paradigm change, but very few have the courage and passion needed to do what it takes in a timely manner.* Of course, unless the GP has the necessary sense of urgency and the stomach for fundamental change then you shouldn't expect the portfolio company CEO to succeed with a turnaround. In the case of Sheridan, it involved plant closures and large redundancies, off-shoring of all manufacturing to China and Pakistan, creation of an agile design and marketing culture, among other challenging shifts. As it happened, we had months, not years, in which to achieve these goals. In this, we and management failed.

4. *Special returns require special angles, so look for the special angle you have or can bring to the deal.* In the case of Austar there were two: bringing 'clean hands' to the vendor, enabling us to solve a problem with the junk bondholders' position; and discovering a pioneering legal concept of 'international comity', which enabled a transaction otherwise impossible.

   If you hope to make exceptional returns for your investors, like six times your money as in Study Group International (SGI), then you better have a special angle. This can be a special person with insider knowledge, a synergistic bolt-on acquisition and/or new products and services. With SGI we had the successful ex-CEO in our team and we developed a new product (international study centres) with dramatically higher growth at higher margins.

5. *When talented operating executives keep beating their own stretch targets, don't get in their way.* First understand and agree what the key drivers of performance are in any particular business, then agree with management what metrics will be used to report on these drivers. If management keep beating their numbers—for example, ARPU and customer churn at Austar, margin per tonne by customer at UMH, free cash flow per student at Study Group—then let them get on with it.

6. *The 'blind date' institutional selldown process can provide an outstanding and efficient exit outcome.* Especially relevant to publicly listed securities, where continuous disclosure provisions may place constraints on a bargaining process, this overnight auction process was pioneered by the Caliburn advisory firm.

7. *Have the courage to know when to stop flogging a dead horse.* This is a repeat of Lesson 5 in Part One of this book, learned in the Rumentek experience. I have repeated it here as it is such an important one.

On the one hand, you don't want to give up on an investment just because it is proving more difficult than you expected. And you owe it to all the stakeholders, employees, creditors, lenders, management and investors to not give up prematurely. You are acutely aware that reputation is hard-earned and easily lost.

But, on the other hand, any decision to chase the deal with more cash must be disciplined by the basic fiduciary responsibilities you have to your own investors. So avoiding embarrassment that you got it wrong with this investment, just hoping that things must surely improve, never wanting to give up too soon—these are some of the emotional inputs that should not be allowed to trump objective realities. It is actually a lot harder *not* to chase good money with bad . . . As disappointed as we were with the outcome of the ADR deal, we did at least limit our loss to just 10 per cent of our investment.

8. *If you mix a bucket of clear water with a bucket of muddy water, you finish up with a bigger bucket of muddy water.* Mixing a profitable small-store format business with a loss-making big box format

retailer was a dumb idea in the case of ADR. They had different store management, different merchandising and different customers. They were, and always will be, different businesses requiring different things for success.

This experience might be compared with the success experienced by MFAs multiple acquisitions of brands and businesses that were quickly integrated within the existing IT and sales platform servicing existing customers of the larger parent company.

9. *A well-executed sale process begins on day one of your ownership.* The online data room provided to us when we acquired SGI was constantly updated thereafter by the company's very astute CFO. The importance of this point was underscored by the number of questions tabled by the bidders, namely 710 during due diligence. These were answered promptly and with a minimum intrusion on management time.

Of course, you cannot always pick the ideal timing for the investment exit. The corollary is that it makes sense to be ready should an attractive opportunity suddenly appear. This may manifest in the form of the IPO market window opening, or an unexpected approach by a major trade competitor.

Certainly when Bright Foods approached the Manassen company, management were already prepared with accurate, contemporary and comprehensive due diligence materials. This provided the buyer with reassurance that they were dealing with a professional team.

10. *Be prepared to embrace cross-border complexity in the deal, not shy away from it.* Cultural, time zone, currency, tax and other such challenges do reduce the field of credible buyers. With our offices in Sydney, Brisbane, Singapore and New York, we were well suited to the geographies and prospects in the UMH, SGI and Austar deals. All three of these earned us approximately six times our initial investments.

11. *Sometimes it is well worth 'staying around the hoop' because the ball might just bounce your way, if you are patient enough.* In the UMH case, we worked and waited eighteen months as the markets

declined and the vendor's price expectations were realistically recalibrated.

A similar period of courtship was involved until the Accolade deal landed. We remained in contact with the vendor while it reviewed its exit options, all the while winding back its exit value expectations. It is a refreshing reminder that even in this high velocity life we all lead, patience can indeed be a virtue.

12. *Look for whether you can alter a price-taking business into a price-making one by differentiating service and/or customising product specification.* If you can, you will probably be able to buy low and sell high. The UMH management team delivered on both service and product differentiation, so enabling rapid earnings growth with existing and new customers.

In recent years most wine producers have become price takers in over-supplied markets where demand is dominated by the mega grocery chains. Accolade Wines will need to learn from UMH's success in moving some of its products to price maker status.

13. *People still make the difference, and do not let anyone tell you otherwise!*

I realise you already know this and I am really only reinforcing Lesson 7 in Part One. Every so often timing can prove to be the principle determinant of fortune or tragedy. And, of course, insightful analysis and comprehensive due diligence are essential for any GP to deliver sensible investment performance through the cycles. But in my direct experience with more than 70 VC and PE deals, superior returns (better than four times your money inside five years) are only delivered by outstanding portfolio company CEOs. Only a great CEO can turn a good company into a great one.

Victor Hugo elegantly defined 'genius' in *Les Misérables* as 'a creature with a telescope in one eye and a microscope in the other, rummaging about in the infinitely large and the infinitely small'. Each and every one of the successful CEOs featured in this book exhibit this characteristic.

PART THREE:

Creation of the GP manager

It is a beautiful morning on Sydney Harbour, fresh with that clear, crisp air that heralds early spring in Sydney. I am in a comfortable deck chair on the stern of *Archina*, a truly lovely 60-foot timber ketch that is the joint pride and joy of me and Joe Skrzynski. Built at Careening Cove in Sydney back in 1932, *Archina* sailed in the very first Sydney to Hobart yacht race in 1945 and more recently in the fiftieth anniversary race to Hobart in 1995. Now an annual classic in the international offshore racing events calendar, after competing in seven of these 640-mile 'slogs' I have finally worked out that I probably don't need to do another one. Or maybe just one more.

Right now Joe is approaching in the tender from the Rose Bay marina. This morning's plan is to continue our deliberations regarding the ongoing transition of ownership and decision-making to our younger partners. Now that both of us are in our sixties, and enjoying the twenty-fifth year of our business partnership, surely we can figure out how to work more 'on' the business rather than 'in' it, spend more time mentoring our younger partners and less time worrying about how to control everything. Shouldn't be too hard, should it?

Unfortunately, the PE sector worldwide has few examples of successful succession. To be fair, the sector is a relatively young one with probably not less than 90 per cent of all GPs formed during the past fifteen to twenty years. This arithmetic almost guarantees that GP succession will be one of the major challenges for the sector worldwide in the decade ahead.

A morning on the aft deck of the yacht, away from the office and interruptions will surely help Joe and me to show that succession is possible and even enjoyable.

The anatomy
of the GP

The DNA of the CHAMP Private Equity management company evolved from the petri dish of venture capital, cross-fertilising with expansion capital deals and small-scale management buy-outs that had been successfully completed in the predecessor AMIT Nos 1, 2 and 3 funds. A common preoccupation through all of these activities was backing great managers, going for growth in sales and cash profits, and never being over-greedy at exit time.

The modern general partnership (GP) needs a team of executives who can execute on the following seven core requirements:

1. RAINMAKING: A nose for new deals, and how to find them.
2. DEAL ANALYSIS AND EXECUTION: Ability to value a company and buy it for a sensible price on sensible terms, including arrangement of a sensible level of debt to support the acquisition structure.
3. IMPROVING THE PORTFOLIO COMPANY: Knowing how to help management make their companies great, not just good.
4. SELLING THE PORTFOLIO COMPANY: Recognising when it is time to sell and knowing how to achieve a fair price.

5. MANAGEMENT OF THE GP: Managing project teams, coaching junior staff and leading by example.
6. SERVICING THE INVESTORS: Not only with profits but also timely and accurate information and building strong relationships.
7. FUNDRAISING: Being able to present the case for why investors should entrust you to do a great job with their savings. Building this trust over many years is essential.

A GP will only achieve top quartile performance, as measured over successive funds and fifteen years or longer, if its key team of executives possess excellent capabilities in all seven of these core competencies. There are past and current examples of GPs who achieve top quartile performances in a single fund, but there are only a few who can show this performance over longer cycles with successive funds. This is inevitably due to a weakness in one or more of the seven competencies listed above.

At CHAMP, during the most recent decade of our operations, we have concentrated on recruiting and motivating a talented team of executives who in aggregate deliver these core competencies. This team is presently comprised of as follows:

2	Founder directors
5	Managing directors (including finance director)
3	Directors
4	Associate directors
5	Associates
19	

This professional executive team of nineteen is supported by an admin and accounting group of six, with further secretarial support from eight other assistants; a total staff of 33. In addition, there is a separate team of ten investment professionals led by Su-Ming Wong managing the CHAMP Ventures funds.

CHAMP's finance director, Barry Zuckerman, is the inaugural and five times repeat winner of the industry AVCAL award for best financial reporting to investors. He is also Australia's representative on the international agency responsible for establishing best practice valuation and reporting standards for the PE industry.

CHAMP operates from its head office in Sydney, with a satellite office in Brisbane, a four-person team in the Singapore office, and usually one associate director seconded to the New York office of CHI.

So what makes an ideal GP executive? If we ran a gene array scan, what would we find in the DNA structure of our existing executives? Of course, in an idealised PE world they would all be clones of me . . . just kidding. What you want, of course, as in most professional services companies, is a mix of talents and ideas producing sustainable and hybrid vigour. Most experienced GP execs will ultimately be competent and interested in all seven of the key competencies, but few if any will be excellent in and passionate about them all. Nor do they need to be, in my view, but it is essential for the GP to encourage and accommodate a working balance and a culture of mutual respect for the different skills among the executive team.

In the executive committee of six (excluding the two founding directors, whose involvement nowadays roams across all activities in a mentoring/coaching way) there are:

- 4 main 'rainmakers' (competency 1)
- 6 involved in new deal analysis and acquisition (competency 2)
- 6 active with portfolio company improvement (competency 3)
- 6 involved at portfolio exit time (competency 4)
- 2 heavily involved in GP internal management and investor reporting (competencies 5 and 6)
- 3 frontrunners with fundraising (competency 7)

Of the nine associate directors and associates, all devote most of their time to the analysis and due diligence involved in deal assessment (competency 2) and also the activities of competencies 3, 4 and 6.

There is no single blueprint for the 'correct' balance of talents. But I do believe that without an excellent talent bank in *all* seven competencies, the GP will sooner or later struggle and disappoint itself and its investors. And this leads me to now discuss what has so often been the elephant in the GP room, namely the matter of founder succession.

GP management
succession

When asked by an admiring investor at a recent annual general meeting of Berkshire Hathaway about his future plans, Warren Buffett, now in his eighties, told the investor to be careful what she wished for. He recalled a similar question about 45 years earlier when he was congratulated on the continuing profits and dividends and asked by the anxious investor: 'But how long are you going to stay around for?'

Succession is rarely a straightforward matter. Incumbent managing partners, be they founders or otherwise, often overstay their use-by dates, and often leave talent vacuums underneath them since they had been calling all the shots themselves for so long. Younger partners and others involved with the firm will usually feel embarrassed, churlish or too intimidated to promote serious discussion about succession, particularly so if the senior partners are the founders and shareholders.

In the year 2000, we began the very successful transition of management and control of the venture capital and expansive capital business of AMIL. Our partner Su-Ming Wong was keen to build on this legacy business and establish Champ Ventures as the leading GP in this niche of the PE market. We agreed a protocol for ensuring no confusion or competition could occur between the investment activities of Champ PE and Champ Ventures. This key protocol ensures that the maximum size equity cheque for CV is below the minimum size for CHAMP.

CHAMP maintains a minority shareholding in CV. These two GPs have standalone professional teams in adjacent offices. Su-Ming is supported by his two senior partners, Stuart Wardman Browne and Greg Smith. This leadership group brings a collective scar tissue and commercial savvy to the task. Assisted by an additional team of seven seasoned professionals, they have racked up a most impressive investment record with the CV Fund 5 and CV Fund 6. As a result the new CV Fund 7 successfully closed its fundraising target of $475 million in mid 2012.

Following the successful transition arrangements with Su-Ming, Joe and I then turned our attention to the challenge of transition within CHAMP itself. The CHAMP I Buyout Fund had been raised in 2000. This was followed by CHAMP II, the 2005 vintage $1 billion buy-out fund. At that time the GP ownership was 50 per cent with myself and Joe, and 50 per cent with our New York partners at CHI. The carry economics was split 75 per cent to the Australian team and 25 per cent to the NYC team. 'Carry' is the term used in PE to describe the profit share that normally accrues to the benefit of the PE fund manager, the GP. The carry is a share of the profits derived from the funds' investments after all of the invested capital in the fund has been returned to the investors, the limited partners (LPs). Typically, carry will be set at 20 per cent of fund profits.

In 2002, Joe and I reached a verbal understanding with our senior Australian team members. We made it clear that prior to the launch of our next fund, the CHAMP III buy-out fund, we would enter good faith negotiations with regard to the economics and shareholdings in the GP. We were enthusiastic to achieve such a transition for three important reasons, discussed in the following sections.

CHAMP: Life after Joe and Bill

Having spent decades of our lives building a pioneering and respected firm in the Australian PE market, we wanted to be confident CHAMP Private Equity would continue to succeed and expand long after our retirement. In other words, both Joe and I as partners and founders want to leave a lasting legacy of which we can be proud.

We have witnessed the break-up of other PE firms around the world and indeed in Australia. Characteristically, these have been bank or other institutionally owned PE management companies, 'insto models' as compared to what I call 'owner-driver' models where the GP execs own and run the business. In the insto models, sooner or later two issues come to a head and cause the disintegration:

- The first is a fundamental non-alignment between the relevant inputs and outputs, between the management and the profits. In the beginning, the institutional sponsor may provide a very important seed-funding and money-raising role for the first fund. As a result, the sponsor would keep the majority of the economics while the PE execs were actually doing all the work. This non-alignment inevitably leads to the key execs leaving the insto firm and starting their own shop across the road. In Australia we have seen that happen many times—for example, when the Grant Samuel PE team left to form Archer Capital, when most of the Gresham PE group left to form Ironbridge, and the Quadrant executives parted company with Westpac.
- A second issue resulting in the demise of the insto model is the non-core status of PE within the bureaucracies that own them, and the fundamental strategic thinking of major banks and financial holding companies. The career path for ambitious executives to get to the top of Macquarie or Westpac or ANZ would never be via the non-core and unimportant PE division of the bank.

  Nor could there ever be a satisfying solution to the misalignment of interests with third-party investors in a PE fund managed by an insto GP. The investors want to know that the motivations and rewards of the GP execs are totally and only tied to the performance of the PE fund they manage. Third-party investors become unnerved if the futures and fortunes of the GP execs are seen to be tied to their sponsoring bank employer.

For one reason or another, we have seen most of the Australian banks tinker with and ultimately withdraw from PE: there was NAB with its ill-fated Paternoster Partners venture in the early 1970s, and Westpac initially with its BLEC (Business Loans and Equity Capital) venture with the pioneering UK PE business, 3i, in the early 1980s, and later with Quadrant Capital (Quadrant is now a successful owner-driver model, independent of the bank). And then came ANZ with its ANZ Ventures division, which was launched with a flurry in the early 1990s only since to be wound down.

We did not ever want to see any of this happen to CHAMP!

Essential precursor for investors in CHAMP III

As we moved through the investment of the CHAMP II funds, it became increasingly clear we needed to finalise our succession planning. Not only to acquit our responsibilities to our younger partners but also to reassure potential investors in CHAMP III that there was indeed a strong bench of management other than just Joe and Bill.

Investors want to know who they are backing as management not only of the next fund but also the fund after that. For them to bother completing their forensic inquiries and due diligence, most serious investors in PE are looking for a long-term relationship where they may be invited to make repeat allocations to funds, backing people they know and trust. All pretty obvious.

A PE fund usually has a finite life of ten years, by which time investors expect fund investments to have been realised with all capital and profits returned in cash. The period within which the GP is allowed to invest the capital committed by investors is usually the first five years. For this reason, and for other practical business reasons, we had already devolved responsibility for the major investment tasks in CHAMP II to the senior executive team. Neither Joe nor I were on any of the portfolio company boards, and the investment project directors were always one of CHAMP's partners at a managing director level. In this way, we wanted to be able to demonstrate that an investor in CHAMP III would be backing the successful management team already in place in CHAMP II.

The standard project team for the analysis, recommendation and execution of an investment is usually comprised of three execs: a managing director, an associate director and an analyst. This analysis and due diligence will normally require the engagement of accountants, lawyers, industry consultants and key practitioners with operational experience relevant to the business enterprise concerned. The CHAMP project team of three is usually expected to stay with that investment for the several years needed for improvement and growth. That same team will also want to see the ultimate exit completed successfully. Investors take close interest in these projects and want to know who has been responsible for successes (and failures) and who will be responsible for investment management going forward.

I have more to say about all of that in the fundraising section that follows. But for now, let me just share with you the rhetorical riddle surfaced by Warren Buffett's remarks mentioned earlier in this chapter. On the one hand, investors wanted to know Bill and Joe would be staying around for CHAMP III, and, on the other hand, wanted to be reassured that Bill and Joe were not actually essential to the success of CHAMP. The investors needed to see that the younger team had sufficient hands-on experience and appropriate incentives, including proprietorship, to ensure they would stay the course for the life of CHAMP III, CHAMP IV and hopefully beyond. The transition we have achieved in our GP is best summarised under two areas, economics and governance.

Economics

Table 15 shows the movement in shareholdings and profit shares (carries) from the CHAMP founders (Joe and Bill and CHI) to the Australian executive team. This transfer occurred prior to the start of the CHAMP III fund in 2010 and represents a significant shift in the economics, the share of the spoils, of the GP. It reflects the founders' desire to motivate and reward the younger partners for their increased role and effort in ensuring the ongoing success of the CHAMP funds.

It should be noted that the Australian shareholders include all managing director and director level executives; carry participants include all shareholders plus associate director level executives. Carry participants are obliged to subscribe their own cash in the fund pro rata with all other investors. Since the GP agreed to invest \$3 million in the CHAMP III fund, at the same price as all other investors, each partner in the GP contributed pro rata to his or her carry participation—for example, a 10 per cent carry participant is required to invest \$300 000 of his or her own money. This significant commitment further reassures investors that they have the full attention of the GP management team.

Governance

The essential governance structures are circumscribed by the CHAMP board of directors, and the remuneration committee of that board (REM). The board is majority controlled by the Australian team; it is the investment decision-making authority for new deals, for follow-ons and for exits. The board is also responsible for the approval of annual budgets and business plans.

Table 15: Transition of GP economics

	Shareholdings in GP		Carries (GP profit participation)	
	Pre-CHAMP III	Now	Pre-CHAMP III	Now
Australian founders	50%	25%	32%	22%
Australian execs	Nil	50%	43%	62%
Subtotal Australia	50%	75%	75%	84%
CHI	50%	25%	25%	16%
	100%	**100%**	**100%**	**100%**

The board is comprised of all members of the executive leadership team, plus two representatives from CHI and an independent director, currently Nick Greiner. The board is also currently chaired by me.

The REM committee of the board is comprised as follows:

- Nick Greiner, AC, chairman
- Joe Skrzynski, AO, a CHAMP founder
- Leonard Harlan, a CHI founder
- Cameron Buchanan, a rotating executive committee member
- Barry Zuckerman, CHAMP finance director.

The REM committee has the important responsibility of determining annual salaries and bonuses, based upon recommendations from the three CHAMP members of REM and advice from external consultants as required. Any aggregate increase in salaries and bonuses greater than 15 per cent in any year requires board approval. Any changes to individual carry allocations is a separate focus requiring approval from a committee of shareholders.

These important transitions in the economics and control of the GP were designed to fairly reward those expected to do the heavy lifting, namely the Australian executive team, while still incentivising the founders and CHI to continue to remain fully committed to the success of CHAMP.

This design was 'road-tested' with a number of CHAMP's lead investors prior to being inked. And in the CHAMP III fundraising process, all of the details were provided to investors.

It is fair to say that the internal process of agreeing and negotiating this transition was at times frustrating, relationship-testing and emotionally draining for many of us. While the new cake had been baking for several years, it was the final details of the icing and the size of the slices that tested the digestive mechanisms for all parties concerned. But in spite of the number of chefs involved, the final product has proven to be a healthy one.

Our partners in NYC, John Castle and Leonard Harlan, had not embarked on such a transition phase within their own firm. They were older than me and Joe, so why should we be thinking about transitioning ownership and responsibility to younger and less experienced partners? And to be fair to John and Leonard, the CHAMP partnership agreement of ten years ago was struck with Bill and Joe, not with others, so why fix what ain't broke? They were also raising a new fund, the CHI #5, without any fundamental shifts in partner economics and governance, so why should CHAMP embark on such changes now?

For the reasons outlined in this chapter, we had a different perspective and initially had some difficulty selling this to our NYC partners. The expression 'if it ain't broke don't fix it' is as popular as it is misguided. Most machinery needs care and maintenance, most needs periodic upgrades and most ultimately needs replacement with better technology. Most partnerships need the same 'fixes' over time.

It is fair to say that Joe and I feel vindicated by the complete success of the CHAMP III $1.5 billion fundraising. This is not to say that our template is appropriate or optimum for CHI or anyone else, but it is increasingly clear, in this ever-tightening PE capital market, that succession planning will now be a front and centre issue for leading investors worldwide. I am also confident that John and Leonard will work with their younger partners in NYC to find a sensible solution prior to the next CHI fundraise.

Working *on* the business more than *in* it

A third reason for our interest in securing a positive and sustainable transition of the GP was our personal ambitions to spend relatively more of our time working *on* the business rather than *in* it. By this I mean having more time to mentor members of our team, to play constructive devil's advocate roles in the team's due diligence and analysis process, to worry more about strategic threats and opportunities in our portfolio companies and indeed in the CHAMP GP itself.

Learning to let go, to delegate with confidence, to trust with confidence, to not undermine by second-guessing and micromanaging—these are the sorts of challenges a founder must successfully overcome if he or she is to become fully effective working on the business and creating space and opportunity for younger partners to flourish. I am addressing these components myself and looking forward to improving on some old habits. Joe is too; only time will really tell.

In this our twenty-fifth year of business partnership, Joe continues to be a one-man analytical powerhouse. Quick to indentify the key drivers in any industry, keen to focus on any uncontrollable risks such as government regulation, technology disruption or weather dependency, Joe is always able to assist CHAMP's project teams to efficiently frame the right questions for due diligence.

After twenty-five years of such a strong business relationship and bonds of personal friendship, it is perhaps not surprising that I can pretty much tell what Joe will think about a new deal when it comes into the shop, and vice versa. When people ask me why I stay so actively engaged in the business, my answer starts by pointing to the strength of and my confidence in this special partnership with Joe. Add to that my enjoyment of the camaraderie of the wider CHAMP partnership, the stimulation and excitement that is the very essence of PE, the enormous buzz from assisting the performance growth in our portfolio companies, the pride of ownership in CHAMP as the Australian pioneer of PE, and the satisfaction of delivering profits to our investors . . . these provide ample reasons!

The art and science
of fundraising

Venture capital and private equity investing is not for everyone. For starters, the VC investor needs to contemplate an average waiting period of about ten years before realising any returns. The PE investors' time horizon might be closer to five years. For both cases, the investors' money is relatively illiquid compared to other alternatives like cash or deposit, publicly traded company shares, or other publicly exchanged securities. The investors' funds will be considered to be at greater risk, ranking behind the claims of creditors, mortgagees, and other regulated preferences.

As a result, the VC and PE managers sensibly seek to raise their investment funds from off-market wholesale institutions, rather than on-market retail traders and investors.

Prior to 2000, the supply of such funds was about 100 per cent domestic. By 2012, about 70 per cent of PE funding is being supplied by international investors, primarily pension funds, endowments, and sovereign wealth funds. This rapid shift has accompanied the increased sophistication and investment performance of the Australian PE sector.

Timing for a new fund

Like most PE funds, the CHAMP funds are structured as ten-year limited life funds, during which the GP has five years in which to invest the committed capital. And not until 75 per cent of the fund's allocated capital has been invested (and/or committed to be invested) is the GP allowed to begin marketing another fund. This is an understandable protection for investors who might otherwise worry that their GP was forever out marketing new funds rather getting on with the job of investing existing ones.

And so it was that towards the end of calendar year 2008 we approached the planning for the launch of CHAMP III. The CHAMP III fund is actually the ninth fund with which the partners in the CHAMP group have been actively involved. Since 1987, eight funds had preceded it: the AMIT Nos 1, 2 and 3; the AMWIN Innovation Investment Fund (IIF); CHAMP Ventures #5 and #6; CHAMP I and CHAMP II. The CHAMP Ventures #7 fund, a $475 million fund raised during 2011–12, is the group's tenth successful fundraising, bringing aggregate funds raised to more than $4 billion, $2 billion of which raised since the GFC when LPS have been busy reducing the number of their GP relationships.

Given the typical management fee structure of a fund, the GP faces a 'cliff' by the end of year five in terms of operating income stream. The typical PE fund is expected to be fully invested by year five and thereafter the management fees decline rapidly. So by year four of the fund's life the GP will be wanting to give serious thought to the prospects for raising another fund.

CHAMP I was a 2000-vintage fund, a pioneering dedicated buyout fund for Australia. Lesson 9 in Part One of this book—timing is more important than analysis—was developed from my experiences with early VC investing, and in particular our experience in the 1990s with the dotcom boom and bust. But it is a lesson that may apply just as aptly to fundraisings.

Our very first institutional fundraising, the 1987 vintage Australian Mezzanine Investment Trust (AMIT No. 1), is a quintessential example. This was the first institutionally subscribed PE fund in Australia. Joe and I had obtained five 'soft circle' commitments from five Australian institutional investors in September 1987. Three were large corporate super funds (Shell, BHP and CRA), one was the New South Wales State Superannuation Board, and the fifth was AMP. None had ever made a PE investment to that date.

One of our core propositions in our presentations to these investors was that public equities markets at the time were heading for a correction, and that this would dramatically increase the demand for and attractiveness of private equity. In the very next month came a 'correction' all right: the stock market crash of 1987 when 20 per cent was knocked off public markets in a shuddering 48 hours. This extraordinary event constituted a MAC (material adverse consequence) in our draft contract with these five investors. Of course we reminded them that one of our core propositions had just unfolded rather sooner than we could have hoped. Only one of our five investors, AMP, pulled out, and so began the $30 million pioneering AMIT No. 1 fund. This 1987 fund did indeed benefit from the fall in acquisition prices that followed the stock market collapse—timing may not be everything, but it surely makes a big impact!

In the introduction to Part Two I describe various factors that led to our decision twelve years later to launch the CHAMP I fund. By then there was considerable 'science' supporting our case, including the analysis of buy-outs completed by us and others in Australia during the prior decade. There were also the buy-out fund precedents from North America and Europe along with a compelling analysis of the preconditions then supportive of the need for a dedicated fund in Australia.

But there was also much 'art' involved in developing the case for CHAMP I. Important was the creation of our partnership with the NYC-based buy-out operator CHI, and there were also our long-term relationships with investors here and abroad that actually made possible the timing of what was then considered a very bold initiative. Indeed, I believe the surge of offshore interest and money into the Australian PE markets subsequent to the formation of the CHAMP I and

CHAMP II funds was in large part due to the example set by Harbour-Vest, the international leader in the PE fund of funds business at that time. An investment in a 'fund of funds' provides the investor with a convenient and wide portfolio spread, as the name implies. Rather than investing in a single PE fund, or themselves endeavouring to directly select a number of PE funds, many institutional investors elected to invest via a specialist fund manager, via that manager's fund of funds. Harbour-Vest's demonstration of faith was key: faith in the Australian economy, in the thesis that buy-outs would indeed work well in Australia, and in the integrity and quality of the PE managers and the supporting infrastructure of lawyers, accountants, investment banks and lenders, all necessary to a long-term viable and sustainable PE sector.

The PE division of the John Hancock insurance group was acquired by a Harvard Business School classmate of mine, Brooks Zug, and his friend Ed Kane and renamed HarbourVest in the 1970s. HarbourVest was an early mover in the PE fund of funds business internationally. Joe and I had many meetings with HarbourVest executives over a fifteen-year period before they ultimately took the plunge into Australia via CHAMP in 2000.

In the mid-1990s, one of the younger HarbourVest partners, Philip Bilden, moved his family from Boston to Hong Kong to head up the Asian business for the firm. He had started out in PE at a very young age, with a Midwest SBIC (small business investment company) before completing his MBA at Harvard. From there he lobbied hard and long to join the exciting business run by Zug and Kane out of Boston. Son of a distinguished naval officer, phlegmatic and unflappable, Philip is very much a 'lead by example' sort of guy.

Philip proved to be an astute judge of people and markets; he avoided the early over-exuberance in Asia that cost US and other PE investors so dearly in the 1980s phase of 'get into Asia at any cost'. Philip also politely and adroitly eschewed early invitations into China and, in doing so, did his investors a huge favour.

When I asked Philip why he had started out in the Midwest SBIC, he explained that his girlfriend had taken a job out there. Having since got to know Tricia Bilden, I would suggest that, save for Philip's decision to invest in Australia via CHAMP, this was undoubtedly the best decision of his life!

Philip's quietly diplomatic style and grace make him very much the gentleman's gentleman in PE circles. Widely respected and always courted as a keynote speaker on the international PE conference circuit, Philip could be easy to underestimate. He is in fact a shrewd and tenacious operator, tough when he needs to be but always measured and fair in his dealings.

And so it was a huge signal when Philip recommended that HarbourVest become an anchor investor in the CHAMP I fund. He was the early mover for offshore funds into Australia and others soon followed. His confidence also emboldened some of our Australian investors, which in turn fulfilled the expectation of other offshore investors wanting to see 'Aussie skin in the game'. This 'Aussie skin' came in the form of institutional investors and their advisors who had already participated in our previous smaller funds. These included funds advised by the Wilshire investment advisory team, headed by the effusive and engaging Ovidio Iglesias. Telstra Super, Unisuper and Emergency Services Super Scheme were important early investors in CHAMP I as advised by Ovidio. A stickler for transparency and timely reporting to investors, Ovidio could occasionally test one's patience but was always looking for a win–win solution for his investors and the GP. No longer with Wilshire, Ovidio has established his own boutique PE advisory firm, Continuity Capital Partners.

Another very influential Australian advisory firm, Quentin Ayers, brought Funds SA and SERF (the Stevedoring Employees Retirement Fund) in to CHAMP I and so assisted in building our list of highly pedigreed local institutional investors. Like Ovidio Iglesias, the two principals of Quentin Ayers, Gary Lines and Ralph Suters, had been involved with our prior funds over many years. Quietly spoken, appallingly polite and never to be rushed, they were strenuously forensic in their due diligence, and have been strong and consistent supporters of us and the sector.

It would be hard to find others during these early years who have done more that Iglesias, Lines and Suters to educate and independently advise fund trustees and managers about PE allocations in Australia.

The support of these advisors and their investors continued into the subsequent 2005 vintage CHAMP II buy-out fund. Capped at a maximum of $1 billion, this fund was oversubscribed by two and a half times, making it the first time ever that we had to reject several applications and ration many others. This proved to be a very difficult challenge in terms of managing relationships, a challenge I was not in fact anticipating. I had spent the previous 30 years of my commercial life annoying and begging investors to make allocations to venture and private equity, and here in 2005 I was knocking them back! How could that be?

One again, timing played an important role, but no more important than the demonstration effect of the CHAMP I fund's performance between 2000 and 2005. The fund had outperformed most other 2000-vintage funds in the rest of the world. It had completed investments in the media sector and in the quintessentially Australian sector of mining services. Exits already achieved by Bradken (three times money) and Austar (six times) were superb demonstrations to doubting investors that the buy-out business could indeed succeed in Australia.

Furthermore, the Australian economy continued to power ahead with year-on-year positive GDP growth numbers outpacing virtually all other developed nation economies. Australia's proximity to Asia was at last being understood as a special advantage; many investors wanting to participate in the growth markets of Asia could see that a low-risk way to do so might be via Australia.

So the combination of CHAMP I's performance and the continuing robust performance of the Australian economy made the timing of our CHAMP II launch in 2005 most propitious.

But how about the timing for the CHAMP III buy-out fund? On holidays in September 2008 Lea and I were making the most of a warm sea breeze as our chartered Dufour sloop skipped between the island of Elba and the Italian mainland, unawares that the world and CHAMP were heading into the storm of a global financial crisis.

Our credentials from CHAMP I and CHAMP II would assist; our professional team was unchanged and keen to ride again with a new fund. This was a team that had demonstrated strong discipline in terms of the acquisition prices paid for the CHAMP II portfolio, and a continuing focus on operating performance improvement as the priority, not financial engineering with excessive debt used to fund the deals. The following figure illustrates these points quite dramatically.

Figure 3 shows that the average price paid by our competitors was 8.4 times EBITDA compared to CHAMP's average price of 6.0 times EBITDA. And to finance the deals, our competitors borrowed much more than we did, on average 5.5 times EBITDA compared to CHAMP's 3.5 times EBITDA.

The portfolio was well balanced and performing strongly, so the stars were aligning sensibly for the launch of our next fund. But with the emergence of a global financial crisis, maybe this time the 'timing gods' were not on our side.

Figure 3: Middle market buyouts, average multiples paid: 2005–2009

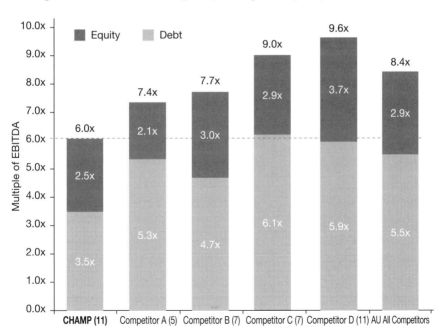

Note: Numbers in brackets represent size of sample used to calculate average.
Source: UBS, CHAMP analysis.

The CHAMP III fundraising

As events transpired, the timing for the launch of CHAMP III was far from optimal. Indeed, some of my colleagues saw it as the 'launch from hell'.

We prepared our information memorandum, assembled the obligatory data room, and formally opened initial discussions with our key investors towards the end of 2008. But the rumours of impending bubbles bursting in the real estate mortgage markets, in collateralized debt obligations (CDOs) and in stock markets around the world were looking more and more likely to be proved true. Some of the key events leading up to this situation are provided in the following lists.

In the United States:

- *February 2007:* Downturn in US housing numbers.
- *May 2008:* Bear Stearns problems result in sale to JP Morgan.
- *September 2008:* US Government steps in to control Fannie Mae and Freddie Mac.
- *September 2008:* Lehman Brothers files bankruptcy.
- *September 2008:* Bank of America buys a troubled Merrill Lynch.
- *September 2008:* US Government steps in to provide liquidity to American International Group (AIG).
- *December 2008:* US Government makes loans to bail out General Motors and Chrysler.

In Australia:

- *August 2007:* RAMS Home Loans collapse post IPO.
- *December 2007:* Allco Finance in administration.
- *June 2008:* Babcock & Brown in administration.
- *November 2008:* Australian Government guarantees the banks.

In Europe:

- *April 2007:* UBS and Credit Suisse announce multibillion dollar writedowns.

- *September 2007:* Northern Rock given liquidity support from the Bank of England.
- *April 2008:* Bank of Scotland and RBS undertake largest rights issue in British history, £12 billion, to shore up balance sheet.

How can you launch a fund in the middle of a global financial crisis, at a time feared to be greater in potential impact than the Great Depression of 1929? In particular, what could this extraordinary turmoil mean for the PE sector? The buy-out business depended on leverage, on the availability of bank debt, so with the collapse of banks and withdrawal of credit around the world, did this spell the end of the buy-out business model?

Even worse, if that were possible, could our investors be shanghaied from supporting our new fund by the 'denominator effect' in their portfolio? That is, most of the institutional investors in Australia and offshore limited their investments in alternative unlisted securities, including PE, to a modest percentage of their total investments in all asset classes; for most super and pension funds this limit ranges between 2 and 10 per cent. So if the value of their publicly listed securities falls by 25 per cent, this can suddenly cause an apparent and unwitting over-allocation to PE.

These and similar concerns were indeed top-of-the-mind issues for our target investors. Furthermore, and unsurprisingly, the turmoil created a widespread fear: where was the bottom, and just how bad could this be? It is to be expected in such times that the appetite for new investments shrinks and decisions are deferred.

So our timing could hardly have been worse. The fundraising was a very demanding slog of almost 24 months duration. This compares with the wonderfully timed CHAMP II fund, which was a six-month slam dunk in comparison. Yet again, this experience resonates with Lesson 9 on timing in Part One.

Building investor support and engaging a placement agent

Our three AMIT funds, the AMWIN Innovation Investment Fund, the CHAMP Ventures #5 and #6 funds, and the CHAMP I fund were all raised without the services of a placement agent. So after seven successful fundraisings by ourselves, why did we see the need for a placement agent in the subsequent fundraisings from CHAMP II on?

Essentially, as the size of the fund target reached $1 billion we knew we needed more and more investors from an increasingly sophisticated and global PE capital market. And we needed the best investors, those who would likely be repeat investors. We needed to access investors from Europe, North America, the Middle East, Asia and, of course, Australia. We would seek to create diversity also through the type of investor, not only by geography. A mix of pension funds, endowment funds, funds of funds and sovereign funds could give us a strong base of support, less vulnerable to the cyclical swings in the fortunes of any one investor group.

Given the above objectives, it was also clear that we did not have the intelligence network to ourselves optimally resource such a global exercise. Accordingly, in 2005 we conducted a tender process and selected the MVision placement agency from among half a dozen specialist PE agencies.

A London-based breakaway from the Merrill Lynch PE placement business, MVision was founded by the distinctive, somewhat eccentric entrepreneur Mounir Guen, aka 'Moose'. Moose's eccentricity and at times hyperactive lifestyle is best understood by his background. Born to an English mother and a Tunisian father, a double-PhD diplomat who at one time also served as minister of finance at the IMF, his parents' pursuits meant that Moose grew up travelling from place to place, seeding shallow roots, managing multiple house moves and learning to entrepreneurially fend for himself. Along the way, Moose's parents separated and his early adulthood was then spent in New York. Later, while studying economics at the LSE in London, Moose met his wife to be, Caroline, daughter of the larger-than-life CEO of the Wilkinson Sword group, John Bloxcidge. London became home . . . at least for a few years.

Moose joined JP Morgan in the United Kingdom and assisted in managing a Saudi investment fund. Subsequently in 1988 he joined Merrill Lynch, which had developed a well-regarded PE placement business led by Jerry Greene and Phil Poole, where Moose focused on finding investors for non-US funds. Always most comfortable being the boss, Moose eventually left the large Merrill corporate structure and MVision was born as an independent boutique PE placement agency in January 2001.

The MVision plan was and is to be very brand loyal, backing 'local heros' in different geographies. Now in his early fifties, Moose can justly boast that MVision has closed more VC and PE funds and raised more PE money globally than any of his competitors around the world. Would I recommend Moose to others? Yes, but never to my closest competitors!

So what did we get from MVision for our millions of dollars in placement fees in CHAMP II and CHAMP III? At least the following five services:

1. Access to a large, pre-qualified number of institutional investors
Many years ago I visited the offices of a European pension fund to give my investment pitch. After about twenty minutes or so it emerged that the senior investment officer had thought mine was an Austrian fund. Only one syllable out, but unfortunately he had zero allocation for PE in the Asia-Pacific region. This is an extreme illustration of the importance of the pre-qualification work that a placement agent can do and so avoid time wastage for all parties.

MVision has probably introduced us to literally hundreds of pre-qualified investors worldwide.

2. Market intelligence
GPs like CHAMP come to market only once every four years or so. MVision is in the market full-time on behalf of multiple clients. So the knowledge base of who the key investment decision-makers are, the likes and dislikes among different investors, particular concerns about Australia generally or CHAMP people or investments particularly, changing allocations to PE, the holiday schedules of the relevant investment committee's chairman . . . these are 'soft' components where a plugged-in and professional agent can actually make a difference.

Market intelligence also includes 'hard' facts about our competitors such as actual fees, terms and conditions being negotiated in the market in real time. While it is realistic for a GP to meet the market on terms and conditions required by the investors, it is also important for the GP to understand the trade-offs so as not to move to the lowest common denominator of all such investor requests.

3. Third-party sales force
A good agent like MVision knows you inside out, warts and all. They will push you to articulate and assemble the hard evidence of how you originate, value add, monitor and exit your investee companies. They will give you 'no holds barred' feedback, including what people are saying about you. This objectivity helps the GP sharpen its pitch; importantly, it also enables the agent to promote you to investors in a third-party endorsement way.

4. Closing
When it comes to fund closings, the agent can play an important role. Most limited partners have a formal investment committee process. HarbourVest, for example, will normally run a fund allocation decision through three investment committee (IC) meetings prior to any positive decision about whether and how much to invest. A good and well-informed agent stays tuned in to what issues are raised in these IC meetings and what may be worrying various IC members.

Once again, the role of the effective agent is part art, part science—part is gathering and analysing the facts about the investors and their requirements, part is managing expectations, relationships and timing.

Of course, the agent can only facilitate and advise. The investor wants to deal directly with the GP, probably with every executive, often with multiple visits to the GP offices separately from the electronic visits to the GP data room. The investor will make reference calls with bankers, portfolio company CEOs, executive employees and others. But our experiences in good capital market times with CHAMP II, and in bad capital market times with CHAMP III, confirmed that the agent also played a mission-critical, value-adding role.

5. A big improvement in the mix of key PE investors

The CHAMP III fundraising came at a time of general retreat from the PE asset class by most Australian superannuation funds. Fortunately, the expanding appetite among many of the world's major sovereign wealth funds (SWFs) more than offset the Australian investors' reticence.

The Aussie super fund retreat was due to several factors:

- the denominator effect
- fear of a liquidity run as super members exercised their member choice options
- indecision generally given the GFC
- international diversification.

Nonetheless, we were successful in retaining many of our existing super fund investors and gaining one or two important new ones. In aggregate, these Australian super funds committed $407 million, or approximately 27 per cent of the total fundraising. Three of Asia's leading SWFs plus the major SWF in the Middle East provided a further $385 million, or approximately 26 per cent of the CHAMP III funding.

This happy result was produced by the CHAMP fundraising project team of Ben Sebel, David Jones and Barry Zuckerman. They were assisted by Joe and me and by many other members of the professional team, and the entire effort was aided and abetted by Moose and his MVision mercenaries in Europe, Asia and North America.

Figure 4 illustrates the diversity of the investor base in the CHAMP III fund. Four sovereign funds, three of which are Asian, now make up just over 25 per cent of funds subscribed. The other large investors are comprised of leading Australian superannuation funds, offshore pension funds and offshore fund of funds.

We are very proud to have earned the confidence of such investors, and especially pleased that so many of them have grown with us as repeat investors in sequential CHAMP funds. All the art and science of fundraising will ultimately come to little without the support of these investors, in good times and bad.

Figure 4: CHAMP III investor types

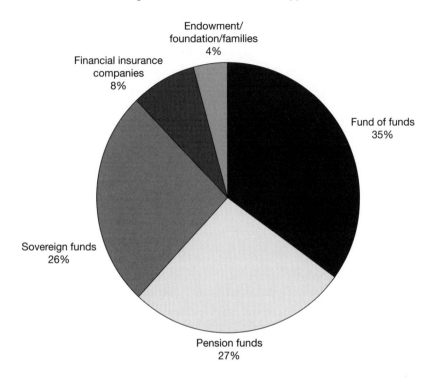

PART FOUR:

Looking ahead

We have just flopped over from 2010 into 2011 and are now enjoying our regular first week in January in the exceptionally beautiful New South Wales village of South West Rocks. For many years now we have rented with the Gray family two lighthouse keepers' cottages on top the Smoky Cape promontory, the second-most easterly point on the Australian coastline. The cape was named by Captain Cook when sailing north from Sydney in May 1770; the elegant and prominent lighthouse was erected in 1891.

Today, my very good friend and frequent sailing companion Professor Peter Gray and I are watching the sizeable fleet of yachts competing in the annual Sydney to Coffs Harbour race. The boats and their crews are enjoying near perfect spinnaker conditions in a frisky 25- to 30-knot southeasterly breeze and following seas.

As we watch, Peter asks whether I see this fast and seemingly trouble-free race as a suitable metaphor for the Australian economy's cruise out of 2010 into 2011. Peter, a highly accomplished biotechnology scientist, is in charge of the rapidly expanding Australian Institute for Bioengineering and Nanotechnology in Brisbane. Like a lot of professors, he often asks you questions to which he already knows the answers.

On this day, 2 January 2011, the Australian dollar has broken through parity to reach a then high of $US1.02 (a record since the free float of the Aussie dollar in 1987). Coal, iron ore and several other commodity prices are still strengthening as Australia powers into the new year on the back of a resources boom. Demand from Asia, in particular China, Japan, and India, looks certain to drive this boom for several years yet for the low-cost but high-quality minerals companies in Queensland and Western Australia. The tough question and the hard challenge for Australians is how do we prepare for the time when this commodities boom ends?

To return to our yacht race metaphor, the crews on these boats are actually well equipped and prepared for when the wind inevitably changes. When the wind swings 180 degrees they will drop their spinnakers and hoist their other power converters, called headsails, which enable them to sail closer to the wind. And if things really get rough they also have a set of stormsails to hoist and weather the storm.

But how will an already struggling Australian manufacturing sector cope with the headwinds of a high exchange rate, increased import competition and a diminishing workforce of those with the requisite engineering and fabrication skills?

So my answer to Professor Gray was consistent with what he already knew, namely that Australia's top economic performance would likely continue for much of the current decade. However, unless significant effort and investment now finds its way into new growth sectors—like renewable energy, biotech and bio-medical devices, agribusiness and tertiary service sector enterprises—we should not expect such economic performance in the following decade.

Introduction

This book has documented some of AMIL and CHAMP's failures and successes. Happily, the successes have dramatically outweighed the failures. Importantly, when we have sold our portfolio companies, they were almost always in far healthier condition than when we acquired them. I believe that this is the acid test for the sustainability of venture capital and private equity.

In looking ahead to the next decade, I believe the role of and need for private equity in the Australian capital markets will steadily grow. Private capital will continue to provide solutions that public markets cannot. This has become patently clear following the global financial crisis of 2008 to 2010, since exacerbated by the spluttering of the Eurozone markets.

What then are some of the questions and issues of particular relevance to Australia?

Why bother with venture
capital in Australia?

In July 2011 I was invited to address the Thought Leaders Dinner in Brisbane, hosted by the Australian Institute for Bioengineering and Nanotechnology (AIBN). The AIBN, the inaugural director of which is my good friend Professor Peter Gray, is on the University of Queensland precinct and in a short ten years has grown a 500-strong research faculty and staff.

Professor Gray had provocatively challenged me with a question: 'Why shouldn't Australia just give up on venture capital?' After all, we are successful and early adopters of new technology, so why don't we just shop the world and import what we think we need?

For a country that owes its very beginnings to quintessential venture capital, this question struck me as paradoxical. After all, high-risk money had funded the uncertain journeys of discovery by Cook and others in the late eighteenth century—this was gutsy venture capitalism on the part of the British Admiralty and Treasury, pure and simple. Still it is a good conversation to instigate, even though I know that a 'copycat Australia' is the very opposite to the innovation leader Peter wants this country to be.

A bit more historical perspective. It was not until 200 years after Cook's entry into Botany Bay that Australia had its first VC company, a business I started in 1970 and precociously named International Venture Corporation (IVC). Among its founding shareholders who ponied up the initial $500 000 investment capital were Rod Carnegie and Baillieu (Bails) Myer. Two years later, Hill Samuel (soon to become Macquarie Bank) provided another $2 million.

Since those early days, a number of Federal Government programs have targeted the market failure in our capital markets, manifesting in a dramatic shortage of risk capital for the commercialisation of Australian inventions and early-stage development of innovative companies.

While there have been some stand-out individual success stories, like Cochlear, ResMed, LookSmart and Seek, the investment returns for institutional investors in VC funds have been lacklustre when measured over the past two decades. As a consequence of this, and following the experiences of the GFC, the institutional investors in Australia have gone on a VC strike. And yet in the United States there has been something of a VC renaissance: after the collapse in activity prior, during and after the GFC, the March quarter of 2011 saw approximately $8 billion of new money raised by VC funds in North America.

And who would have thought that after search engines and electronic shopping it would be social networking that provided the next tearaway returns for VC investors? Facebook, for instance, with its $100 billion IPO valuation in 2012. In my day, friends were people you actually knew . . . not anymore it seems!

So, should Australia bother with VC? Should it just accept that its apparent strength of research and discovery cannot be coupled with risk capital and commercialisation? What's wrong with being a rapid adopter of other people's technologies anyway?

Let me try to explain a couple of reasons I hope that Australia *does* bother with VC. There are obvious national interest reasons for Australia to maintain and advance its basic engineering and IT skills, including defence. There are also less obvious public health and safety reasons, evidenced by Australia's successful border quarantine protection against such things as footrot. Then there's the capability to develop vaccines against the random threats of such things as SARS and swine and bird flus, and the prowess and importance nationally manifest in our innovations with vaccines, most recently the first cancer vaccine (against cervical cancer) developed by Professor Ian Frazer and now produced by CSL Limited for worldwide distribution.

Borrowing from my learnings over the past decade as chairman of the Garvan Institute, I believe Australia does rank highly in the international stakes of medical research. Its discoveries in vaccines, cancer biomarkers, diabetes, immune disorders and inflammatories, nanotechnology, stem cell technology and much more have all established Australia as a credible competitor and contributor to medical research worldwide.

We have an extraordinary capability in the R part of the health and medical R&D (research and development) process. No other sector in Australia can boast a more internationally competitive or relevant quotient of intellectual capital, and it would be delinquent of policymakers and all of us were this pre-eminence in R not supported and exploited by an appropriate level of D.

Why bother? Because the worldwide demand for improved treatments and cures for major diseases is huge, and this demand will continue for decades ahead. Australia could capture a share of this, but only if it can access the VC to also fund the D in the R&D process, from lab and clinic to marketplace.

One of the greatest races in all human history was that between the US bioscientist Craig Venter and the syndicate of governments led by the United States to be the first to sequence the human genome, identifying and sequencing the DNA make-up of the approximately 25 000 genes that are contained in every one of the 100 trillion or so cells in each of us. In 2001, both competitors in this race succeeded with a dead heat after several years and at a cost of some $3 billion; today, such a sequencing can be completed in weeks, not years, for perhaps as little as $20 000. And it is increasingly likely that this cost will drop to just a few hundred dollars within another two years or so.

This phenomenal explosion in accessible knowledge will deliver the era of genomic medicines. It will make pathology of disease possible at the molecular level, taking analysis and understanding of individual cancers and other diseases way beyond that which traditional cellular and blood-based pathologies can ever do. Probably within the next decade this will mean that personalised medicines—for example, chemotherapies designed for a patient's unique physiology and specific cancer mutation—will be available. Pathology of blood and tissue will now be complemented by pathology at the molecular level. Australian researchers and clinicians can and, in my view, must participate in the development of this truly exciting era of genomic medicine. This will require medical school graduates skilled in bioinformatics with the computational abilities to organise and analyse the mega volumes of DNA sequencing data. And the medical efficacy will require the interpretive skills of clinician pathologists accredited to advise physicians, oncologists and patients about treatment options.

I believe there is an awakening and understanding of this opportunity at both a national and state political level, and a bipartisan one at that. The Federal Government's health policies now embrace the need for translational outcomes—that is, for research (both lab- and clinic-based) to demonstrate the transfer of discoveries in new drugs and methods of prevention treatment and care. Thus, a demonstration of improved health outcomes in patients is required to justify taxpayers' expenditure on health and medical research, be it capital for equipment and research facilities (such as microscopy, imaging, assaying, sequencing and bioinformatics) or the recurrent salaries and staff support for the researchers and clinicians doing the work in university and research institute labs, in hospitals and other health delivery places.

This new policy thrust makes sense for Australia but the riddle currently remains: namely, an absence of the development funding in the R&D process that translational research by definition requires. This funding is vital for prototyping and proof of concept, for human clinical trials, for the requisite patenting and IP protection, and for the participation by clinician scientists and allied health professionals otherwise prevented from undertaking research, usually because their hospital employers require them to conduct an ever-increasing number of procedures.

The health industry in Australia is roughly $140 billion in size, close to 10 per cent of the gross national product. Within that figure, health and medical research may be estimated at around $3 billion per annum including the $800 million research funding budget of the National Health and Medical Research Council (NHMRC). Only $10 million per annum of this NHMRC funding is set aside as development grants, just over 1 per cent.

Our research scientists in universities, medical research institutes and elsewhere often refer to their 'valley of death'. This is the place where the research money runs out and there is negligible development funds with which to develop proof of concept, prototypes and evidence from early stage trials. Without such validation, discoveries are not investment-ready for venture capitalist or big pharmas. I do not argue the case for governments to fund the entire process from validation through to market commercialisation. But a bridge across this identified valley of death is the only way our research scientists will get to the other side of the 'valley', where the venture capitalist, biotech companies and big pharmas hang out.

I've had only a modest involvement in biotech investing, including companies like G2 Therapies Limited (now in Phase II clinical trials with Novo Nordisk in Denmark with its C5a antibody to rheumatoid arthritis) and EnGeneIC Limited (now in early Phase II trials at the Peter MacCallum research hospital in Melbourne with its unique nano-particle drug delivery system for cancer tumours). But my experience confirms the following reality to me: in establishing a viable portfolio pipeline of new drugs, treatments or medical devices, the VCs and big pharmas simply don't have to and won't invest in early clinical valida-tion and development work. Their choices from around the world are so many, and the risks (both in dollars and time lines) so high, that these investors can sensibly wait for the later-stage opportunities to present themselves.

Australia does need innovation and venture capital to help get more of this into existing industries and new industries. Long may our wonderfully endowed mining sector thrive but without produc-ing improvement throughout our entire economy, without a dramatic increase in the commercialisation of our innovation, Australia will eventually slide down the national prosperity chart.

The opportunities must include the biosciences, products and services for a future renewable energies industry, innovative products and services for the resources sector including agribusiness, internet intensive retail services, and media and communications businesses. All of these exciting prospects require venture capital. In my view, an immediate intervention by Federal Government to stimulate institutional support for VC is warranted. Implemented thoughtfully with 'sunset clause' reviews, such an intervention would provide a stunning innovation dividend over the next two to three decades.

Will the PE business model survive?

For many reasons, the PE business model will not just survive—it will thrive! There are supply-side and demand-side explanations for why this is so.

On the demand side

Here's the basis of it: public markets often just cannot, and should not, compete with private alternatives.

Arguably, the limited liability public corporation is the single greatest invention in the last 200 years. A gift of the British legal system, this construct allowed the accumulation of risk equity capital on a scale that enabled the industrial revolution and the step function in worldwide productivity and growth that followed. Investors big and small could co-invest and spread their bets in a portfolio of exposures; managers and directors could be allowed to make honest mistakes without incurring 'unlimited' liability for their risk-taking with other peoples' money. Today we take this clever invention for granted, but perhaps in our zeal to preserve its sustainability we have allowed the regulators to circumscribe and cobble the apparatus.

Let me be clear that I remain in awe of the basic public company concept. In return for the protections and powers 'licensed' to companies, our society has increasingly required that the basic values and behaviours required of its citizenry be mirrored in those of its companies. So pursuit of profit is okay provided the environment is not damaged, health and safety is not compromised, and fair markets are protected from collusion and insider trading or other forms of corruption, and so on. This sophisticated construct has served us well and will continue to do so. However, by its very nature, its sophisticated complexity and regulation will often neuter entrepreneurship and innovation.

With the extraordinary development of the limited liability public corporation came the separation of ownership and control, first researched by Berle and Means in their famous 1932 treatise *The Modern Corporation and Private Property*. Simply put, ownership of companies has become widely spread among individuals and investment entities, most of whom never know or meet the managers who actually operate their companies. Control and management have diverged, and with this separation comes the challenge of maintaining alignment of both parties' motivations, interests and time horizons.

Just who are some of these public company owners . . . and who are the independent directors representing? Are they responsible to the hedge funds and others placing long/short bets on the share price movement, or institutional investors hugging the market index, or superannuation funds seeking yield via frank dividends, or mum and dad investors looking for capital gains? By law, the directors are supposed to be acting in the best interests of all shareholders equally. But with such a confusing array of shareholder expectations, how is this really possible?

Such a challenge is dramatically reduced in the case of a PE-owned business. The owner-driver company, a sole proprietorship where the owner is the manager, is by definition never burdened by this alignment challenge. A PE business, owned 100 per cent by PE and the operating management team, also enjoys the power of this focused alignment of owner–manager interests.

So a company that needs a major overhaul of its business model, perhaps from an in-house local production to an outsourced offshore one, or a three-year downsizing phase, or a major acquisition of a key competitor for sustainable scale economies, or a major investment in product development and redesign . . . in all or any of these scenarios, the private company is almost always better positioned to act urgently and to cope. Management and owners will be motivated by what their business might be valued at in, say, five years' time, not the next quarter or two under the second-guessing gaze of stock market analysts.

This difference in 'expectation horizons' has been spotlighted by the global financial crisis. The irksome display of multi-million dollar salaries and bonuses paid to senior management of failed companies— like Enron, Lehman Brothers and American International Group in the United States, and Allco Finance, Babcock & Brown and Centro Properties in Australia—are just a few of the countless companies where the owners (and creditors) lost all or most of their money! This of course is just the tip of a misaligned iceberg. The new dean of the Harvard Business School, Professor Nitin Nohria, has described this as a shocking abuse of the 'value added' concept. Nohria derides a cor- porate system that tolerates management receiving a share of 'value added' *before* such value can be measured and monetised for other stakeholders. This non-alignment is endemic to public companies, not PE companies. The PE portfolio company management only cash in their equity entitlements as and if the owners do. And the GP manager of the PE fund only collects its equity entitlement as and if the fund investors are first paid their share in cash.

For these and other reasons, the demand for PE will continue to grow strongly. Consider some other examples of why this is so:

- The company (public or private) that cannot sell to or merge with a large competitor for antitrust/ACCC reasons may choose to access private equity.
- The company with founders who may simply be unwilling to sell to an arch rival may find PE their only solution.
- A management team of a division or subsidiary, ignored or regarded as non-core by head office, might obtain board approval for a management-led buy-out financed by PE.

- When public equities markets are in retreat such that IPOs and new rights issues are no longer available, many companies may choose to seek PE.

The post-GFC years through 2012 are an example at the time of writing where PE is providing a shock absorber role, with provision of risk capital where public markets fear to tread. For example, CHAMP's public to private acquisition of the outdoor media company oOh!media in March 2012, and Quadrant's 50 per cent acquisition of the outdoor advertising business APN in May 2012, plus a large number of PE acquisitions and equity capital provision during 2010 to 2012. Apart from the mining sector, this was an IPO market vacuum period.

The requirements for 'continuous disclosure' for publicly listed companies is rightly regarded as an essential ingredient for maintaining fair markets, minimising the likelihood of insider trading and/or ill-informed buy and sell decisions. At the same time, such disclosure requirements will often intimidate managers from taking decisions essential for the long-term prospects of their business but which involve pain and losses in the immediate short term. Thus a public company CEO may struggle to convince himself or his board that a plant closure should not be delayed, even though the company's next two quarter earnings will be negatively impacted. His board will be concerned that such a move would likely lead to a rapid fall in the company's share price, damaging its prospect for a much-needed capital raising.

The same company, if unlisted and owned by a PE company, would not have these dilemmas and inhibitions. The decision to close the plant wouldn't have anything to do with the share price, or what shareholders and stock analysts have to say about the next quarter's earnings downturn. It would be a decision all about what is best for the business in the medium to longer term.

This difference in time horizons leads me to another important illustration of the benefits of the private model over the public one: from June 2008 to June 2012 (the four-year global financial crisis of our modern capital markets era), the CHAMP portfolio valuations increased by 35 per cent while the ASX All Ordinaries accumulation index declined by 2 per cent. Do the maths!

On the supply side

When the equities bubble burst upon the arrival of the GFC in 2008, many journalists predicted that this spelled the end of the PE buy-out model. The argument went like this: with the collapse in the equities market there could be few opportunities for exits via IPOs, so this problem, combined with an inevitable collapse in liquidity and bank credit, would spell the end for buy-outs, since without leverage of bank loans the PE model would never work. This analysis and prediction was of course facile.

The headline PE failures in Australia, such as the grossly overleveraged and overpriced buy-out of Channel 9 by CVC and the unfortunate collapse of the Angus & Robertson, Borders bookshop chain acquired by PEP, were in fact exceptional. More than a hundred other successful buy-outs in the same time period have gone unremarked; their success in terms of job creation, profit improvement and superior returns to investors just don't enjoy the readership attention. A few of these successes have been described in Part Two of this book but go largely unreported in the popular press.

Indeed, I am often asked why PE seems to have a 'poor reputation' in Australia. The popular press likes to write up the occasional high-profile failure, including the occasional IPO price sag experienced post-float (such as the Myer company floated at around $4 by TPG and which has struggled at a $1.50 mark more recently). Understandably this contributes to the poor reputation. Of course, the objective reputation of actual performance record, not the juicy press commentary, is what really counts in the end. Why else would institutional investment in PE have grown from $30 million when we started out in 1987 to be greater than $10 billion today? Why would the lenders to the sector, principally the four major banks in Australia, be so keen to lend to PE? Why would the superannuation funds and other sophisticated institutional investors be allocating equity capital to PE funds? These are the people who know that PE is doing its job—that is, growing and improving businesses and, as a result, achieving higher investment returns than public equity markets are able to show.

Importantly, the banks who have participated in this remarkable ten years or so development of the buy-out business in Australia have enjoyed very healthy margins and fees for their shareholders (perhaps with the exception of Bank of Scotland International (BOSI), now in withdrawal from Australia). The Australian banks are now the lead players in the PE-syndicated loans market, and all of the four pillar banks are open for business with dedicated teams for coverage of PE. While some of the European banks have been forced to withdraw to their liquidity-stressed epicentre, other foreign financiers such as Investec, GE Capital and HSBC remain actively involved. I am confident that a number of the leading banks in Asia will also increase their participation in Australian PE transactions in the decade ahead.

Certainly the leverage ratios will remain modest compared to some that we saw in the three-year run-up to 2008; multiples of debt at eight to ten times cash flow, and even greater, were sometimes available. These debt levels were never appropriate, but the PE buy-out model does not rely on reckless borrowing (euphemistically described as 'financial engineering'). It does rely on leverage to drive the returns on equity, but only if the debt is sensibly tailored to the earnings growth and cash flow prospects of the business acquired. My partner Joe Skrzynski repeatedly reminded our younger partners that we needed to be our own credit committee; in the ebullient times leading up to the GFC it was often important to exercise restraint by not accepting the debt on offer from some of the banks. In the post-GFC environment, a sensible and typical example of a buy-out funding might be 50 per cent debt and 50 per cent equity, so if the acquisition price is six times cash flow, the debt component of an acquisition funding will represent three times the annual cash flow of the business. Depending on the underlying asset profile, growth prospects, capital expenditure requirements and other considerations, the banks will choose lower or higher limits to their exposures.

My point is this: most buy-outs sponsored by credible and experienced PE firms in Australia represent attractive and very profitable credits for the banks. This business will continue to be an important revenue and profit driver for the banks for many decades to come. Indeed, my guess is that the highest-margin business presently enjoyed by the Australian banking sector is their financing of PE transactions.

Just as important on the supply side is the continued interest of institutional equity investors from here and abroad. The traditional suppliers of PE around the world have been the pooled super funds (referred to offshore as pension funds) together with endowment funds, insurance companies and sovereign wealth funds. These provide the lifeblood flow of equity to the PE funds, where the GP managers in turn invest this equity into portfolios primarily comprised of unlisted private companies.

The appetites of these institutional investors will expand and contract with economic cycles and, more particularly, with the outperformance (or otherwise) of PE investment returns relative to other asset classes. Traditionally these PE investors have sought a spread of 500 points above public equities' returns to compensate them for the higher risk and lower liquidity associated with their allocations to unlisted private portfolios. CHAMP and a few other GPs in the Australian PE sector have provided at least that superior return to investors for many years now.

Benefits of PE investment

Given these basic supply and demand reasons, I believe the best-performing GPs will continue to demonstrate the benefits and rewards from PE investing. The best recent and post-GFC evidence of this view is the successful fundraising by CHAMP (the CHAMP III buy-out fund of $1.5 billion), Quadrant (QPE No. 3 with $750 million), Archer Capital (buy-out fund #2 with $1.5 billion) and CHAMP Ventures (fund # 7 with $475 million). These are all Australian-based GPs and it is a testament to the sustainability of the PE model that this aggregate of approximately $4.25 billion has been raised during a time of such volatility and even panic in world capital markets.

And one more reason the PE model will continue to grow is Australia's good luck of adjacency to the economies of Asia, because Asia will turbocharge the Australian PE sector in the coming decade.

In January 2008 we decided to open a CHAMP office in Singapore. We did so for three basic reasons.

First, for decades we have encouraged our portfolio companies to look to southeast Asia for new markets, for export and import, for bolt-on acquisitions, and for sources of funding where relevant. The majority of CHAMP's portfolio companies have been successful in a diverse range of activities in Asia, from Datacraft achieving the first US dollar-denominated IPO in Singapore, to Austal Ships' rapid growth in supply of fast ferries to China and Japan, to the bolt-on acquisition by International Energy Services of Singapore's largest fuel transport group, to Study Group International's successful establishment of regional sales offices in China, Korea, India, Hong Kong and Singapore, to Sheridan offshoring its sheet production to Chinese mills, and to United Malt's significant expansion of malt exports to Japan.

We wanted to encourage this sort of growth by establishing our own in-market capability to assist portfolio management teams. Our Singapore office is headed by CHAMP managing director Nat Childres, who prior to his decade with CHAMP lived for many years as an M&A lawyer for White & Case in Jakarta and Singapore. Nat was a champion for our ambitious south-east Asian plans. He has a wealth of practical work and life experience in Jakarta, Singapore and Kuala Lumpur; importantly, having worked at MD level in CHAMP's Sydney office from 2000 to 2008, Nat has been able to decant the CHAMP culture to the Singapore office. Nat recruited Shane Gong as a principal executive, who had helped Macquarie Bank open its office in Singapore before joining Rothschilds' Singapore M&A team.

Second, we wanted to use our presence to source primary deal flow for CHAMP that we would not otherwise see. In particular, our objective was to be active in the Singapore, Kuala Lumpur and Jakarta networks in the search for companies relevant to Australia and/or in fields of endeavour relevant to CHAMP's knowledge, experience and success. In September 2012, we agreed to acquire a major interest in Miclyn Express Offshore Limited, a Singapore-based company servicing the shallow water oil and gas sector. This specialist workboat company derives approximately 33 per cent of its profits in Australia and the balance in Asia and the Middle East. We are confident of completing a small number of such buy-outs in the life of CHAMP III and for many years beyond.

Third, we have a deeply held belief in the regionalisation of our PE business. We believe Australian PE expertise can be sensibly deployed in Asia and that the foremost Australian GPs have the appropriate scale, time zone and expertise to play a leading role. In this sense our sector is just one prism through which I see Australia's future in Asia. Ours should be an Australasian business model, one that our investors and portfolio companies alike will come to recognise as a valuable and distinguishing feature of current and future CHAMP funds.

Bring on the Australian republic—please!

If ever Australia should be capitalising on its independence and self-made appeal, surely this is the time. When the old-world governments and methods in Europe and the United Kingdom have so patently disappointed and when the future of Asia Pacific markets shine in contrast, Australia should emphasise its independence and owner-driven status. It should shed the remaining colonial weights and comparisons and be itself, writ confidently.

I was impressed by the two royal visits to Australia last year, one from Her Royal Highness, Queen of Australia, the other from Crown Prince Frederik of Denmark.

Queen Elizabeth is highly respected and well loved by a large contingent of Australians, myself included. However, she cannot possibly represent the interests of Australian exporters or other such interest groups of this nation, nor should she try to. The British royal family can, and indeed does, ably represent British interests in such matters, and rightly so. The Queen might sensibly be chauffeured in a Rolls Royce but never in a Holden Commodore.

The other royal visitor, Crown Prince Frederik of Denmark, underscored this fundamental difference when replying to our PM's welcome in Parliament House. Crown Prince Frederik regaled his audience with the prowess of his Danish subjects' commercial achievements in the alternative energy sector, and plugged the opportunities for Australians to partner with these Danish corporations. All good sense for the next in line head of state of Denmark to do so.

And such a role ought to be possible for an Australian head of state too, but it is only a credible role if that head of state is one of us, an Australian citizen, living onshore, not offshore, and whose primary interests are patently and unequivocally Australian.

For about a decade I served as chairman of the Australian Trade Commission (Austrade). Austrade is charged with promoting Australian export and investment interests around the globe, a challenge which in the main it steps up to with great professionalism. Many of the Austrade offshore posts were then, and still are, co-located with Australian embassy offices. When trade missions of Australian exporters are conducted, these will often involve formal meetings attended by officials of the host country. Toasts are exchanged as a matter of courtesy and protocol; I or the resident Australian ambassador would reciprocate host countries' toasts to the Queen of Australia. On frequent occasions, I would be left to explain to puzzled Asians, Middle Easterners and Europeans why the Queen of England was our head of state, quaintly the Queen of Australia! And yet the monarchists' mantra seems to be 'if it works, don't fix it'. Well, it doesn't work!

When our head of state is travelling outside of Australia, how wonderful it would be if he or she might from time to time be able to positively represent us, whether opening a show for the indigenous Bangarra Dance Theatre in Beijing, or the Sydney Symphony Orchestra in New York City, or a trade show for Australian biotechnology companies in Berlin.

Don't let anyone fool you: what we have now doesn't work and it is not a good look! It simply is an antiquated, inappropriate and embarrassing flaw, which must be remedied. Like all absurd vestiges, it will of course be changed one day, but why not now? I am certain the Queen would not object, nor would she be surprised or offended. My guess is she may even be disappointed that Australia has been so reticent to fully grow up.

Australian private equity will be increasingly involved in Asia as its many Australian portfolio companies expand their market penetration there and as Asian-based deals are directly sought by Australian PE shops. CHAMP was the first Australian PE firm to open in Asia with its office in Singapore in 2008. One day I hope our head of state may actually be invited to speak at one of the Asian capital cities' venture capital and private equity conferences. It would be great for Australia, but impossible for now. Bring on the republic, please!

APPENDIX:

A short history of venture capital and private equity in Australia

We sail into the ancient port of Knidos just before lunch on a beautiful blue and calm Aegean day. It is still June and not too hot. Lying several hours south of the much larger port of Bodrum on the Turkish coast, Knidos is framed by splendid hills on two sides and an isthmus at its end where the Aegean actually meets the Mediterranean. It is a safe and wonderfully interesting anchorage.

As our eyes focus on the hillside we realise that we are surrounded by the ancient ruins of what must have been a thriving and cultured civilisation. At the water's edge, in a prime position like Sydney's Opera House, rests a splendid amphitheatre still in good condition.

What also draws me to Knidos is my curiosity about an extraordinary venture capital project launched by the city officials some 2400 years ago. In those days Knidos actively competed with nearby ports for the custom and trade of all sorts of shipping. The city grew famous for its shops, theatres and professional women; it attracted fishermen, merchants and navy vessels from far and wide.

To further enhance its position, the officials commissioned a massive sculpture of the beautiful Aphrodite, to be erected in the temple of Apollo high above the urban centre. It was an expensive project. Would it work, would the returns be there, and how long before one got one's money back? Questions the venture capitalist is always wrestling with.

Aphrodite was the first known nude statue of a woman and caused instant and considerable controversy. Like it or hate it, you had to come and see it. And so it proved to be a big success—at least until the scandal of the nude goddess brought such disrepute upon the city that the sculpture mysteriously went missing. Today only its impressive round marble base remains and, alas, no trace of the nude has yet been discovered. Nonetheless, the legend of this high-risk, highly risqué venture lives on.

Back in the cockpit after an exhausting hike to the site of the missing Aphrodite, my mind drifts to our own much shorter history of venture capital and private equity in Australia. And so to the appendix.

A short history of venture capital and private equity in Australia

1770 to 1945

The financing of voyages such as Captain Cook's travels on the *Endeavour* in 1768 to 1771 was quintessential venture capital—high-risk money funding uncertain journeys of discovery, perhaps with treasure and booty in return, perhaps with wrecks, lost lives and total loss of capital. This was 'gutsy' venture capitalism on the part of the British Admiralty and the Treasury of the day.

The subsequent settlement of Australia in 1788 was in a way an even more remarkable venture capital project. Transportation of prisoners seemed like a brilliant and cheap solution at the time for an impossibly overcrowded and expensive prison system in London. The jettisoning of prisoners to an offshore facility was an imaginative solution, rendered possible by British maritime technology and seamanship. Yet the British soon learned that they had a tiger by the tail when the costs of building a settlement in faraway Sydney dramatically outpaced any revenue generation. Decades were to pass before innovations such as merino wool and gold discoveries reversed the cash drain on the British Treasury.

It has been said that necessity is the mother of invention. The special requirements for survival in a harsh geography and climate, remote from external solutions, not surprisingly produced a culture of self-sufficiency and inventiveness among early settlers in Australia.

Whitehall had prohibited the building of boats in the colonies since such vessels were considered potential instruments of escape. However, in the best New South Wales tradition, the local authorities turned a blind eye to the entrepreneurial craftsmen who by 1805 had built an amazing 40 vessels. These vessels were essential to the expansion of sealing, whaling and trading, and to meet the demands of new settlements along the Hawkesbury and Parramatta rivers. This innovative maritime tradition has since produced other remarkable seagoing achievements for Australia, including Ben Lexcen's America's Cup-winning winged-keel design, and a world-leading industry of high-speed ferry design and construction led by INCAT in Hobart, Tasmania, and Austal Ships in Perth, Western Australia.

The 'tyranny of distance' also spurred James Harrison to invent the world's first ice-making machine, allowing the start of a meat export trade in 1857. Of similar impact to the agribusiness prospects of the Australian economy was the stump-jump plough. Invented by Robert Smith in South Australia during 1876, this clever mechanical innovation allowed crop production on terrain previously too rough to be economical.

These and other innovations combined with the blood, sweat and tears of convicts and settlers to eventually reverse the Australian 'cash burn' into a surplus for the British. Their bold investment in Australia produced hard-earned venture capital style returns—eventually!

It was to be at least another hundred years, however, before an Australian-based venture capital industry took shape. Before attempting a description of this more recent history I should first say a little more on what is meant by the term 'venture capital'.

The US National Venture Capital Association defines it as: 'Capital provided by firms of full-time professionals who invest alongside management in young, rapidly growing or changing companies that have the potential to develop into significant competitors in regional, national or global markets.' Venture capital activities involve more than just the provision of funding and include the active participation and involvement of the investors in the management and strategic focus of the business. Essential to the concept of venture capital is the fact that investors provide equity, rather than debt, to the investee. Venture capital generally does not include investments into the asset classes of property or capital-intensive projects such as mineral extraction.

Chris Golis includes a useful description in his instructive book, *Enterprise and Venture Capital* (3rd edition, Allen & Unwin, Sydney, 1998). He writes:

> Simply put, *venture capital may be regarded as an equity investment where investors expect significant capital gains in return for accepting the risk they may lose all their equity.* Typically, the investment is either in a privately held company or a publicly listed company that has just started and does not have a track record of producing dividends for investors. The other major form of venture capital investment is in the leveraged buyout of stable, mature businesses. Here the buyout is financed with a larger than usual proportion of debt, placing the equity component in a correspondingly riskier position.

Venture capital investments may be made at different stages of a business's life cycle, including the following:

- *Seed investing:* Investing in an idea, before the formation of the company or development of any product.
- *Early-stage investing:* Capital provided to a company in its first stages of development.
- *Expansion-stage funding:* Funding to help already established firms accelerate their expansion into existing or new markets, prepare them for subsequent listing on a stock exchange, or pre-pare them for sale or for merger with other companies.
- *Management buy-outs or buy-ins:* Funding advanced to assist the acquisition of a business by an existing or a new management team. This usually involves the acquisition of an established, often mature enterprise with equity provided by the venture capitalist and debt of up to 75 per cent of the transaction value

supplied by senior and subordinate lenders (usually banks). In these transactions the venture capitalist acts as the control investor with 80 to 90 per cent of the shareholding, with the management team holding the balance.

A venture capitalist is the name given to the manager of a pooled fund subscribed to by private and institutional investors for the purpose of making a number of venture capital investments. Typically the manager will make ten to fifteen investments in the fund so providing a portfolio of opportunities, each investment expected to be of three to seven years in duration. All investments are expected to be sold within the life of a fund, normally ten years, and all net cash proceeds return to the investors.

Innovation, a process of discovery and development, is the greatest growth driver in any economy, whether of a developed or developing nation. The supply of venture capital is the essential financial lifeblood for this process to flourish. In this regard, the Australian experience is at best a stop-start story.

1945 to 1970

Prior to the emergence of dedicated professional venture fund managers in the 1970s, private capital was supplied from time to time in post–World War II Australia by wealthy private investors. This occurred predominantly in the form of family support for private family-run businesses. No formal market for private capital, as such, existed.

Then, during the 1960s, venture capital was tapped by the public markets in the form of public subscription to a plethora of mineral and oil exploration companies. The companies were speculative explorers and many of their public share issues were rendered popular by the various income tax deductions then available. These tax schemes were driven by a government policy aimed at achieving development of the capital-hungry resources sector, with maximum Australian ownership.

In the early 1960s Australia experienced a huge surge in the minerals sector, with spectacular 'boom and bust' stock market performances. Companies such as the nickel explorer Poseidon experienced share price movements and valuation templates reminiscent of today's publicly traded internet companies. In a period of less than twelve months, Poseidon shares ran from $10 each to $260; within another twelve months they were less than $1.

There is no analysis available to me that objectively measures the cost/benefits of the tax-driven government intervention, but my estimate is that the ore discoveries and their subsequent development well and truly justified the exploration costs and the tax deductions that accompanied these costs. This was a sector-specific venture capital experience that evaporated with the removal of the tax schemes and with the burst bubble of the speculative minerals market boom.

Later on in the 1960s another sector-specific and tax-driven venture capital activity occurred. This time it was based on a public policy aimed at stimulating the development of an Australian film industry. My business partner, Joe Skrzynski, was then very active in that industry and is regarded as the father of the '10BA tax deduction scheme'— tax legislation providing incentives for investors in film production. A significant flow of risk capital was stimulated primarily from wealthy individual investors; between 1968 and 1978 a number of films such as *Sunday Too Far Away*, *Gallipoli* and *Picnic at Hanging Rock* put a fledgling Australian movie industry on the world screen. Of course, there were many failures too in what has traditionally been something of a hit-or-miss business.

The politics of this sector-specific support shifted by the late 1970s when the taxation incentives had largely been removed. Nonetheless, an industry had been kickstarted; Australian directors, producers, actors, writers and cameramen have since continued to build a worldwide reputation for the Australian film industry.

These spurts of sector-specific venture capitalism did not, however, lead to the formation of venture capital funds as such, and it was not until 1970 that venture capital management companies began to emerge.

1970 to 1984

The first Australian venture capital company, International Venture Corporation Pty Ltd (IVC), was founded by me in August 1970. Capitalised with less than $500 000, the shareholders, apart from myself, included David Stone of Boston, Rod Carnegie and Baillieu Myer of Melbourne, Evelyn de Rothschild of London, and various private investors from Sydney including John Walton, Rodney Hudspeth, Gary Bogard, Nick Whitlam and the O'Neil family. American Research & Development Inc. (AR&D) and Memorial Drive Trust (the investment arm of the Arthur D. Little group) were also early shareholders from the United States.

During those early years I received great encouragement from the young and energetic Englishman Christopher Castleman, who had landed in Sydney to head up the Australian arm of the then highly successful merchant bank Hill Samuel (later to be rebadged as Macquarie Bank). Chris sensed there would be an expanding need for venture capital in Australia and an opportunity for Hill Samuel Australia (HSA) to play a role. Over many a late-night glass of his favourite ouzo, Chris and I agreed on a financing for one of IVC's fledgling portfolio companies, Ora Banda Mines Limited. This mining exploration company had discovered a unique deposit of pyrophyllite, a high-quality refractory clay, and needed funds to develop a mining and crushing operation. Castleman negotiated a loan with warrants for this risk venture and subsequently earned a handsome return for HSA.

Two years later, Hill Samuel Australia acquired approximately 25 per cent in IVC and Hill Samuel's CEO David Clarke joined the board of IVC. Like Chris, David knew there would be a huge need for professionally managed venture capital and private equity if Australia was to fulfil its growth potential. The board now comprised Bryan Kelman as chairman, myself as managing director, Ted Vogt representing Textron Inc. (the then owner of AR&D), David Clarke, Rodney O'Neil (of the highly successful O'Neil family business, including concrete and quarrying) and Gary Bogard (a former partner in the law firm, Freehill Hollingdale & Page).

Bryan Kelman was my mentor. Back in the early 1960s, Bryan had moved from his Sydney base, where he had achieved great success as the CEO of Ready Mixed Concrete, to start and run the Ready Mixed operation in the United Kingdom. A civil engineer by training, Bryan wasted little time in building the UK operation to the point where it outgrew the Australian parent. When the CSR company subsequently acquired the Ready Mixed business, Bryan was recruited back to Australia to run the expanding concrete and quarrying division.

I had joined the mailroom of CSR when I left school in 1961, aged sixteen. After mail sorting came stints in the data-processing unit, the accounts department, and sundry other projects. When Kelman joined CSR in 1966 he wanted a young executive assistant and I was fortunate to be chosen for that role, then in my twenty-first year.

Kelman was a complete business executive: an entrepreneur who could accommodate but not be compromised by large corporate protocol, an engineer with loads of commercial savvy and discipline, and most importantly in possession of a very high EQ (emotional quotient) as well as IQ. This EQ was evermanifest; in style he was naturally open and inclusive. No matter how small your role in a project might be, you would emerge from a project meeting fully engaged and motivated to ensure its success.

As Bryan took on more and more responsibility for the expanding winning interests of CSR in the Pilbara and at Gove, I fell into the practice of attending board meetings as his alternate director. Talk about jumping into the deep end! I was privileged to participate in management and directors' meetings, both functional and dysfunctional, at this early stage of my career. Always Bryan showed genuine interest in my observations, recommendations, mistakes and questions. Somehow he found time to counsel me; most importantly, his example was indelible. His ability to see and understand the other side in any dispute before rushing to improve his own position was to be a lasting lesson for me. Getting to 'yes' was often about not saying 'no' prematurely.

IVC was the first venture firm established in Australia dedicated to private capital transactions. Early investments included businesses in aquaculture, road surfacing and concrete, consumer finance and leasing, property services, marine equipment manufacturing, intensive piggeries, off-peak heater manufacturing, Australian film production, laser equipment, minerals exploration and pyrophyllite extraction and processing.

At that time Joe Skrzynski was in charge of Finance Facilities Pty Ltd, the non-property business activities of Sir Paul Strasser. Finance Facilities provided investment support to a number of unlisted entities. These included the first business in licensed taverns, a firm making safety car seats for babies, a chemical coatings enterprise and several others. These and other successes were to form the foundation of Joe's subsequent stellar career in private equity.

Within two years of IVC's commencement another venture firm was formed by Dr Timothy Pascoe, who was managing director. Shareholders included Rod Carnegie and Bails Myer from Melbourne and Chris Abbott from Sydney; the initial capitalisation was approximately $1 million. This company was called Enterprise Management of Australia Corporation (EMA) and investments were completed in the tourism and leisure sector, manufacturing and services. An early success was a transaction backing John Elliott in the acquisition of the IXL jam enterprise.

Like IVC, EMA experienced mixed results in the early years and the board decided to sell off investments and return proceeds. IVC did likewise in the early 1980s, including a distribution in specie in its successful Barlow Marine portfolio company.

Another early player in the private capital sector was John Grant who, in the late 1970s, opened a venture capital management business with the sponsorship of Hambros Bank in Australia. This business continued under the name of Hambro-Grantham, with a focus on small technology companies. Grant was successful in obtaining a licence under the Management and Investment Companies (MIC) scheme referred to later in this section, and in establishing a parallel fund. In the late 1970s, one or two other initiatives appeared, including a company called Australian Innovation Corporation. It was formed to invest only in very early-stage ventures and found the going too tough, with disappointing financial results.

Another institutional player that then emerged was the government-owned Australian Industry Development Corporation (AIDC). Focused primarily on major manufacturing and mining project financing, the AIDC also included private equity transactions among its activities. This provided it with some solid results in the wine and mineral processing sectors during the late 1970s and early 1980s. It also had an outstanding financial success in the 1980s in the Australian Submarine Corporation, building submarines in partnership with Kockums of Sweden. The AIDC's record in smaller high-technology investing was, at best, mixed. Successes included Paul Trainor's pioneering medical instruments company, Nucleus. The AIDC was a patient and brave long-term investor in Nucleus, eventually achieving outstanding profits from its investment when the company was acquired by Pacific Dunlop. The AIDC's investment in Optus was also ultimately a profitable experience. As a non-executive director on the board of AIDC I enjoyed the opportunity and challenge of these large-scale VC investments.

However, many other AIDC investments in computer manufacturers, telecoms equipment suppliers, software development companies and a variety of specialty retailers all proved unsuccessful. These failures forced its pullback from private capital investing in the late 1980s.

Following the lead of the Federal Government, and in response to the politics of the day, several state governments also established investment funds to promote their domestic industries. The major ones were the Victorian Development Corporation, the West Australian Development Authority, the Queensland-based Venture Fund and the South Australian-based Enterprise Investments. Most state funds were launched in the mid-1970s and held equity investments in small-scale businesses, typically investing $0.5 to $2 million. The success of these funds was highly variable and most were badly affected by the 1987 stock market crash. All except for the Victorian Development Corporation have downsized or have been wound up since the early 1990s. State governments today attempt to promote industries in different ways, such as sponsoring technology incubators and encouraging domestic investment from interstate and international IT companies to provide skills and spin-off technologies to the local industry.

Another important institutional effort was led by the National Australia Bank in partnership with Charterhouse from Britain and the A.C. Goode brokerage house. Called Paternoster Partners, this company was formed as a venture capital business and staffed by 'experts' from Britain, but it proved unsuccessful and was liquidated within five years or so. It was to be almost twenty years before the NAB re-entered the venture capital market.

The experience of these pioneers in the first ten to fifteen years leading up to the MIC licence program in 1984 was at best mixed. Some portfolio company successes like Barlow Marine, IXL, Nucleus and others demonstrated that venture capital could indeed work in Australia. Overall, however, the financial returns to investors did not prove compelling enough to shift the attitudes of a still risk-averse institutional investment sector. If anything, the early returns entrenched the 'I told you so' attitude in the boardrooms of the major banks and superannuation funds around the country. Australians, it seemed, were willing risk-takers on the weekends at the racetrack, but from Monday to Friday the boardrooms were decidedly risk-averse. Banks were asset-backing lenders, not cash flow financiers. They were interested in real estate property, not intellectual property. Similarly, the major superannuation fund managers achieved sound enough returns for their superannuants by investing in the top 100 public companies, government securities and inflation-driven real estate. Why should they take the extra risks involved in private capital transactions? Indeed, superannuation fund trustees had onerous responsibilities to their members and could be held liable for investment losses.

It was not until the end of the 1980s that legislation defining the responsibilities of trustees was altered such that trustees could allocate a percentage of their portfolio to various risk categories without being individually responsible for any specific investment loss within any one such risk category.

It was against this background that inquiries were established by the Federal Government. The Crawford study group on structural adjustment in 1979 recommended the creation of an Australian Innovation Authority; the Myers Committee inquiry into technological change in 1980 also recommended government involvement in increasing the supply of venture capital. The Ferris Committee report in 1984, entitled *Lifting the Performance of Manufacturing and Services Exports*, recommended venture capital assistance for high technology exporters.

Various submissions were made to these inquiries by those of us active in the industry at that time, and also to the 1983 Campbell report on the Australian financial system.

1984 to 1990

The Espie Committee (chaired by the late Sir Frank Espie) had been established in 1981 to 'consider and report on the problems facing high technology enterprises in Australia'. Its 1983 report identified several factors inhibiting the supply of venture capital in Australia, including:

- an apparent lack of quality management, particularly in high-technology industries
- poor attitudes towards investment in high-risk, long-term investments, whose appeal was not as great as that of short-term, risk-averse investments
- Australia's lack of technology development, partly as a result of the lack of capital, and also because of tight government controls of many IT industry players, such as Telecom (now Telstra) and the CSIRO
- the failure of government to support small businesses by means of assisting venture capitalists.

The Espie report recommended that the Federal Government be the catalyst in developing a venture capital base domestically, by offering incentives to encourage investment in small businesses. Acting on this, the government established the Management and Investment Companies (MIC) scheme to take advantage of the perceived opportunities that developing high-technology companies were offering in terms of wealth creation and economic growth. Sir Frank, a highly successful mining company executive, would be pleased to observe the success enjoyed by his son Paul, who decades later has established the Pacific Road Resources Fund, a PE fund focused on early-stage mining ventures.

A strong champion for government intervention in the venture capital markets at that time was the Minister for Industry, the Honourable John Button. Button was well respected for his industry development work over many years. He had resisted cries for legislation to compel the superannuation funds to allocate some percentage of their capital into venture activities. While acknowledging that a 'market failure' did exist in the early-stage funding market, he did not believe that a compulsory investment scheme would work in Australia, politically or commercially. He was, however, prepared to try a more limited intervention, hence the MIC program was born.

The MIC program was implemented in 1984 to encourage and promote investment in innovative startup technology businesses, by offering financial, strategic and administrative assistance to venture capital investors. The government did this through the issuing of a limited number of MIC licences to companies that could satisfy the government's strict criteria.

The licensees, listed in Table 16, raised almost $400 million over the life of the scheme.

Table 17 shows the annual performance of the overall MIC scheme, in terms of the amount raised and where the proceeds were directed.

During the scheme's eight-year life, the fourteen licensed fund managers invested in over 150 companies. By the termination of the scheme, the entire venture capital market consisted of 32 different funds with a capital base of $794 million.

Certain of these licensees established 'parallel funds' that effectively leveraged the MIC scheme further by attracting the involvement of a number of institutional investors. Some of the early parallel funds launched by MIC companies were:

- Advent Western Pacific parallel fund, managed by Western Pacific Investment Co.

Table 16: MIC licensees

Company or fund	Fund size ($m)
Austech Ventures Ltd	27.5
Australian Pacific Technology Ltd	29.4
BT Innovation Ltd	22.5
Continental Venture Capital Ltd	95.1
Corporate Enterprise Investments Ltd	0.2
CP Ventures Ltd	40.4
First MIC Ltd	52.4
Greenchip Opportunities Ltd	13.7
Japan Australia Venture Capital Fund	8.3
Samic Ltd	15.9
Stinoc Ltd	26.4
Techniche Ltd	19.3
Western Pacific Investment Company Ltd	29.0
Westintech Innovation Corporation Ltd	11.7

Table 17: MIC investments

Year	Amount raised	Amount invested	Number of new investee businesses
1983–84	Combined with 1984–85	0.1	1
1984–85	79.1	8.5	19
1985–86	41.0	35.5	47
1986–87	69.3	53.3	47
1987–88	40.7	45.7	25
1988–89	15.7	31.8	9
1989–90	58.6	39.1	5
1990–91	87.5	11.3	2
Total	**392.1**	**225.4**	**155**

Note: Totals may differ due to rounding errors.
Source: Management and Investment Companies Licensing Board, Annual Report 1988/89.

- Melbourne Australia Investments parallel fund, managed by Continental Venture Capital Co.
- H-G Ventures parallel fund, managed by First MIC Ltd.

By the end of 1986 the MIC program had achieved apparent moderate success, largely buoyed by investor confidence and strong growth in the overall economy. However, the October 1987 stock market crash destroyed equity markets worldwide. Following the huge losses for many large entrepreneurs and super funds, market enthusiasm for private equity waned. In addition, the impact of the crash meant that most of the MIC funds' existing investments required additional financing, which restricted the amount of capital available to other potential investments.

With the benefit of hindsight, the architecture of the MIC scheme was fundamentally flawed. The upfront tax deduction led to a separation of ownership and control of the funds; the incentive was realised by tax-driven investors regardless of the investment outcomes. Furthermore, the restrictions on how the money could be invested virtually guaranteed future failure. Only investments in early-stage technology companies were permitted; since a maximum investment for most MIC funds was only about $1 million in any one investee, most of the MICs developed extremely high-risk portfolios with no capacity for follow-on support investing.

Nonetheless, several successful investees emerged, including Cochlear, AMRAD and Vision Systems. In addition, teams of young executives entered the industry and 'cut their teeth'; many of these executives remain in the industry today. In this sense, the MIC program was an invaluable step along the way to creating an industry capability.

Secondary sharemarkets, called Second Boards, were established in Australia by all state-run stock exchanges, led by Perth in July 1984. Prima facie, a Second Board was beneficial to venture capitalists as it provided an exit mechanism for investors to realise their investments in cases where a firm had developed but was not established enough to list on the Main Board. The Second Board was also popular with business owners for its more favourable listing requirements, such as permitting companies with different share classes to list. This enabled small business owners to retain control of their business after listing, even if they were not the senior shareholder. Second Boards were not without their undesirable attributes, however, with many businesses listing prematurely relative to their stage of development. The Second Board companies were too small to warrant the attention of investment research analysis and the major institutional investors were uninterested or unable to invest.

By October 1987, 243 companies had listed on Australian Second Boards, having collectively raised $1.4 billion and achieved a market capitalisation of $3.8 billion. In terms of share performance, Second Board companies significantly outperformed the Main Board in the three years leading to March 1987 and their success was buoyed by the growth of the economy. As with the MIC funds, all Second Boards were devastated by the drying up of capital and the increased risk-aversion of investors following the 1987 crash, and eventually they all became redundant.

Corporate venturing also emerged in the 1980s and was attempted by firms such as Amcor, Telstra, BHP and CRA, which typically invested in firms relevant to their own areas of industry. Large corporations tended to invest in venture capital either by allocating funds to internal fund managers, by establishing subsidiary venture capital companies, or by investing in independent venture companies. On the whole, these efforts did not prove very successful.

A more recent entrant in the Australian corporate venturing field was Acer Computers, through its establishment of a $30 million fund for investment in smaller Australian computer companies. Intel also made an allocation to Australia as part of its worldwide venture investing strategy. It is still a little early to judge the outcomes from these initiatives.

The Federal Government has provided many other incentives to small- and medium-size enterprises over the years, typically to encourage investment in the areas of exporting and R&D. In July 1985 the government introduced its R&D concession scheme, which offered a 150 per cent tax concession for businesses with an annual R&D expenditure in excess of $50 000 annually. This scheme has been revisited and reconfigured in 2010.

The Grants for Industry Research and Development (GIRD) scheme was introduced to complement the R&D concession scheme by further encouraging a focus on new and emerging technologies. Three different grants were available, depending on the importance of the investment to both the company and the Australian economy. These were in the form of discretionary grants for small, high-technology firms; generic technology grants for new and emerging technologies fundamental to industry competitiveness; and National Interest Agreements for R&D projects that created national benefits.

Following the Ferris Committee report in 1984, the High Technology Exporters scheme was introduced by Austrade in 1986 to improve the export performance of the emerging companies. Eligible companies could qualify for export industry assistance if they could demonstrate funding support from the AIDC or from an MIC licensee.

The National Industry Extension Service (NIES) was a Commonwealth and state collaboration to aid in the delivery of information, referral and diagnostic services to the industry, and was launched in March 1987. NIES attempted to encourage firms to modernise their management and production systems, with the overall intention of increasing efficiency and competitiveness in local industry.

In 1987, Joe Skrzynski and I came together to form Australian Mezzanine Investments Pty Ltd (AMIL) with the ambition of building Australia's pre-eminent private capital funds management group. Our first fund, AMIT No. 1, was subscribed by a small number of institutional investors with a total amount of $30 million. Our first commitment came from the New South Wales State Super fund; the fund's executive in charge of alternate investments was Philip Kelly, a clear-headed, straight-talking, charming and unassuming original thinker who liked to make things happen. Philip had the support of his chairman, Bevan Bradbury, who bravely championed his backing of the AMIT No. 1 Fund. In doing so Philip and Bevan can be counted as pioneers of Australian institutional support for PE.

In mid-1987, Joe and I had suggested to our potential backers that the stock market was looking overheated and a market correction would likely occur. Such a correction, we argued, would assist our efforts, since smaller companies would no longer find such easy (and, in our view, premature) access to the then overpriced public equities markets. However, we had not expected the depth of the stock market collapse of October 1987. Following this market rout, we provided all our investors with the opportunity to reconsider their commitments to AMIT No. 1; to their credit, and our considerable gratitude, only one of the five pulled out.

Not long after, and under the auspices of Bond Street Investments Pty Ltd, Macquarie Bank indicated its intention to expand its private equities business. With David Clarke as its chairman and the popular, irreverant Sandy Lockhart as its chief executive, Bond Street later became Macquarie Direct Investment Management, with its first fund, the Macquarie Investment Trust No. 1, subscribed to $51 million early in 1988. Macquarie continued to successfully expand its activities as one of the better performing private capital managers in Australia at that time.

It was some years later that bank-owned private equity models like the Macquarie one began to falter and fall out of favour in Australia and around the world. They did so for a mix of reasons. First, career paths for upwardly mobile banking executives were typically transaction-driven; the path to the top of the executive ranks might track through retail banking, corporate finance and mergers and acquisitions divisions, never via the longer time frame of a private equity division. Second, institutional investors in bank-managed PE funds began to realise that their interests were never as closely aligned as with those of 'owner-driver' managed funds. The partners in a private and independently managed PE fund (like AMIL, later to become CHAMP) earned their salaries and profits entirely and directly from their investment record. If their investors made a profit, so did the managers. This was never as direct or as clear in the case of the bank execs in charge of the bank's PE division. A PE executive might earn a considerable portion of his or her annual bonus from an overall banking pool and only part from the PE performance. PE investors don't like those indirect and opaque incentive structures.

As a direct result, the next decade witnessed the complete withdrawal of ANZ, NAB and Westpac from their modest participation as VC and PE managers.

1990 to 1999
Pooled Development Funds
The MIC program was officially replaced by the Pooled Development Funds (PDF) program, which was announced in the Federal Government's 1992 Economic Statement. This program aimed to improve

the access of small- and medium-size enterprises to domestic private equity, by offering registered PDFs tax concessions and other investment incentives. The PDF program was introduced in an attempt to remove some of the problems inherent in the unsuccessful MIC scheme, such as lack of flexibility and absence of incentive to institutional investors. A significant tax incentive provided to investors had been the exemption from capital gains tax on any sale of shares by investors in a PDF. To satisfy the PDF program, funds had to abide by a number of regulations.

The flexibility of the *Pooled Development Funds Act 1992* allowed changes in the program to occur, and several of these have helped to promote the scheme since its inception. In 1994 improved tax incentives were offered to allow the distribution of dividends to be either tax exempt or applied to a dividend imputation system. This change attempted to further encourage investors, in particular superannuation funds, to invest in PDFs, for which the tax benefits were previously negligible due to existing tax regulations. The continual registration of new funds intensified competition among fund managers and increased the overall pool of available capital. As a result, rapid growth in PDF capital raising and investment occurred, despite difficulties in attracting overseas investment due to prohibitive tax regulations.

In 1998 the PDF Act was again amended and, for the first time, the government permitted share buy-back schemes to increase the liquidity of the investments for investors. The amendments also allowed super funds to fully own PDFs so as to further encourage domestic and overseas super fund participation, where previously they could own only up to 30 per cent. Additional changes enabled PDFs to offer loans to a maximum of 20 per cent of their capital base, where previously loans could not be made at all. PDFs were also permitted to merge, as long as cash was not paid out by either PDF in the course of such a merger.

To July 1998, 66 registered PDFs had invested over $155 million from a total pool of raised capital of $279 million. Table 19 gives the details. To date, the impact of PDFs on the venture capital industry has been modest, both in terms of capital raisings and investee performance. The regulatory restrictions on the activities of PDFs have contributed to this outcome, including the inability of PDFs to invest in large companies or in foreign-owned entities. Nonetheless, the PDFs did deepen the venture capital markets.

Co-operative Research Centres

Historically, Australia has punched well above its weight in terms of scientific breakthroughs. However, it has also punched below its weight in terms of commercialisation of breakthroughs. Its Nobel prize-winning contributions to penicillin, x-ray crystallography, xerography (forerunner of Xerox), the black box flight recorder and many other world firsts have been commercialised by others.

In response to the 1989 ASTEC report, *The Core Capacity of Australian Science and Technology*, which recommended the development of interdisciplinary science and research centres, the Federal Government established the Co-operative Research Centre (CRC) program in May 1990. The program aims to bring together public sector bodies, higher education institutions and industry, through the formation of large and integrated teams, in order to facilitate specialised research. The specific objectives of the program are to:

- contribute to economic and social development and the establishment of internationally competitive industry sectors through support for long-term, high-quality research
- commercialise the benefits of research

Table 18: PDF investments

Year	Amount raised during year ($m)	Cumulative amount raised ($m)	Number of PDFs	Cumulative number of investee companies
1992–93	20	20	5	0
1993–94	15	35	11	37
1994–95	26	61	26	59
1995–96	74	135	40	89
1996–97	29	164	51	120
1997–98	115	279	66	147

Source: Pooled Development Funds Registration Board, *Annual Report: The Pooled Development Funds Program*, AGPS, Canberra, 1994–98.

- increase skills through training and education of graduates and researchers
- promote the efficient use of R&D by strengthening research networks and building specific centres to conduct research.

There have been several selection rounds since the program's launch in 1990 and, although early CRCs were heavily government-funded, the private sector has become increasingly involved. The range of CRCs today is evident by examining the CRC website, www.crc.gov.au.

CRCs are generally established under contracts that run for seven years. They are selected by the Minister for Industry, Science and Resources on the advice of the selection committee, which in turn is advised by expert panels.

Although not intended to be profitable entities, some CRCs have generated external earnings, primarily through providing contract research. In 1996–97 this amounted to $46 million, which represented an increase of $11 million compared with the funds earned in 1995–96. Participation in the program grew impressively and by 2000 included over 250 Australian and international companies, 61 state government departments and agencies, 35 universities, 24 CSIRO divisions, eight Commonwealth research agencies, eight rural R&D corporations and numerous other organisations.

An example of a successful centre is the Australian Photonics CRC, which brings together the Universities of New South Wales, Sydney and Melbourne, the Australian National University, and industry players including Telstra and Siemens. The CRC co-ordinates over 80 per cent of R&D in photonics communications and, since 1991, has enabled telecommunications firms to increase the capacity of optical fibre networks by a factor of ten! The success of this CRC led to an extension in funding to further support the technology, with eight additional partners joining the program in 1997. Two years earlier, in 1995, the CRC founders established a startup company, Indx, at the Australian Technology Park in Sydney. Indx has won several major contracts, including a deal with Fujitsu to supply optical cable to link Europe and the South Pacific.

Co-operative Research Centres may prove to be a growing source of products and ideas for the venture capital market in future years. The test of commercial relevance that the industry participants bring to CRC priorities should produce a marked improvement in the rate of commercialisation of Australian scientific breakthroughs; however, this ambition has not yet been met.

START scheme

In April 1997, then prime minister John Howard, in his small-business statement, officially approved the START scheme, an investment encouragement program with five major components, one of which specifically targets the venture capital industry and is called the Innovation Investment Fund (IIF). The IIF was established to complement the Pooled Development Funds program and is a major AusIndustry initiative designed to encourage the commercialisation of Australian high-technology companies by matching every dollar privately raised with two dollars from the government. The IIF specifically targets technology companies and attempts to fill the void left by venture capitalists focusing on developed businesses, rather than emerging and startup investments. The initiative followed extensive consultation with the Australian Venture Capital Association and a review of similar programs in the United States, Israel and elsewhere.

Provision of incentives to private sector investors so they will bother with the higher risks and costs involved in early-stage technology investments is basic to the aims of the IIF. Lessons drawn from the earlier MIC scheme led to a much improved architecture for the incentives provided. Rewarding actual achievement at the back end rather than providing tax deductions upfront and requiring private money to actually be at risk alongside the government funds were two important improvements.

A fund's life is expected to be ten years, with a minimum of half the capital being invested in seed, startup or first-round funding. In return for its provision of funds, the government requires repayment of capital plus the bond yield plus 10 per cent of the profits of the investments. Under the initial proposal, $130 million in funding has been committed by the government on a two for one matching basis with approved venture capital managers, thereby creating $195 million for new technology company investments.

The IIF program is an innovative move and represents the most significant government initiative taken to encourage early-stage investment since the MIC scheme in 1984. The amount committed to the program has made the government the largest single investor in the early-stage venture capital industry and has been a successful step towards re-establishing a venture capital industry geared to provision of startup and early-stage capital.

In December 1997, five companies were allocated licences under the IIF. These were Allen & Buckeridge Investment Management, AMWIN Management (a joint venture between Australian Mezzanine Investments and the Walden International Investment Group), Coates Myer & Company, Rothschild Bioscience Managers and Momentum Funds Management.

The other components of AusIndustry's R&D START scheme support business research and development by providing grants and loans to firms. The government initiative pledged to provide $700 million over four years (from 1998) for small- and medium-size enterprises (SMEs) to undertake industry R&D and related activities. The four other components were as follows:

1. *Core Start* provides assistance of up to 50 per cent of project costs through grants and loans for R&D-based investments by SMEs.
2. *Start Plus* targets larger businesses and offers up to 20 per cent of project costs for firms with a group turnover exceeding $50 million.
3. *Start Premium* provides a repayable amount of up to 56.25 per cent of project costs and is intended for high-quality research projects.
4. *Start Graduate* grants are awarded to companies with revenues under $50 million to employ a graduate to undertake R&D-related research in collaboration with a research institution for up to two years.

All of the grants were offered to support R&D projects in Australia for up to three years, with grants being given on a competitive basis. In R&D START's first round of funding in April 1997, sixteen projects were offered a total of $44 million.

To some extent these various research-based programs 'politically' replaced the previous R&D syndicate investment programs, which were brought into disrepute by a preoccupation with rewards to investors from the excellence of financial engineering rather than the excellence of the science funded.

Other schemes

Another government initiative in venture capital was the Keating Government's establishment of the Australian Multimedia Enterprise (AME) in 1995 as part of its 'Creative Nation' policy. AME was to provide $45 million for investment in multimedia projects and concept developments, with the primary focus being directed towards CD-ROMs and online services. AME's aim was both to promote the growth of technology companies domestically and to provide research and literature on the status and nature of technology-based industries in Australia. By 1998 it had funded more than 90 Australian projects, benefiting over 300 practitioners. However, throughout its government-owned life, the scheme was the subject of constant criticism for not having outlaid anywhere near as much as the $45 million it had initially pledged.

AME was sold to Allen & Buckeridge in April 1997, having invested $15 million in various projects. Earlier in that year, the government reclaimed $16 million in a share capital return from AME, and reclaimed a further $13.3 million from Allen & Buckeridge in a share buy-back following the sale. The government justified the sale of AME by claiming that the Innovation Investment Fund was larger and better targeted at startup companies.

Following the failure of the Second Boards during the 1980s, the Australian Stock Exchange (ASX) again attempted to show its commitment to growing businesses by establishing the Enterprise Market in April 1998. This internet-based business introduction service aimed to facilitate capital-raising for Australia's estimated 10000 SMEs, which, in 1998, were seeking an estimated $5 billion in funding through a single national market for non-listed businesses. The service targets 'business angels', or wealthy private investors, who might otherwise not be informed of potential business opportunities. The Enterprise Market was designed to enable firms to list company information online; the market would then work with existing business introduction services to create a single 'business angel' market in Australia, as is the case in the United States. This initiative has since lapsed.

A Yellow Pages survey of small business revealed that, in 1997, business angels invested in excess of $1 billion in 6800 businesses, and the angels were becoming an increasingly important source of finance for startup and early-stage companies.

'Incubators' became another approach. They were state government initiatives to create mini-Silicon Valleys, to bring developing high-technology companies and resources together in order to provide the wherewithal—resources, knowledge, skills and so on—needed to facilitate collective growth of the tenant firms. In return for rent and a small amount of equity, the incubators provide sponsorship and promotion, which might otherwise be unavailable to small firms. Examples of incubators are the Australian Technology Park, a Sydney-based collaboration between the University of New South Wales, the University of Technology and Sydney University. Another is the Playford Centre in South Australia, which is sponsored by the South Australian Government, Microsoft, Oracle and EDS Australia. Since opening early in 1998, the Playford Centre had already assisted more than 50 South Australian-domiciled IT companies, including Camtech and Maxamine, by the year 2000.

The Australian Venture Capital Association (AVCAL), formed in April 1992, represents and promotes the venture capital industry in Australia. Its members come from the majority of funds managers, investor groups, lawyers, accountants, merchant bankers and others who are associated with the industry. AVCAL's charter aims to 'promote the Australian venture capital industry and encourage investment in growing business enterprises'. Its objectives include promotion of professional and ethical standards and the provision of a unified voice for the industry. AVCAL is actively involved in the production of PricewaterhouseCoopers' *Economic Impact of Venture Capital*—an annual survey publication that provides important information on the impact on small business and the Australian economy—and is a partner with Arthur Andersen conducting other annual surveys of venture capital activity in Australia.

By 1999 the venture capital market had grown to well over 40 professional investment groups, which collectively managed hundreds of funds with, in aggregate, over $2.7 billion. By comparison, in 1993 seventeen investment managers controlled only $507 million (1993 Arthur Andersen/AVCAL survey of development capital; 1998 AVCAL venture capital survey). The growth of venture capital had been enhanced by regular media reports highlighting the impressive growth and profit levels often experienced following investment. In the 1990s, companies backed by venture capital significantly outperformed both the economy and the top 100 ASX-listed stocks in terms of sales, profits, exports and employment growth. Figure 5 indicates the significant influences that venture capital funding had on the overall growth and development of companies that received investment.

Although expansion capital and management buy-ins/buy-outs accounted for over 80 per cent of venture capital investment activity, the proportion of investments in seed, startup and early expansion was slowly increasing, largely due to encouragement from the government through the IIF program. As had been the case for most of the 1990s, manufacturing and technology firms were the largest recipients of venture capital and, in terms of geography, New South Wales and Victoria received over 60 per cent of the capital awarded. (*AVC Journal*, September 1999).

An Australian Venture Capital Association survey indicated that, at June 1998, over $1.7 billion was invested in 221 businesses, with 50 new businesses being the beneficiaries of new funding in the 1997–98 year. These beneficiaries were spread over many sectors and regions, as Table 19 demonstrates.

By far the most important thrust in the venture capital industry in the 1990s came from the private sector. The major funds managers

Figure 5: Comparison of growth data: VC-backed companies and top 100 ASX companies, 1992–96

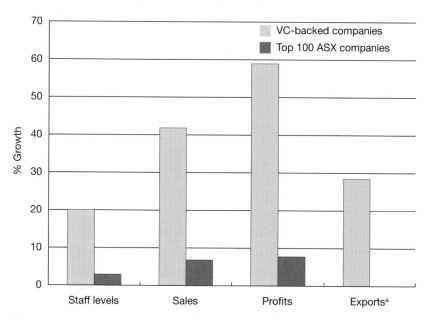

Note: ᵃ Top 100 companies data n/a.
Source: *The Economic Impact of Venture Capital*, Coopers & Lybrand Economics Survey, 1997.

in 1999 are listed in Table 20. Many of these venture funds managers developed large teams of full-time professionals and were able to deliver attractive returns to investors.

Further evidence of the increasing interest in and depth of the Australian venture capital sector in the 1990s was the emergence of 'business angel' networks. As noted earlier, an 'angel' is typically a wealthy businessperson who, with other such individuals, may provide seed capital to young entrepreneurs with good ideas and emerging companies. These angels may provide more than just money, lending their own experience to assist entrepreneurs to develop their business models. Networks of angels are likely to invest in early-stage efforts before a venture capital company provides funding.

Table 19: Breakdown of venture investment by industry and region

Industry	Number of deals Number	% Total	Value of deals Value $m	% Total
Agribusiness	15	4.73	35.91	5.27
Communications	25	7.89	30.18	4.43
Construction/housing	7	2.21	6.00	0.88
Distribution	10	3.15	21.49	3.15
Environment	6	1.89	2.76	0.40
Food/beverages	6	1.89	25.48	3.74
Health/bioscience	30	9.46	30.33	4.45
Information technology/software	55	17.35	61.01	8.95
Manufacturing—consumer	7	2.21	21.94	3.22
Manufacturing—industrial	39	12.30	239.45	35.14
Media/entertainment	14	4.42	42.23	6.20
Resources/mining	30	9.46	53.96	7.92
Retailing	7	2.21	8.46	1.24
Services—business	32	10.09	42.80	6.28
Services—consumer	7	2.21	11.73	1.72
Technology	10	3.15	16.24	2.38
Tourism/leisure	17	5.36	31.54	4.63
Total	**317**	**100.00**	**681.51**	**100.00**
Region				
New South Wales	115	36.30	213.35	31.30
Victoria	81	25.60	263.95	38.70
New Zealand	16	5.00	42.80	6.30
Queensland	17	5.40	35.39	5.20
Western Australia	52	16.40	58.43	8.60
South Australia	10	3.20	17.42	2.60
Tasmania	3	0.90	1.61	0.20
Australian Capital Territory	2	0.60	2.35	0.30
Northern Territory	2	0.60	7.62	1.10
Asia	2	0.60	0.06	0.00
Africa	1	0.30	7.80	1.10
North America	12	3.80	29.25	4.30
South America	1	0.30	1.00	0.10
Europe	3	0.90	0.48	0.10
Total	**317**	**100.00**	**681.51**	**100.00**

Source: Australian Venture Capital Journal/PricewaterhouseCoopers Survey, 1999.

Table 20: Australian venture capital firms, 1999

Top 25 fund managers and listed firms	Capital ($m)	Top 25 private and captive firms	Capital ($m)
AMP Business Development Funds	343	AMP Asset Management— Resources	900
Macquarie Direct Investment	311	AMP Life	312
Deutsche Asset Management	291	UBS Capital	150
Rothschild Arrow Private Equity	226	AMP Asset Management NZ (NZ$)	110
Catalyst Investment Managers	185	Emerald Capital (NZ$)	100
BCR Asset Management	155	RMB Australia	100
Australian Mezzanine Investments	133.7	Lombard Group (NZ$)	100
Westpac Development Capital	125	Leyshon Group	80
Hambro-Grantham Management	115	Aboriginal & Torres Strait Islander CDC	64.1
AusAsean Management	110.2	Nomura/JAFCO Investment	60
GS Private Equity	103	Oceania & Eastern Group (NZ$)	55
Gresham Private Equity	102.5	Citicorp Equity Capital	50
Advent Management Group	100	National Australia Investment Capital	44
Lion Selection Group	100	Direct Capital Private Equity (NZ$)	35
Allen & Buckeridge	87	Resource Finance Corporation	35
Macquarie Technology Funds	78.3	Acma Australia	30
Development Capital of Australia	65	Australian Technology Group	30
CVC Investment Managers	62	Fairgill Investments	25.5
Technology Venture Partners	60	Flinders Capital	22.5
Pacific Equity Partners	50	Nepean Capital Partners	20
Gresham Rabo Management	49	Salisbury Group (NZ$)	20
Australasian Media & Communications	47.5	Accord Capital Investors	16
		Manufactured Construction Systems	9
Greenchip Funds Management	47	Loftus Capital Partners	8
AMWIN Management	41.2	Mercantile Mututal Investment Management	7
Coates Myer & Co.	41.2		
Total	**3028.6**	**Total**	**2383.1**

Source: *Australian Venture Capital Journal*, October 1999.

2000 to 2012

The period 2000 to 2012 witnessed several basic shifts in the Australian PE landscape:

- a rapid growth in the leveraged buy-out segment, growing to approximately 75 per cent of all PE activity by 2012
- a continuing presence of expansion capital activity
- a levelling out in the performance of, and support for, venture capital activity

- the emergence of a secondaries market with an increasing volume of transactions between one PE fund and another.

The percentage allocation to PE investing by Australian super funds has declined since the 2008 onset of the global financial crisis. Now less than 1 per cent of cumulative assets, these savings institutions are virtually 'on strike' in 2012 with respect to new commitments to venture capital.

The following figures illustrate some of these shifts. Figures 6, 7 and 8 chart cumulative figures, and the line indicates the trend in average size of investment. As shown in Figure 8, while fewer transactions were completed in PE in the recent post GFC years, the average size of investment has increased. The VC chart in Figure 7 shows an opposite trend.

Figure 6: Superannuation funds committed to VC and PE as a % of total assets

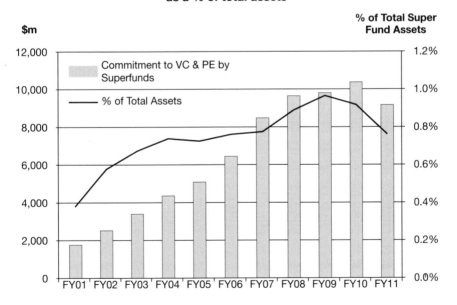

Source: ABS

Figure 7: Superannuation fund investment in investee companies, VC

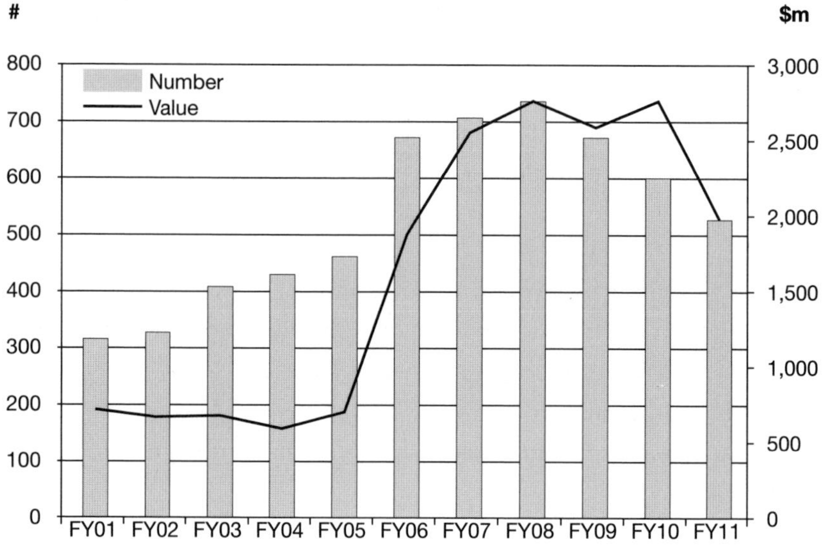

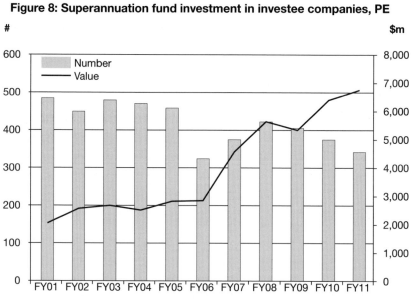

Source: ABS

Figure 8: Superannuation fund investment in investee companies, PE

Source: ABS

In the twelve years since *Nothing Ventured, Nothing Gained* was published, we have witnessed explosive growth in the size and the role of PE buy-out funds in Australia. In 2000 there may have been about $1 billion in funds available from domestic PE shops, including CHAMP's pioneering CHAMP I Buyout Fund of $500 million.

Since then, approximately $22 billion has been raised by Australian PE funds (see Table 21).

In the same period, the 'P' in PE has become very public in the press. At times it seemed that journalists were hell bent on performing their 'fourth estate' duty by exposing publicly the private activities of private equity people with pejorative labels: privateers, barbarians at the gate, marauders, assets stripper and financial engineers to name a few.

Press scrutiny with some colourful and unbalanced language contributed to a number of public inquiries. This public scrutiny motivated the industry association, AVCAL, to compile a research report entitled: 'The Evolution of the Australian Venture Capital and Private Equity Industry'. At the time of this report's release, AVCAL's CEO Katherine Woodthorpe commented that 'every national regulatory body in

Table 21: Amount of funds raised by fiscal year, Australia (in AUD millions)

Year	Venture capital		Private equity		Total	
	Amount	No. of funds raising capital	Amount	No. of funds raising capital	Amount	No. of funds raising capital
FY2002	57.24	3	611.61	3	668.85	6
FY2003	161.82	5	391.30	5	553.12	10
FY2004	96.09	5	1,631.11	5	1,727.20	10
FY2005	349.87	6	1,447.01	18	1,796.88	24
FY2006	120.60	4	4,073.84	15	4,194.44	19
FY2007	356.73	4	8,639.71	19	8,996.44	23
FY2008	333.40	5	1,833.01	15	2,166.41	20
FY2009	174.89	9	1,429.31	16	1,604.20	25
FY2010	158.00	13	1,207.92	10	1,365.92	23
FY2011	120.00	3	2,222.71	11	2,342.71	14

Source: AVCAL PEREP_Analytics, Thomson Reuters, AVCAL Analysis
Notes:
1. Fiscal year means the year ended 30 June
2. Venture Capital refers to Seed, Early Stage, Balanced VC and Later Stage VC funds.
Private Equity refers to Growth/Expansion, Generalist, Buyout/Later Stage, Turnaround, Secondary and Mezzanine funds.

the financial markets, and the Senate in 2007, found that PE was positive and healthy for the Australian economy'.

Between 2004 and 2008, most of the established PE firms from offshore discovered Australia. Of course, several of CHAMP's and PEP's limited partner investors had already 'found' Australia and had seen firsthand that the Aussie buy-out business was alive and well. CHAMP's Austar media deal was one important demonstration of how PE could improve a business and deliver six times profits for its investors.

Additionally, the major US and European investment banks were already well established in Sydney and Melbourne. The likes of UBS, CSFB, JPM, Merrills, Deutsche, Goldman Sachs and Rothschilds had all rapidly developed their PE practices dedicated to servicing the Australian PE markets. And so it was only a question of time before the major offshore PE houses would be encouraged to our shores. Blackstone, KKR, CVC, TPG, Carlyle were some of the 'big guns' seeking targets in antipodean hunting grounds. In the mid-2000s, global funds under management by these five alone exceeded $250 billion . . . and others followed their lead Down Under, including Permira, Providence, Unitas, Terra Firma and Navis.

What quickly captured the imagination and angst of the Australia press and public was that no Australian company was too big a target for this new breed of buyers. The icons of Australian capitalism were apparently 'up for grabs' in the heady boom market days from 2005 to 2008.

So it was that KKR had a run at Coles, one of the two oligopoly supermarket chains, and TPG with others at Qantas, CVC at media enterprise Channel 9, KKR at Channel 7, TPG at Myers Retail, one of the two largest department store chains, and TPG jointly with Carlyle at Healthscope hospital group. All of these transactions were greater than $1 billion each in size.

This rapid pursuit of famous Australian entities proved to be a 'shocking' experience for Australians of all persuasions—politicians, journalists, workers, mums and dads. The flurry of acquisition attempts was aided and abetted by overzealous lenders and intermediaries in an inglorious orgy of fees and bravado. It was an era of excess, of prices bid too high, of debt made too easy, of greed trumping common sense . . . and it would lead to the inevitable days of reckoning sooner rather than later. The IPO float price of Myers at $4.10 delivered a tidy profit to TPG investors, but unfortunately the shares never rose over issue price and at the time of writing languish well below $2.00. Caveat emptor you can say, but this style of exit does not endear PE to the wider community!

Meantime, the CVC group has battled with its Channel 9 media purchase from day one. Having paid a double digit EBITDA purchase price this debt laden deal has delivered a huge equity loss for CVC of approximately $2 billion. To CVC's credit, it has stayed the course of managing the deal. But once the Channel 9 acquisition deal of approximately $2.3 billion was acquired by the hedge funds Apollo and Oaktree, CVC was destined to lose control. Indeed by mid-October 2012 the hedge funds converted their debt into equity and became the proud owners of an iconic Australian media enterprise. This debt conversion to equity values the enterprise at 9.2X estimated FY2013 EBITDA.

In the immediate period ahead, there will continue to be a strong presence of the offshore PE group in the larger end of the Australian PE markets. Potential acquisitions of Billabong, Pacific Brands and Perpetual Trustees are rumoured, and there will be more to come in that $500 million to $2 billion enterprise value range.

While the Australian press has concentrated on some of the failures in VC and PE, it has done little to illustrate the successes. And by success I am not just referring to returns for the PE fund investors, primarily pension funds (see Figure 9), but also successes measured in terms of jobs created, exports, taxes paid, new products and services developed.

Analysis of these important positive metrics is presented in the AVCAL research to which I previously referred (http://www.avcal. com.au/documents/item/148).

Table 22 of PE and VC investment performance prepared by the independent and Boston based advisory group, Cambridge Associates, demonstrates the decade long superior performance of Australian PE compared to various stock exchange indexes. This is an impressive performance of resilience as it spans the period of the 2008 to 2009 global financial crisis.

Figure 9 shows government funds of just over $1 billion invested in PE and VC as at June 2011. The principal component of this government

Figure 9: Source of PE and VC funds, FY11

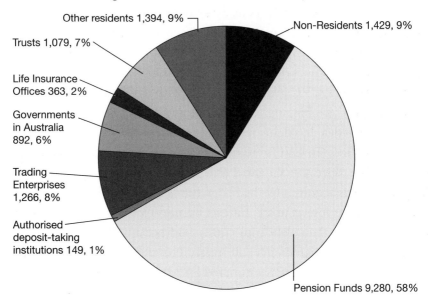

Other residents 1,394, 9%

Non-Residents 1,429, 9%

Trusts 1,079, 7%

Life Insurance Offices 363, 2%

Governments in Australia 892, 6%

Trading Enterprises 1,266, 8%

Authorised deposit-taking institutions 149, 1%

Pension Funds 9,280, 58%

involvement has been via the Innovation Investment Fund (IIF). The IIF program is a VC stimulus mechanism introduced by the Federal Government in response to the perceived 'market failure' in innovation and early stage venture development in Australia.

The IIF program enables the Government to deliver important incentives to private investors via a matching funds formula, and by a preferred capital structure enhancing the risk/returns profile for private investors. This program has successfully encouraged funding from otherwise risk-averse institutional and other private investors. As a direct result, 15 funds were established between 1998 and 2011, as shown in Table 23.

The IIF program is completing a Round 4 of allocations due late in 2012 or early 2013, which should add another $100 million of Federal funding into the VC sector.

In recent years, the majority of IIF investing has been in the life sciences, information technology and communications, and renewable energies sectors. It is too early for any definitive assessment of the program to be made.

Table 22: Cambridge Associates LLC Australia/AVCAL index returns for the period ending 31 December 2011

Index (A$)	1-Quarter	1-Year	3-Years	5-Years	10-Years
Cambridge Associates LCC Australia Private Equity & Venture Capital Index (A$)[1]	2.42	7.85	7.11	3.29	7.52
Cambridge Associates LCC Australia Private Equity & Venture Capital Index (US$)[1]	8.22	7.59	21.31	9.20	14.04
S&P/ASX 300 Index	2.05	(10.98)	7.67	(2.39)	6.14
S&P/ASX Small Ordinaries Index	(0.60)	(21.43)	11.83	(5.18)	6.48
UBS Australia Bank Bill Index	1.21	4.99	4.37	5.49	5.44
UBS Australian Composite Bond Index	1.94	11.37	6.31	7.40	6.46

The Cambridge Associates LCC Australia Private Equity & Venture Capital Index is an end-to-end calculation based on data compiled from 51 Australia private equity and 20 Australia venture capital funds, including fully liquidated partnerships, formed between 1997 and 2011.
[1] Pooled end-to-end return, net of fees, expenses and carried interest.
Source: Bloomberg L.P., Cambridge Associates LCC, Standard & Poor's, Thomson Datastream, UBS AG and UBS Global Asset Management.

However, our own early experience is encouraging. In 1998, with our CHAMP Ventures colleagues lead by Su-Ming Wong and in partnership with the offshore venture management group Walden and Partners, we established the first IIF called AMWIN Management Pty Ltd. This was a $40 million fund including the government money provided on a two for one basis. The government money was entitled to a return of its capital with a modest interest rate together with 10 per cent of the fund's profits. From the private investors' perspective, this capital structure provides a powerful incentive to participate and succeed, to put up only a third of the capital for 90 per cent of the profits.

AMWIN was a highly successful fund, particularly with its investments in the LookSmart search engine business, the SEEK job search startup and the Gekko mining equipment company. As a result the returns to the government from AMWIN alone paid back the entire Round 1 allocations by government to all five IIF participants.

I think an extension of the IIF scheme is justified and still required as one important response to a continuing market failure—that is, a failure to develop and commercialise more of the nation's innovation.

Table 23: IIF licence companies

Round 1 - 1998 (Capital Commitment A$m)	
Allen & Buckeridge Investment Management Pty Ltd (A$41.25)	
AMWIN Management Pty Ltd (A$41.25)	
Coates Myer and Company Pty Ltd (A$41.25)	
Momentum Funds Management Pty Ltd (A$31.15)	
GBS Venture Partners Limited (A$42.50)	
Total	**197.40**
Round 2 - 2001 (Capital Commitment A$m)	
Start-Up Australia Ventures Pty Ltd (A$39.21)	
Four Hats Capital (A$50.00)	
Neo Technology Ventures Pty Ltd (A$31.70)	
Stone Ridge Ventures Pty Ltd (A$35.69)	
Total	**156.60**
Round 3, Tranch 1 - 2007 (Capital Commitment A$m))	
Cleantech Australian Fund Management Partnership LP (A$50.00)	
Brandon Capital Management LP (A$40.00)	
Total	**90.00**
Round 3, Tranch 2 - 2009 (Capital Commitment A$m)	
Yuuwa Management LP (A$40.00)	
OneVentures Management Pty Ltd (A$40.00)	
Total	**80.00**
Round 3, Tranch 3 - 2011 (Capital Commitment A$m)	
Brandon Capital Management LP (A$40.00)	
Carnegie Venture Capital Pty Ltd (A$40.00)	
Southern Cross Venture Partners Pty Ltd (A$40.00)	
Total	**120.00**
GRAND TOTAL	**644.00**

Source: The Department of Industry, Innovation, Science, Research and Tertiary Education

The IIF program has helped create a platform of sophisticated technology investment management. It will be a shameful waste if we fail to leverage this skill base in the decade ahead.

2012

Global upheaval in capital markets since 2007 have tested investment products and investor nerves worldwide. What began with a rout of overleveraged and overexposed banks and financial institutions has now spread to a whole of system currency risk, the Eurozone. These major issues continue to threaten the stability and predictability of world capital markets. The underlying strength of the Australian economy, with its dependence on new Asian markets rather than older European ones, is of some comfort. Certainly the profitability and credit rating of the Australian banking system is providing some underpinning of confidence to an otherwise very 'skittish' and risk-averse domestic investor base.

The successful PE fund raisings by CHAMP in 2010 ($1.5 billion), by Archer in 2011 ($1.5 billion), and by Quadrant ($750 million) and CHAMP Ventures ($475 million) in 2012, confirm that the markets are still open for PE, at least for top quartile performing fund managers. This cannot be said for VC.

At the same time, public equities markets in 2011 to 2012 have provided poor support for companies seeking capital solutions via share placements or initial public offerings. The longer these constraints prevail, the greater will be the demand for and efficacy of private equity.

A very strong and sophisticated infrastructure now exists in the form of dedicated PE sponsor groups in the legal, accounting, banking, insurance and advisory firms nationally. This will service the established GP managers and their major investors for Australia and offshore in a continued expansion of the Australian PE sector in the decade ahead. This growth is likely to manifest in relatively new sectors of activity for PE. In this regard Figure 10, showing recent 'sector breakout' by PE in the United States is instructive.

I believe these sectors will also witness increased involvement by Australian PE with technology intensive enterprises, including life sciences companies. We will also see a rapid increase in Asian-based transactions in the portfolios of Australian PEs. McKinsey, in its recent report entitled 'Private Equity Asia-Pacific: is the Boom Back?' reported that the number of PE deals completed in Asia in 2010 was 500; in 2011 the number was more than 1200.

By value this resulted in the Asia-Pacific market now accounting for 21 per cent of global private equity, closer to the region's estimated 28 per cent share of global GDP. At this date CHAMP is the only

Figure 10: US PE sector breakout (in US$ billions)

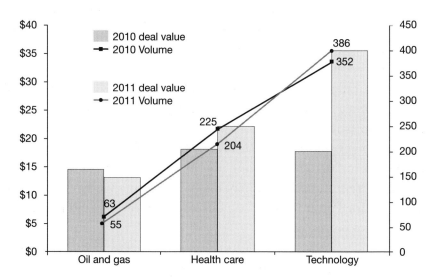

Source: Dealogic Jan 2012

Australian GP who has established an office in Asia but more will surely follow. Australian PE is well placed and well experienced to participate in this growth—as my next edition in ten years' time will hopefully chronicle!

Index

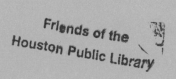